FAT MAN
ON
A ROMAN ROAD

Tom Vernon cycles so that he can see the world, and the world can see him. The world does not usually have much difficulty in doing this, since Tom generally weighs about nineteen or twenty stone: but he likes to meet it casually, before it can put on its Sunday best for the man from the radio. He says: 'In a car, you go to meet people: on a bicycle, they come out to meet you, by chance.'

Tom was an obscure member of the Peter Cook/David Frost generation at Cambridge, and has worked in theatre, the arts and the BBC. He has been an Elizabethan minstrel, a charity and pressure group organiser, a classical music producer, a teacher at a Jewish comprehensive school, a PRO, a radio show songwriter, the best-known Santa Claus in Britain, and a guide at Wookey Hole Caves. Now he is some sort of arty-craftsmany hybrid, writing and making TV programmes.

He's probably much the same as a lot of other Englishmen, except that he's fatter, rides a bike and writes about it, and loves oddity. He likes to think that he has an eye to see things, though, and a heart to care about them, and sometimes a knack of writing them down. He never has any idea what is going to happen next.

He is the author of the highly successful *Fat Man on a Bicycle,* also based on a BBC Radio 4 series and available in Fontana.

Also by Tom Vernon:

FAT MAN ON A BICYCLE

Illustrations by
PETER FREETH

FAT MAN
ON
A ROMAN ROAD

TOM VERNON

A bicycle exploration of Britain and the British
from the bottom left-hand corner
to the top right-hand corner of the Roman roads:
Topsham to Musselburgh,
the full story of the journey
of the BBC Radio 4 series
FAT MAN ON A ROMAN ROAD
and episodes in
FAT MAN AT WORK

Fontana/Collins

First published in Great Britain
by Michael Joseph 1983
First issued in Fontana Paperbacks 1985

Made and printed in Great Britain by
William Collins Sons & Co. Ltd, Glasgow

TO JENNY

I can do without celebrity: I'm happy with simple things –
Woods, a river in a valley, an ordinary brook . . .
. . . OK, if you can come out with a reason for everything,
If the future's a walkover to you (and never mind the row
That the forces of evil are kicking up outside) – that's fine.
But I'll show you a lucky man, a happy man –
He's the one who gets on with the country gods:
Pan; old Silvanus; and all the company of Nymphs.

Rura mihi et rigui placeant in vallibus amnes,
Flumina amem silvasque inglorius. O ubi campi,
Spercheusque, et virginibus bacchata Lacaenis
Taygeta! o qui me gelidis in vallibus Haemi
Sistat, et ingenti ramorum protegat umbra!
Felix, qui potuit rerum cognoscere causas,
Atque metus omnes et inexorabile fatum
Subjecit pedibus, strepitumque Acherontis avari!
Fortunatus et ille, Deos qui novit agrestes,
Panaque, Silvanumque senem, Nymphasque sorores!

GEORGICA LIB. I I
p. Virgilii Maronis

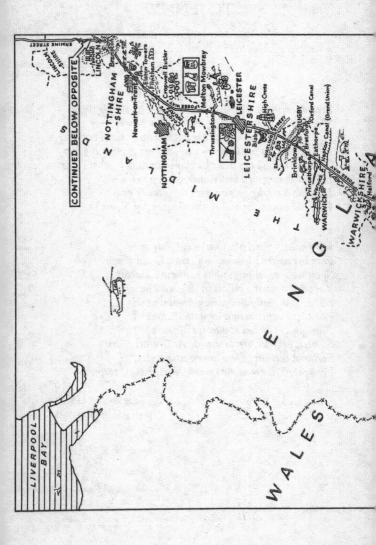

CONTINUED BELOW OPPOSITE

ERMINE STREET

LINCOLN

N NOTTINGHAM-SHIRE

Newark-on-Trent

Belvoir

Cropwell Butler

Elton Towers

Flintham

FOSSE WAY

Melton Mowbray

NOTTINGHAM

Thrussington

MIDLAND

LEICESTERSHIRE

LEICESTER

Blaby

High Cross

RUGBY

Brinklow

Bretford Oxford Canal

Princethorpe

Eathorpe

WARWICK

Napton Canal (Grand Union)

WARWICKSHIRE

(Halford)

FOSSE WAY

ENGLAND

WALES

LIVERPOOL BAY

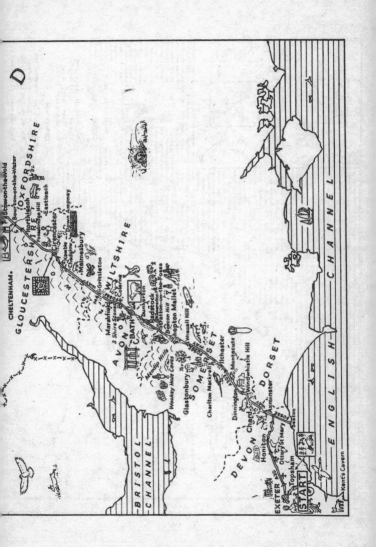

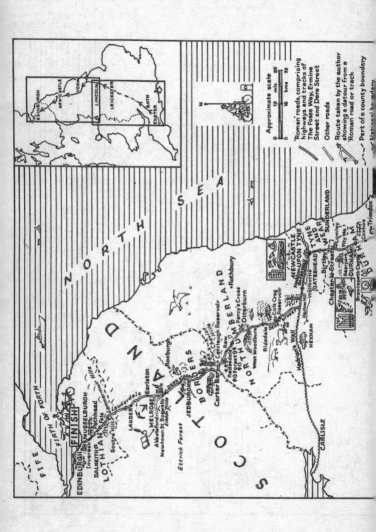

ENGLAND

Swaledale

NORTHALLERTON
Hornby
Ainderby
Brompton
Appleton Wiske
Middleton St George
Hutton Hills

Thirsk

NORTH YORKSHIRE
Easingwold
Copmanthorpe Shelton
YORK
Vale of York
Boothens
Bishopthorpe
Market Weighton
Sancton
Hoyton
North Newbald
Brough
HULL
HUMBERSIDE

IXTH LEGION

Whitton
Winterton
Winteringham
Appleby
Broughton
ERMINE STREET
Casnby Corner
SCUNTHORPE

GRIMSBY
Brigg

DONCASTER

LINCOLNSHIRE
R.A.F. Scampton
Holton-cum-Beckering
LINCOLN
Branston

FROM ABOVE OPPOSITE

IRISH SEA

LIVERPOOL BAY

WALES

CONTENTS

STRAIGHTFOREWORD

I wanted to look at Britain and meet the British: I did not care much about the Romans whom I do not like even as much as they deserve. The trouble with people who build empires is that they usually want to build them out of people like me – which is a form of togetherness I can do without.

In their desire to get straight from here to there, however, the Romans invented the most random thing possible: a road that does not curl with the landscape; goes out of its way to see no sights, meet no particular people, visit no special places; and which therefore comes by chance on all of these. I took to the Roman roads on my bicycle so that I might do the same.

This book is a picture of a diagonal strip of Britain as Britain was in the brooding, unprosperous summer of 1982 (and picture it is, for though I make radio programmes with my ears, I start thinking about the world with my eyes). It is about individuals I met (because I did my best not to meet the other sort of person) and tries to express their value and to relish their quirks, as both appeared to me.

It is also an attempt to make some general sense of England and the English (for though I ended my journey in Scotland, it would be impertinent to say much about the Scots on so short an acquaintance). When I made my first trip *Fat Man on a Bicycle* from Muswell Hill to the Mediterranean, I lunched in Rambouillet with an enthusiastic internationalist, Dr Plante, who said to me: 'For a man to love another country, I think he must first love his own.' It set me wondering whether my own country and its people *were* lovable. In this journey, I thought I might find out.

I followed my route in the spirit of 'more or less' – i.e. adventurously enough, but not slavishly – riding, or tramping, an assortment of road surface from triple-carriageway to river bank. The route went more or less from one corner of the coherent part of the Roman system to the other – though there are isolated patches of Roman road further north and west. It began in Topsham in Devon (once a Roman port) and soon took to the Fosse Way (it is Foss Way on the maps, but the common usage you see written up on houses and farms has the 'e'). I travelled up through Somerset, the Cotswolds and the Midlands to Lincoln; up Ermine Street to the Humber and across to York; north to Durham and Newcastle; along Hadrian's Wall to Dere Street and thence to Scotland over Carter Bar, ending in Musselburgh, just east of Edinburgh.

Fifteen centuries of history resonated along the road. As I went, I felt that I travelled not only through a present place but through the twilight of two empires: and even though I do not care for the Romans much, I could not help recapturing a little of that sense of wonder you feel as a child in a country of twisty roads, when a grown-up shows you a highway that goes straight, and tells you that even beyond the horizon it is straight, still.

There are many people to thank for their help apart from those who appear in the text, either named or described: the Ordnance Survey who sorted out a set of their 1:50,000 maps which are one of the crowd of quiet achievements which make it feasible for the British to affect modesty so often; Faber and Faber Ltd who lent me the file copies of those of their Shell County Guides that are so sadly out of print; to Huntsman's, Savile Row, who made me an exceptionally prestigious pair of shorts; to F. W. Evans the bicycle-makers; Friedman Wagner-Dobler who rescued two chapters from the ravings of a crazed computer; and to all sorts of people who helped with information, including many in tourist offices, companies, and local councils; to my wife Sally whose judgement is often much better than mine; to Cathy Mahoney, Ros Bartlett, Jay Andrews and Sharon Banoff at the BBC who spent hours on the telephone researching, apart from other things; to Monica Sims, Richard Wade and Alan Rogers; to those who helped with the BBC Radio 4 programmes which told the story of the journey; to Barbara Kronig and William McPhil of BBC TV's Costume Department who lent me a toga and showed me how to put it on; to all those people who gave me information and help that I would have liked to credit more adequately in the text but could not without spoiling the flow, notably Dr Valerie Maxfield, Cllr Walter Daw, Stephen Morland, Peter Addyman, Francis Daly, Clive Wilkin, the Rev. Sidney Adamson, George Colville, George Kergan, The Honest Lads and Lasses and Town Band of Musselburgh, also a fisherman, fishwife, fishmonger and fish-filleter of that town; and, above all, to my producer, Jenny De Yong, who is really the co-author of this book, since she made everything happen.

Tom Vernon, Muswell Hill, July 1983

THE ROAD
AT WINDWHISTLE HILL

I missed a turning after Axminster, and had to go down into Chard past Breeches Farm, and a field of very bare sheep without any. It was an afternoon over-exposing and under-exposed – chilly for July, and the clouds had turned lead-colour, and sagged just after I had joined the Fosse Way. There was no one about in the grey tea-time apart from a lad and a girl out with the dog and an ulterior motive; not a soul to warm their legs in the bus-shelter in the front wall of the Tytherleigh Arms, where they have built a seat on the radiator of the beer-cooler to comfort folk in winter, and although the dull light gave it the feeling of opening time, the Tytherleigh Arms was shut up.

Chard was gloomy, and bumped at me with villainous potholes. Stiff and tired after the first day of real cycling, I crawled up the long three miles of hill out of town, ignoring the insolence of an undiscriminating rabbit that sat on the road watching me coming and could not be bothered to run away. There was a house, once a pub, that still had its board out: 'The Old Happy', it said. I wheezed, and was not.

'You'll try this on a coal lorry, one day,' I said sourly to the rabbit when I was almost on top of it. 'STEW! GORRAH!' The rabbit left in a hurry: it was the smallest of satisfactions.

But then I came to the guard of giant beech trees that watches over the parkland of Cricket St Thomas to the south, and the Windwhistle Inn – where those same beech trees are painted on the sign bending in a high wind against a very pink sunset, and scattering their leaves like frightened birds: and there was my road again. It was 'unsuitable for heavy goods vehicles' and therefore eminently suitable for cyclists, a lane plumetting down the side of Windwhistle Hill. At first it seemed too rambling to be Roman but when I turned away from the precision of the beech trees and the smooth park grass, and looked north across the motley West-Country farmland, I saw that after its tumble downhill, in the distance there was a line of tree and hedge too long for a field boundary, too straight for a river – the Fosse Way, on its way almost three hundred miles to Lincoln.

It was a tiny, careering little lane, where no bicycle brakes would hold a twenty-stone man, and a stream went down the sides – a single-track road, a friendly road where the ferns came rushing down the banks to meet you: there were hazel nuts in the dusky branches above me and, although the surface was none too good, those breakneck bumps somehow seemed less impersonal than the municipal jolts of Chard. Sometimes it rolled with the country, sometimes it was sunk so deeply below the nut-branches that there was little more than moss that would grow on the banks: and it was joined, often, by even tinier roads coming in at funny angles, as if they had aspired to meet it in days long ago, when there was very little else to join.

I passed a pretty, mullioned house of yellow stone, with apples hanging quietly over its wall and an unquiet dog in its garden: it was built right on to the road for company, in the days when a road meant someone to chat to, rather than a horde to roar at you, smog you, and run you over. I was going through the outskirts of Dinnington, until I looked at the map, and discovered that it *was* Dinnington. It was after the Rose and Crown, which had a brown and white goat in its garden, monarch of all it surveyed from its perch on an old stone sink, that there were humbler hedges and a subsiding switchback of little hills through fields that smelt of cows, and something sweet from the hedges. One final jungly tunnel – even down to the creepers dangling from the trees and whipping at me with their ends – and the road surface turned brown and fizzy-sounding with sand washed from banks which implied rabbits. Sure enough, within a mile, there was a blue Land-Rover backed into a gateway and a bearded gentleman equipped for sport with a leather waistcoat, a rather large shotgun, and a rather small black and white dog, hardly larger than the brace of bunnies he was swinging by the ears.

'Can you tell me what happens at the end of the road?' I asked, tending to sound like a moral precept from *The Sound of Music*. 'There's a bit on the map where it seems to go into little red splotches.'

'That's like the old Roman road,' said the bearded man. 'Footpath, right-of-way, trackway – it just goes straight on. Could get through on a bike, but not advisable: you turn there, brings you into Stratton, and then you can go straight through to Wigborough, Wigborough to Norton, Ham Hill – wherever else you want to go.'

'Edinburgh, actually,' I replied, seizing my opportunity to be nonchalant.

'Oh,' said the bearded man, with not quite enough respect.

I left hastily, before the nonchalance wore off, speeding through the flat country before the dusk turned to darkness, for I had no lights: to where Jenny and supper were waiting at the Montacute Arms.

THE START AT THE END
OF THE EXE

TOPSHAM to MONTACUTE

I stood on Topsham quay, trying to put on my toga. It was like wrestling with a washing line, including washing: Jenny held one end, the photographer held the other, and I was in the middle.

'Wait,' I said, 'I can't do it like this: I'll have to park the bicycle. Are you sure you can't remember what they said in the costume department?'

'It's got dirt on it,' observed the photographer, who was having some difficulty managing both the toga and his cameras.

'Bloodstains,' said Jenny. 'It was in *I Claudius*. It's a used toga.'

Fifteen hundred years before, there might have been someone around knowledgeable enough to ask, since Topsham was a Roman port then. In my time, however, it was simply the most south-westerly point I could find to begin my journey from one corner of the Roman roads to the other. So I parked the bicycle, and thought back to the toga instruction evening in BBC Television Centre.

'Oh, now I remember,' I said . . .

There had been the softly-spoken wardrobe mistress and William, who was something of a wardrobe master, if his silk shirt and cashmere pullover were anything to go by. It was odd how he and I were wearing similarly shaped garments, but he looked clothed, and I looked bundled. A toga, I had thought, might be more flattering to the fuller figure.

'Shall I take my clothes off?' I had asked. The wardrobe mistress was very definite from behind her spectacles that it would not be necessary: at least it solved the question of what to wear underneath, which is potentially even more absorbing to a Roman than to a Scotsman. (The Romans had tunics and shifts according to the weather.)

'I never know what people do in wardrobes,' I apologised. The toga came out of a cage where it was penned in with an assortment of stuffs too brightly-coloured to be let out: indeed, it was alarming to think of the threat of all those doublets, caveman outfits, Santa Claus costumes, gorilla suits and farthingales being liberated onto the streets of Shepherd's Bush without a dramatic context – little different in fact to having real Elizabethans, cavemen, gorillas and Santa Clauses wandering about.

It seemed that I was about to experience the sartorial sensations of a Roman senator: apart from the bloodstains – which everyone knows from such works as *I Claudius*, *Caligula* and *Julius Caesar* to have been the invariable consequence of holding public office at that time, and which remain the flip side of ambition to this day – the toga was a posh person's toga, with a band of Tyrian Purple round the hem. Except that it was not purple, but a kind of browny-red – authentic, they told me, for they had been to Pompeii and recreated the subtlety of the ancient colourings they found there with natural dyes, even though that sometimes meant that they had to take the costumes apart before they could put them in the washing machine.

William and the wardrobe mistress began to perform a complex scarf dance with the toga, at opposite ends of the room.

'It should be two-and-a-half times the height of the gentleman who's going to wear it,' William said. 'The shape is elliptical.'

Whatever was going on seemed to have very little relevance to the main participant. 'You're folding it up, and I'm not in it,' I pointed out.

'Coming to you now – makes it manageable.'

'Arms straight down . . .' They went three times round me, widdershins, and I was wearing a toga. Interestingly, the sartorial contrast between me and other people I had seen wearing togas was roughly on the same level as that between myself and William when wearing casual clothes: plainly, there are some people born to look like the sort of parcel the Post Office complains about, and nothing can alter it, not a toga or – probably – even a suit of armour or a grass skirt.

'Very nice,' said the wardrobe mistress in kindly tones. 'Of course, it generally makes people look tall.'

'I couldn't run for a chariot in this: isn't there a belt, or suspenders, or something?'

'You need to walk properly,' William told me, 'very erect. Gather it on the left shoulder – and the weight of the folds keeps it into the neck. If it should slip, you can hitch it up again – there's a knack to it – and your right hand is free for oratory.'

It seemed that a toga dictated the pace of life for its wearer: I wondered, idly, whether trousers and skirts did the same, and whether it made a difference if they were tight or loose, short or long. But there appeared to be no problem in bending over: you could do practically anything in it, except work. The toga's one concession to ergonomics appeared to be a fold like an extra stomach at the waist, in which you could tuck away bits and pieces. It made me feel like a kangaroo.

'You'd have a smaller tunic for an orgy,' said William.

'I think they do now,' I replied, 'but a toga would be good for ablutions, don't you think? You could wash any part without taking your clothes off.'

'You shouldn't have a beard, of course: they didn't, even though they didn't have very good razors. You could have it plucked.'

'Thank you very much for showing me the toga,' I said. 'I think I've got some idea now.'

The wardrobe mistress jiggled with a fold in an attempt to make it seem less like a crumple. 'There, the bloodstain's nice and prominent. There's no problem putting it on, but you need two people.'

'Just a couple of slaves,' said William.

'I'll keep an eye out for a pair,' I had said.

'. . . oh, now I remember, it's all right,' I told Jenny and the photographer, 'we just need more people.' Fortunately, a Topsham family out for a morning stroll was just about to become entangled in the cryptic garment, which stretched from the waterside over the quay and across the road to the garden wall opposite. We thrust the toga into an assortment of hands.

'Would you like to help me a moment? We're just trying to sort out a toga.'

'It's one of those damn-fool things,' said the mother of the family, looking down at her end. A window banged open under the eaves of the cottage opposite, and a pretty woman looked out like Rapunzel in the fairy-tale, except that she wore a dressing-gown and had her hair done up in a towel.

'Not damn-fool at all – well, of course it is, in fact, but not really, because . . .' A car went past, we had to move the toga, and the family seized the chance to escape.

'I don't suppose – ,' I began to the lady in the window.

'Hold on a moment,' said Rapunzel: 'don't do anything. I'm going to get my camera.' She disappeared. We waited. She returned. We all waited. Eventually, there were more passers-by: a party of yachting-people on their way to their boats. I explained how the wearing of a toga might be relevant to a man just about to cycle up the Roman roads.

'Give you five miles before the sheet gets caught in the chain,' offered Rapunzel.

'Anyone can see it's not a sheet. It's too big and, besides, it's elliptical. Look,' I said to the yatchsmen, 'you fold it in the middle so that one curve hangs down about a foot further than the other, then you change places round me, and I'll tell you the rest while you're doing it.' I ducked under the toga and stood waiting. Nothing happened.

'Where are you?' queried the yachtsman on the far side.

'Here.'

'Oh, I thought you meant over here.' Eventually we got it on: it looked even more like an exploding parcel than it had at Television Centre, but the tassel on the left-hand end which just touches the ground to show the correct length hung just right: and neither Rapunzel nor the professional photographer seemed to mind.

'Can I come up and talk to you?' I asked Rapunzel in her dressing-gown. 'For the BBC, you know.'

'Come tomorrow, then you can meet my husband as well,' said Rapunzel, complacently. 'Are you really going to wear that on a bike?'

'No way. What, and end up like Isadora Duncan?'

When the photographer had gone, the toga came off perfectly easily. We started work, recording mud.

'Mud?' I said.

'It will be marvellous in stereo,' said Jenny, who is an enthusiast for sounds as every radio producer ought to be. The mud was certainly loud enough: it made a sort of sucking, whistling inward squelch right along the edge of the river where the tide was out. We had £3000-worth of a brand-new-rather-small-tape-recorder with us, and we christened it with mud. As I marched down to the end of the breakwater with it, a group of women chatting on a bench expressed their interest to Jenny. They told her they had never seen anyone recording mud before: more than that, they had never even seen anyone listening to the stuff, but now she mentioned it, it did sound funny, didn't it? They fell silent, and we all listened to the mud together, as the reels went round.

Topsham was pale grey in the morning, the yachts still asleep in the river with their sheets bundled up, the white stride of the motorway bridge silent and misty in the distance upstream, a grey sheen on the sea at the horizon, visible from the small gravel beach at the end of the Strand, a road which goes nowhere else. It is there that the Dutch houses stand under serpentine gables, upon them the calm of Queen Anne and a succession of peaceful lives since their bricks came from Holland as ballast: further up, the cottages are no less decent, but more higgledy-piggledy, with a greater tendency for their upper storeys to put to sea from wooden bay-windows like the sterns of ramshackle galleons.

With the Clyst and the Exe flowing together into an estuary below the town, and the hills across the river, Topsham feels like the sea in the middle of fields. There was even one of that increasingly rare breed of amphibians, a ferryman, Stan Pym, plying his dinghy across the Exe all year long, except the couple of times when the tide runs at five or six knots and defeats his outboard, and his holidays – when people usually call him out anyway. He carried me over to the far bank – which is not so much a bank as the edge of Exeter Canal – and was in no great rush.

'Nobody tells me what to do,' Stan told me. 'Anyone says they're in a hurry, I tell 'em to go and catch a bus. I'll never be a millionaire, but I haven't had a cold for eight years, and there's a waiting list for my job. Strangers come and say "I'll take over" – mind you, that's when the sun's shining.'

He had developed a sixth sense for a customer. He would sit in his kitchen, and something would make him look up from his paper, through the window, down the hall – and there would be a fare on the far landing. In every sense, he was at home – back in Topsham after thirty years away as a master-builder in Exeter, content to be one of a line of men who had been going backwards and forwards without getting any-where since the Middle Ages.

'Don't you get bored?' I asked him.

'There's four hundred boats out there to look at, and I know the shape of every one of them. There's the seagulls, swans, cormorants taking fish, young ducks getting bigger till they fly away. See that large fly on the water there? You watch.'

I watched. A fish came up to the surface in a gleam of watery silver, snapped it up, and gleamed below again.

'Bored? How can I be bored?' said Stan. We got back to the

Topsham bank and he let me off, to walk up past the Ferryboat Inn and back into the town.

Topsham is a calm and picturebook place: its rent to the Crown is one red rose a year, and one of its postmen has Edward VII whiskers and rides his red bicycle with royal dignity. (So does the other postman, only without whiskers.) It is not a proud place, but it has pride. An old rhyme goes:

> *Exeter was an airy down*
> *When Topsham was a busy town.*

'Topsham's the most peaceful spot on earth,' a passer-by told me. 'George Gissing wrote that. A Japanese business man read it, and then he came to see for himself. All that way, and he said Topsham was as he imagined. I remember Lavender Boyce, the old navigator, told me that in all the world he'd never seen a better sight than the sun setting over Topsham steps.'

The passer-by was Roy Wheeler, a governor of the primary school he had first entered at the age of six, who was on his way to give out prizes at its swimming gala at the community pool, which was making the noise that swimming pools always do — a continuous scream half-way between Guy Fawkes' Night 'Ooooh' and the unexpected strangulation of a close relative. Its sides were crowded with diminutive school chairs and thin children who shivered like dogs out of the water and went 'Aaah' when they got in. It was plain to see that the pool was a cherished amenity: a very proud pool brush hung disdainfully on hooks along the side like an aristocratic moustache, and a more prosaic notice said: 'We don't swim in your toilet: please don't WEE in our pool'.

In the past, the playground of Topsham children was the river: sewage went into it then but, dirty as it was, they did not suffer the 'funny tummy' you get from the cleaner waters now. There were children who had been too poor to buy bathing costumes who made imitation ones out of mud when they came out of the water: but they did have Harry Luscombe, who had swum the Bristol Channel, to teach them to swim — although the local boat-builder told me he had never learned, in spite of being on the water so much and in spite of his name being Bert Trout.

In those days, there was more to catch in the river. Children would get the skeleton of a fish and go after crabs with it: go eel-clatting – threading a rope of worms, hanging it out from a boat, and shaking the eels off into an umbrella. One man used to go through the shallows on all fours, picking up flatfish with his hands and threading them by their gills on a string tied to his belt and passing through his legs so that he moved with a tail of live fish behind him. Salmon boats came up to the churchyard wall, sometimes with a hundred fish in a catch (half a ton or so, for Exe salmon run up to eight or nine pounds in weight).

There had been three times the fish when the Exe was dirty, I was told by the Pym brothers, Denzil and Kenneth, whose family had been salmon-fishers for five or six hundred years: what with that and the great number of cormorants – no longer controlled as they had been, by the placing of a five-shilling bounty on each beak – they themselves only found it worthwhile to be part-time at the salmon fishing.

'Twenty-three years I was full-time, and if I could go again, I wouldn't change it,' said one brother. 'Once in a boat, I'm a hunter. I quarrel with my brother: I've had a salmon jump out of his haul and into my boat (there was a dispute about that for two years). Another time the boat sank with four of us so that we were hanging on his boat – and he was knocking our hands off with the oar, 'cos he couldn't swim. The competition goes on until August 16 – that's close season: then I can't wait till February. You try an early morning then – boat covered in frost, icy seat, icy ropes: one day I got so cold, I had three days sitting in a chair afterwards – I couldn't move.'

They lived in a semi on the outskirts of town. The wall of the living-room was ornamented with pottery heads designed to demonstrate national characteristics and sabotage international understanding: there was a Mr Pickwick, two stalwart lifeboatmen and a toby jug for Britain, a chef for France, a sinister Mexican, and a fierce-looking Pathan with a turban and teeth. Jenny and I sat on a sofa of light tan leather that screamed and raspberried as you shifted your bottom.

Neither of the Pyms was keen on fresh salmon: one of them had fried up a slice five or six years before, but had not fancied it. When they cooked it for a regular customer – the fire brigade would have salmon for their annual dinner, for instance – the art was to bring it to the boil with a knob of butter and a tablespoon of vinegar, simmer it for ten minutes only, and leave it in the water until the next day.

'All I put on after is pepper and vinegar: if it costs all that money, what's the use of cooking it wrong?'

'But what's the skill in catching it?' I asked.

It was in knowing the ways of the fish, the tides and the geography of the river, they said. They had in their heads a whole atlas of strange names for various parts of it – the Blue Door Hole, the Clock, the Pit, the Mud, Black Oar Mud, Black Oar Full Length. None of which information would be any help to me, they thought.

'You'd be in danger: a person of your weight would sink in the mud and never get out again.'

'I'm hunting on dry land tonight,' I said. 'On Woodberry Common. It's the annual meeting of the Topsham Nightjar Society.'

'What's a nightjar?' asked the salmon-fisher's daughter.

'A flagon of cider at the Lighter Inn, I expect,' said her father.

Jenny and I lunched at the Lighter Inn off something called 'Crab Mornay', in which a mixture of crabmeat and cheese sauce had been plonked down on a foundation of gobs of mustard the size of a half-crown: it was very strange.

'Everything OK with the crab?' asked the Lighter Inn, cheerfully.

'Lovely, thank you.'

'Hypocrite!' said Jenny.

'Well, you tell them then. Go on. Go on. There you are: typically English. Eat your mustard, and serve you right.'

Nothing went by the Lighter Inn as we sat before it: nothing moved on the quay where no cargo had been landed since a boatload of lemons and onions eight months before. It did not seem like the port that sent more ships to the Newfoundland fishery than any other in Britain, save London, in the days of William III.

In the heyday of the coastal trade and boat-building in the last century, the great shipping family of Topsham – local magnates and master-mariners both – were the Holmans.

Dorothy Holman still lived along the Strand, with the museum she created at the back of the house in the sail-loft built by her great-uncle, Captain Thomas. She had had her ninety-fourth birthday the previous week.

It was difficult to find Miss Holman because her house was one of those houses which are all outside wall, and it is only when you get inside that you find a garden, old trees, and a house like country Chippendale – unpretentious, but of great quality. Her companion opened the door, a personable blonde in tight Bermudas.

Miss Holman was half-way up the stairs to her museum when we arrived, and had to hurry down again on stick and walking-frame. She was therefore in something of a tizz, as far as a well-brought up Quaker lady of ninety-four can be: which was, to ask if we were the people from the BBC come to frighten her. Had she but known it, I was more apprehensive than she was for I feared she might be deaf, and it is even more difficult to cope with the hard of hearing in a radio interview than it is in ordinary conversation. You shout – the tape recorder goes into paroxysms of over-load: you drop your voice – they can't hear: so you shout, and it starts all over again. It is extremely wearing.

'You can't be frightened by a man in shorts,' I said.

'Sorts?'

'Shorts. Shorts! SHORTS!'

'Oh yes, she's got her shorts on,' said Miss Holman briskly, in admiration of her companion's Bermudas. 'I know you're famous, but I'm so old-fashioned, I never listen to the radio, and I never watch the television.'

'Don't blame you: neither do I,' I said, with perfect accuracy on both counts.

'You're famous, aren't you?' said Miss Holman, returning to the attack. Successfully: I was embarrassed. 'Famous?'

'Well . . .' I had no idea what to say to the allegation. 'Only a bit,' seemed up to the capacity of Miss Holman's hearing-aid: but she liked to get things straight.

'Other people tell me you're famous,' said Miss Holman, not letting go. 'I'm only sorry I don't listen to the radio.'

'Right.' There was a short pause, during which I cleared my throat. 'Congratulations on your birthday.'

'I get more and more astonished to think I'm still alive,' said

Miss Holman, unblandished. 'When I was a child people made a lot of me; when I grew up they didn't notice me; now I'm old they're nice to me again.'

I decided that the only thing to do with this ninety-four-year-old was to treat her as if she were fifty years younger, only at a higher volume. The trick was to ignore the fact that the body was frail, and had to concentrate on the personality that made her bob her white hair and green Alice band as if she were trying to shake her thoughts into proper place by force, and wagged out her words in bursts. She was one of the rather small group of people for whom conversation means listening, thinking and replying (for most of us, it means picking up a cue as an excuse for talking): and she listened, as she talked, energetically – peering through her glasses as if she hoped for an insight through her eyes as well as ears.

Her family had come to the town from Cornwall in 1660, she told me, and since that time had been master mariners – there was nothing braver or more difficult than that, she thought. Her great-grandfather had founded the family fortunes, having first gone to sea on a whaler at the age of five: in later years, he was famous for his rudder, I gathered: I could not be quite certain why, but suspected he might have invented it.

Miss Holman was born in 1888, and christened in the Methodist chapel the family built to spite the vicar: but even in her childhood Topsham was in decline, along with its ship-building – which had been celebrated, among other things, for having invented its own way of making nails. Before, the yards had stretched from one end of the waterfront to the other although she remembered as a little girl looking up at a sailing vessel in the dry dock jutting out its bowsprit and dangling its cables all over the road.

'It was very poor then; lots of old ladies and nobody to ask to children's parties.' She brought out pictures of her childhood taken by her uncle while Queen Victoria was still alive: a picnic the size of a small army camp on Woodberry Common – everyone much dressed up, and standing very still in a casual pose.

'We used to go up in a big brake. It wasn't much fun – all old ladies in bonnets. Look at those baskets of food! Sandwiches, Devonshire cream – couldn't have a party without it: my father had two thousand acres and we used to get fresh cream and butter from the farms. That's me – ' (a calm little girl looking serious under wide eyebrows) '– don't I look bored? That's my cousin, and that's the little maid – she's the only pretty one.' She was not pretty, she was exquisite; standing utterly remote among all the old ladies in bonnets who were certainly not exquisite at all. I wondered what had become of her: but who would know what had become of a servant, however beautiful?

'I don't know who she was,' said Miss Holman, and laughed a high laugh. I said I could not imagine what it must have been like to have servants; to have to share your house with a non-kindred spirit who would, in turn, share it out round the entire neighbourhood via Cook next door, and the grocer's boy.

'They used to gossip about us in the kitchen, I know, because they had a parrot, and the parrot would say, "Been a rumpus, Bert!" My grandmother used to say to her gardener, "What do you find to *do* all day?" – and the poor man had been working till dark, but he just smiled: he was one of the very nice Topsham people.'

'But didn't you think it was all a bit unfair?'

'It didn't occur to me till later; I didn't think it unfair when I was young, because it was *done*. We thought it very important to be nice to them. A lot of people weren't. But the one thing that I thought was terrible was that when you called a horse cab, a poor lad would run along with you for perhaps a mile to get sixpence for helping your luggage down; everybody used to drive them away as if they were pests, or they'd have to carry up the heavy bags straightaway, when they were all out of breath, right up to the top of the house.'

Miss Holman was very obstinate with her armchair for trying to keep her in one place too long, then exceedingly firm with her stick, and took me out of the drawing-room with its flowery white-painted furniture dusky with antiquity into the kitchen, all white tiles and scrubbed table. The indicators for the bells still hung above the door – which is not unusual in old houses, even in 1982 – but the bells still worked. She opened the kitchen cupboard, on the back of the door was pinned a notice – her own instructions to the cook written almost fifty years ago in very neat writing, though the paper was yellowed and the ink faded to brown. The cook began her day by cleaning the cooker and doing the boiler.

'Then . . . ''7.15 am, front steps and door-handle; drawing room'' – oh, the cook did that! Would you believe it?' The list went on all day and well into the evening: there were also specific tasks for each day of the week. ' ''Re-paper cupboards'' – I did think hard, didn't I? just as if they were automatons: ''Clean visitors' shoes at once!'' – oh, it *is* funny!'

'You certainly seem to have been an efficient housekeeper.'

'I'm a black and white person: things are right, or things are wrong,' said Miss Holman, and went on to remark that she used to get very cross with the suffragettes for being undignified. 'I was sixteen in those days, and I used to think ''How awful!'', tying themselves to railings and that sort of thing.'

'But aren't you glad they did now?' I asked.

'Oh, now I feel quite differently: belonging to the Society of Friends, my life's effort has been to behave decently, but I see now that you can't get anything without making a terrible fuss, making a fool of yourself. That's the trouble.'

'Yes, it is,' I said.

There was no sign of anybody making much of a fuss in Topsham. It seemed that life there was as innocent as the flowers painted all over the school wall to brighten the playground. Yet in the Britain I had come from there were three million out of work, a war only just over, and the IRA blowing bandsmen and horses to pieces in London parks. Jenny had been to the glove factory which lives in an old chapel behind the main street, and where one woman reads stories and poems in Devon dialect while they work: they were sewing gloves with scarlet linings. One of the girls said to Jenny, 'That stands for blood, the blood of soldiers.'

While the rest of the world was killing people – this was also the time of the massacre in Beirut – in my two days in Devon I had seen no more sign of civil disorder than a vandalised telephone box, and was in hopes of coming upon a couple of minor graffiti to make me feel more at home – although in the policeman's column in the parish magazine, I saw that scarcely a month went by when there was not at least one act of minor law-breaking, and in the same issue a local councillor was calling for the reintroduction of the birch and capital punishment because some girls had taken a wicker gate off its hinges and 'badly damaged' it.

Topsham, however, seemed to be uncommonly intimate from the enormous list of local nicknames I came across in Miss Holman's museum: almost two hundred and fifty of them, parents and grandparents of the Topshamites I had already met to judge by the names. It must surely be a sign of familiarity, I thought, to call someone Pongo, Pincher, Lovey or Whacker Pym; Chugg-Chugg Amos; Squad-Pie Burgess; Goaty Edworthy; Rumpsey Fellows; Tommy-Teapot Gale; Boogsey Hole; two Holmans – Blow-Hard and Draughty; Pollons, Flannel, Bensoline-Billy, Tommy-Lump and Whizz-Bang Luxon; Gong Osborne; Buckety Palmer; Coe-Handbag Pennells; Camshaft Pulman; Pistol Quick; I'll-Tell-Um Wannell; Bunkum Bowers; Popsy Hedger and What-What Chestnut.

I could hardly see how any 1980s town could be as close as that, but even if latter-day Topsham was a community split several ways, I could hardly see the join. Some people were richer than others, or of a different class: some people were outsiders – there being the usual immigration pattern of small, attractive towns near a city and a university – and these people found Topsham's own nickname 'the Chelsea of Exeter' particularly offensive.

'Here's a real *Guardian* reader,' said Jenny, as we walked through the town towards the Annual Meeting of the Nightjar Society. 'Greenpeace and CND on the windows, and Save the Whale on the door.'

But generally in Topsham, it seemed, the cutting-edge of social injustice had been blunted, the rich did not show off their wealth, the outsiders were mixing in, and the different classes performed their complex dance of inter-relationship in which anybody may change position at any time, provided they end up where they started. The only apparent division between folk was that some say Top-sham, and others Tops-ham, according to whether they were working-class local, or middle-class local: and even here it was less important that you get it right than that an outsider should get it wrong.

Francis Luscombe explained to me how to pronounce Topsham as he sat beneath his apple trees in the cool of the evening just across the road from the salmon-fishers, who had said it the other way, and took me down to his cellar to show me the model of the town at the turn of the century that was due to be presented to Miss Holman for her museum: it had been four years in the making by the Topsham Society, of which he was chairman, and was the size of a model railway layout, with sponge rubber trees. (I have always been interested in how you make model trees, since they are the things which were absolutely impossible to do as a child, if you remember.) He was kind to my comparative ignorance of nightjars, producing a book of reference that had a picture of something that looked like a small, airborne mailbag with spots.

'Oh, it's one of *those*,' I said. 'How, precisely, do we watch it?'

Greed was to be its downfall, it appeared, as is often the way of the world. It was fond of moths, so all we had to do was to find a place where there were nice juicy ones and follow them around until the nightjar came to eat them: then we would all watch, and it could do absolutely nothing about it since, having its mouth full, it would be unable to tell us to sod off. I got the idea at once: there seemed to be nothing to it.

Other nightjar hunters arrived with boots and binoculars, making up a little band about the size of a small chamber orchestra. We piled into cars and drove off into the dusk, in which Woodberry Common was waiting for us, a place of humps and furze, crossed at random by sundry tracks of mud and pebbles, with no vegetation more domesticated than ferns, convolvulus, the dried seedheads of cow-parsley, and purple-pink thistles. On its crest was a clump of fir trees like the hairs on a wart.

Handbrakes rasped and doors slammed. There seemed to be an awful lot of cars.

'I'm afraid we're in competition with the Small Aeroplane Group. So if you hear a high-pitched buzz, it's a model aeroplane and not a nightjar.' We heard a high-pitched buzz. 'That's not a nightjar,' said Francis Luscombe.

'Are you a naturalist?' I asked.

'I'm just a local layabout.'

'Are these all local layabouts?'

'These are all highly-informed birdwatchers.'

He was the sort of man who is always ready with a little joke, a self-deprecation and a jolly-along to make people feel at their ease, so that it comes as a surprise to realise that they are running the show rather better than you could. He bubbled around the nightjar-hunters like a party host as we waited for the last car. It was all as good-humoured and wholesome as a combination of *Wind in the Willows* and *Happy Families*: he was Ratty, the good chap, the organiser; the bird expert was Brian Baker, the fishmonger (who told me that Topsham also has a Mr Fisher, the miller).

'This is Trevor Bartlett: he's an expert on badgers.' Badger had a lean, Lutherian face with deep-sunk eyes that gleamed slightly in the twilight.

'Good evening, ladies and gentlemen: what a wonderful turn-out!' said Ratty of the Riverbank, welcoming all us littler animals to the Wildwood. 'It is three minutes past nine, so I think we'll just trek our way easily and quietly across country.' We trekked off quietly past the aeroplanes, which were not quiet at all.

'Worrroww-worrroww-worrroww,' went the aeroplanes, like a pack of flying tigers.

'Yes, that is a disturbance,' said Ratty, 'but they haven't got navigation lights to fly at night.'

'Have *we* got navigation lights?' I asked, ramming my sandalled feet into a gorse bush.

'We rely on glow-worms,' said an attractive young bunny next to me.

We strode into the emptiness of the common. The area is unusually good for bird-watching because of the variety of habitats – estuary, farmland, heath, reed bed, water meadow, cliff, garden: and the part we were on seemed to be unusually good for midges. After about half a mile, we came to a ridge above a small plantation and stopped in the middle of the furze by the shadowy presences of a few pine trees: here all the midges that were in danger of being left behind caught up, and fresh ones arrived. We spoke in whispers, for fear that we should disturb them or the nightjars at their respective dinners. The dinner next to me said that nightjars had very large mouths: they just flew through the air and scooped up moths.

It sounded easy enough, but I thought it would probably need a pretty good eye, as well as a big mouth.

'Definitely, a very good aim,' said Brian Baker. The nightjar was also a punctual bird – chirring to call out its territory at the same point in the right sort of evening so precisely that you could set your watch by it, if you remembered to add on five minutes a week to allow for the advance of summer. It was not too shy – if you drove slowly on a summer night, you could pick it up in your headlights, warming its belly on the hot road.

'Or if you drive fast, you can pick up the pieces,' I suggested.

We waited. The model aeroplanes had gone home: the common was an expanse of scarcely-textured shadow, the sky hardly lighter. The only sounds were a shifting of boots among heather and subdued slappings.

'There! To the left!' It was a sound like a distant sewing-machine, the chirring. It was to the right, then behind, then faint, but all around. The birds were about to fly. Everybody peered hard into the darkness.

But it was not a bird that I saw. Close by, beneath the silhouetted pines, there was a hooded figure. It was the Black Monk. No – the light from the skies gleamed on its eyes and it was a Vampire. No – its teeth flashed, and it became a graduate in lycanthropic studies from the University of Transylvania. The figure approached.

'I spend a tremendous lot of time up here at night: sometimes I go home with my face covered in bumps,' said Badger, who had put up the hood of his anorak to try to ward off the midges. 'Mammals, that's my main interest. Anything nocturnal – bats, foxes, badgers. My love is of badgers and it stemmed from there. The only sort of birds I really get interested in are the owls – and obviously the nightjar tonight. There's something nice about being out on one's own on a summer's evening when it's dark: the crowds have gone, and you're left. It's marvellous; it's just you and Nature. And the midges.'

We waited. The chirring shifted. There was the quick whistle of the flight call. Suddenly, there was the soft flap of wings overhead, and a shadowy, hawk-like bird wheeled over us. Whether it was all the expectant waiting, I don't know, or the hope that since it had its mouth open it might scoop up some of the midges, but it was like the excitement of a piece of music that returns to its theme after a long time away, and as haunting when it had gone.

'Well you did see one: last year we didn't see any at all,' said Francis Luscombe as we all headed back towards the parking place past a darkened car containing another form of wild-life which was probably more surprised to be watched than the nightjar, even though everybody was most conscientious in looking the other way, and I only squinted most discreetly out of the corner of my eye to see if I could make out what was going on inside.

'Most interesting,' I said. 'And the nightjar was wonderful. Really it was.'

I was soundly midge-bitten as I made my way back to the quay the morning after the nightjar before to talk to Rapunzel and her husband at Drake's Cottage. The Drake in question was a baker, she told me with ruthless honesty, though it was nice if the tourists thought otherwise: and her name was not Rapunzel, but Annette van Oppen.

'Top-sham, or possibly Tops-ham, is like a different planet,' I said to her: and she said that there had just been a fair so perhaps there was a remnant of festivity in the air. She took me into a house that felt like a cross between a sailing ship and a windmill – it had been enlarged from the original three rooms, Richard van Oppen told me, by digging down five feet and putting in an extra floor, because they could not go out or up.

'We don't do building works in this house, we do mining works,' he said, and what he appeared to have found was history. He even knew the dates of the very bricks: there was dressed stone from Roman times, but the earliest brick was 1420, sun-dried: later, you could see that this one had been fired on gorse, this one had been moulded wet (with the clay exploding), this one squeezed drier – and so down to the Hancock brickworks, which flourished in Exeter in the last century. Such casual, domestic history seems to me to be the hallmark of Britain, much more than political history or what those who have a political or social advantage to gain from it call Tradition. Flashy ceremonial is for tourists, the grand sweep of events for scholars; for ordinary people, there is more satisfaction in hoarding fragments of the ordinary past, little bits of concrete history – or, in the case of the Van Oppens, little bits of the history of concrete.

'We're a race that likes to talk about the past,' continued Richard van Oppen. 'I think if you're proud of the past, you're proud of the present – and that makes for a proud future'. It was rhetoric, but he was a quietly-spoken man and it was meant. I had the feeling that it might also be true, certainly in Devon.

'The secret of happiness is to be content with life, and here it has a measured beat to it,' said Annette. 'The restless leave – like Drake. It's not that West Country people don't care about the rest of the world, but they get it in the right place. Top of the list, West Country people put their own business.'

It all sounded to me as if in Topsham, and its big neighbour Exeter (for no small town in England rules itself any longer, since the reorganisation of local government) I had found a microcosm of England. More, a microcosm of an ideal England – not without flaws in the present (and even more in the past), but as good as a practical Englishman might reasonably expect.

Richard was just telling me how the ghosts of Roman soldiers and sailors were to be heard roistering in the night beneath his window (unless it was people coming back from the pub) when there was a toot outside the window. I looked out, and saw Jenny's little grey Alfa-Romeo waiting.

'That reminds me,' I said, 'I have to get to Edinburgh.'

I said goodbye, and went down to get the bicycle off the roof-rack. It was new and shining black, one of the last frames made by Harry Healey, who died a year after I wrote about him in my first book *Fat Man on a Bicycle*. I had named it in his memory, and since he could not be stopped from writing aphorisms all over the walls of his workshop, and since I was off up the Roman roads, I had called it The Roman Philosopher.

It was a high-tech bicycle: it carried a digital mileometer containing a four-bit computer which was Japanese and in-scrutable. The instructions were even more so, but it was comprehensible that every time you got off the bike you had to detach the computer, for fear somebody should steal it. You could then continue to carry your journey round with you, in the form of what may have been miles, kilometers, or something Japanese.

I was prestigiously-equipped all round: literally – for the necessities of publicity had not only forced me into an occasional toga, but had written words all over my T-shirt, and bought me the most refined and expensive garment I am ever likely to own, a pair of Savile Row shorts.

I had not previously realised that there were people in the world who paid £200 for a pair of shorts, nor was I yet one of them: but I had the shorts, which were blue corduroy and as comfortable as one might expect of a garment which had been ripped apart and re-sewn at least three times during the course of its making and fitted as often with the aid of a horse. It was a wooden horse, but not big enough to hold more than an extremely small Greek, and shaped like Tommy the Tank Engine. It was easy to see it was a horse though, because it was surmounted by a large leather saddle (which was in turn surmounted by me). It was all almost entirely surrounded by mirrors, which made it possible for me to see myself from every angle, unfortunately. 'No body is perfect,' Mr Lakey, the cutter, had said very kindly (adding that it was not as difficult fitting the 'overweight' as fitting the very thin – 'At least you can see the problem,' he had said, and I had wholeheartedly agreed).

'Huntsman's' was not really the right class of establishment for such as me, I felt – for I was sure that most of their customers did not enter the portals on bare feet and sandals. It was clear, however, that the shorts were going to last for about as long as the pyramids, and it was delightful to see such care and craft. I am a perfectionist myself – it worries me that many people go through their whole lives with the wrong sort of potato-peeler. The shop had an atmosphere of dispassionate but kindly butlers, of old panelling taken for granted, of immense courtesy and money never mentioned: it was an atmosphere tangible enough to be cut into slices to make thin cucumber sandwiches, and I had commented on it to Colin Hammick, the managing director. 'It's built up over many years, not overnight,' he had said quietly. 'It's the story of Britain, in a way.'

Everything else about my costume rather let down the shorts: my sandals and underwear were exclusive to well-known chain stores: my T-shirt came from a cheap printer of T-shirts – though at least the slogan on it was in Latin. It read: 'Veni, Vidi, Vernon'. What casual passers-by would make of it, I could not imagine.

'If you say it quickly, it sounds like "Welly Wid De Whirr On", or "Funny Wid De Fur On", according to your pronunciation,' Jenny observed.

'I think it's too personal,' I replied. 'We could have made it "Veni, Vidi, Virgil".' (That year happened to be Virgil's 2000th anniversary, and had been generally acclaimed with the enthusiasm which the British public normally reserves for the publication by Her Majesty's Stationery Office of the Comptroller-General's Annual Report and Accounts.)

'Trouble: the casual passer-by would have read it as "Veni, Vidi, Virgin". Or "Weenie, Weedie, Wernon". Or possibly . . .'

'It is time to set off on this expedition,' I said. 'Will you go first, or shall I?'

'After you: it's five miles to Exeter, and I want to be sure you're going to make it.'

I left indignantly and rapidly. There was scarcely time for a quick smell of hay from the fields by the lofty motorway bridge, a garden or two of runner-beans and roses, red flowers bright upon both, before I was in the suburbs of Exeter – the lawns before the crematorium close-cropped as death itself, a corpse of a garden shaven for the last respects. There was a spire rising ahead among the lamp posts, and well before the little grey car had caught up, I had passed the lustreless brick of a set of institutional buildings from our own time and was into the mixture of centuries that survived on the outskirts when the Luftwaffe blitzed the heart of the city, one moonlit May night in 1942.

Despite that, Exeter still has great continuity. There is the warm cathedral and Rougemont Castle; the Guildhall – built above the villa of the Roman governor of Isca, as it was then, so that the well-padded seat of local government sat on the same spot for almost two thousand years. Exeter was always a city of shopkeepers, however, and its prime continuity in recent times has been commercial.

Before the war, Exeter was a medieval town with multiple stocks just beginning to appear in the High Street among the old family shops. A post-war shopping centre rose from their ashes without much architectural distinction that I have ever been able to detect: this was followed by an (inevitably) more modern shopping precinct behind the mighty Victorian columns of the Higher Market, which took some public outcry to preserve.

It is odd that a city which suffered so much destruction by somebody else should continue demolishing itself, but a half-timbered house with a musicians' gallery had just come down for a shoe shop not long before I arrived – people were still talking about it. Exeter has not suffered anything approaching the municipal vandalism of many another city: it keeps a pleasant, relaxed air among gentle hills, but if Devon is the crown of England (as Richard van Oppen described it to me), and Exeter the jewel of that crown, it is in danger of getting rather loose in its setting.

The thing that always worries me about development is that it has its heart in its wallet (usually), or its social conscience (occasionally), or anywhere but in the place where a heart ought to be. Much, much too often it makes people's lives colder when it ought to make them warmer. I couldn't see much warmth in the new parts of Exeter as I wandered round the shopping precinct, and when I met Bob White, out shopping with his wife Lily ('pure as the driven snow,' said Lily), I found I was not alone in my opinion.

'When I was a boy, what we had were small houses and small shops with people up over: now we've got big shops and no people up over,' he said. 'At six o'clock at night, there's nobody here: why don't they build the offices outside, and have people come back into town at night? It's the developers making their money; and some of it ought to go to the city when they've got their investment back. The people who run Exeter are the business people.' He pointed to what he called 'an invisible line' running down the road between the new shopping precinct with its chain stores and the old back streets with their little shops and boutiques: one was for himself and Lily, the other for the middle classes.

'At home, our side of the roundabout is council houses, the other is middle class: and the only way we'll get to mix is when they'll get my wife to clean up their house after they've had a ruckus. That's the way it's always bin, and always will be in Exeter: I reckon I'm as good as anyone, so I don't care.' (However, I thought he must.) 'We're feudal: we never got away from that. We've all got to eat, and sleep, and die: but it's us down here, and they up there.'

At that point, the manager of the shopping precinct came with a henchman to throw out the suspicious man who was actually *talking to people* and *using a tape recorder* on the *private ground* of his company.

'Some funny things happening at the moment, aren't there?' said the manager after he had become polite to the BBC. I agreed.

I went to see one of the Exeter sights that remains – there cannot be much profit to be had out of developing it and in any case you could not pull it down to demolish it, but would have to pull it up. Lucy Mackeith from the local museum took me down into the Exeter underground passages, which are the remains of the medieval water supply system. They are narrow so that the effect is like walking through an endless coffin. Noises and smells – aromas from a coffee shop in particular – filter down from the street in places where there is not much between you and ground level. I thought I smelt beer, but Lucy said that it was two centuries since the Salutation Inn used to drop its beer barrels down on a stone shelf to cool. I was surprised to see the passages so dry – they were airy, with a gravel floor, though otherwise they had most of the disadvantages of caves without any of the advantages. Lucy said that the water ran down the floor of the passages at first, but then they put in wooden pipes. I was just looking forward to seeing them when Lucy said they had rotted, and been replaced with lead.

'I can't show you those, either,' said Lucy: 'they were stolen thirty years ago.' We went back to her museum, past a trio of lively buskers, a young clarinet and guitar and a more elderly violin who said he used to work for the Min of Ag and Fish and Chips: you needed a greatcoat and a couple of pairs of socks in the winter, they said, but otherwise it was a good place to busk, for the police were friendly. He gave the place warmth, and so did the museum.

The Exeter Museum is another Albert Memorial, and like most of the other memorials is rather more interesting than Albert. Lucy's Education Room alone had a reasonantly-coloured picture of a dodo looking as if it had no idea where to go (which it didn't) keeping company with a wapiti, a Bhudda, a badger, a skeleton, and a prehistoric Dentist's Benevolent Society thing called a hesperornis, which resembled a man-eating duck. It had Albert beaten hollow on almost every possible ground – variety, antiquity, and teeth. Albert's only comeback was that, like the dodo, he was extinct: it was not enough.

The room was a children's ante-chamber to the rest of the museum, a toy-box of the mind. And the museum itself was a welcome jumble of inspiration – for in these days of highly professional exhibition design like the smart print of a Sunday supplement, the local museum is often a last refuge of a sane untidiness, since anything that happens to be of interest in the area, anything that happens to have been bequeathed is gathered together often almost as randomly as history itself.

'Do I detect moth?' I asked of a giraffe so tall that he seemed to be trying to get his head out of the skylight above him.

Lucy said that I didn't. 'But under the light, his spots faded so we had a taxidermist in with a paintbrush. We've only got one fake animal: the cave hyena from Kent's Cavern.'

We went to see the hyena, who was rather like a hearth-brush at the back, and looked as if he had not been a very agreeable person to know. Something human seems to get into stuffed animals in museums – the taxidermist stuffs them with more than stuffing, as if they were going into a children's book.

'I noticed that the Bank Vole appears extremely dismayed at having been caught and stuffed while clutching its nose with its feet,' I said to Lucy.

'Wouldn't you?' said Lucy. I remarked that the Short-tailed Vole looked deprived.

I was most taken by the Honiton hippos – an ordinary family from prehistoric suburbia out for the day and overtaken by disaster, as a card by their models concisely informed me:

1 Hippos drink from waterhole.
2 Wallowing in mud, infirm and very young hippos become stuck.
3 Animals attacked by hyenas.

'There they are indeed, yelling, and who can blame them?'
I said, and continued reading:

4 Soon only bones remain.
5 Bones engulfed by downward movement of hillside.
6 1965: Honiton bypass: bones preserved in peat.

There was a brown hippo-sized bone and a hippo-sized tooth in the case: it did not seem much, from the hippo point of view.

'Granny and the kids clobbered at one stroke by remorseless fate,' I observed to Lucy. 'The story of us all.'

'It is,' said Lucy.

I left in the direction of Honiton, via a cup of tea with my maternal aunt Marian, who lives nearby.

'You'll have to have a teabag,' said Aunt Marian, 'there's a spider in the teapot.'

'How long has it been there?' I asked, maintaining my freshly-awakened interest in zoology.

'Ooh, about a year,' said Aunt Marian.

I went out of Exeter past the prison, with its red-brick ziggurat of a chimney; through Heavitree, which gives its name to the brewery; up the hill, down the hill by the Roseland Dairy (Clotted Cream by Post): and it was the country at last, with a smell of blackcurrants from an over-grown market garden, and a clear, weedy stream at Clyst Honiton, watched over by two melancholy little boys short of a fishing rod.

There was nothing on the runway at Exeter Airport except a teaparty of gulls waiting for permission to take off, but the A30 whined and roared and howled with a country rush-hour (which always rush more in the country than in the town, though perhaps more briefly). It was only after Jack-in-the-Green that I suddenly became aware that the road was uncommonly straight. Surprised, I glanced behind with a wobble, to be almost smashed by a speeding car; and though I kept glancing, the succession of motor vehicles intent on asserting their supremacy was too fast for me to see back to where the straight had begun. The only welcome vehicle was a hay-wagon, rollicking on an over-loaded suspension, which blew fragrance in my face long after it was out of sight.

Then, with early evening, the moments of peace grew longer and the late sun shone more golden on the grass, with distant cows strung out in a line, freshly regimented from milking. At the Fairmile Inn, in front of which an unwieldy old man was spinning his cloth cap on his stick like a clown with plates at a circus for the delight of a pink and white little girl (who seemed just as pleased as if it had really been plates), I turned into utter quiet – for the big roads run like torrents through the West Country, but never flood until the traffic spreads at the sea. A lane ran past streamy, thistly fields and untidied-up farms and cottages to Cadhay Bridge, named after the fine, grey Tudor house nearby, and which is actually several bridges and a level crossing too: for the old gates with their great red circles are still in the hedge, twined with creepers as if they were turning to vegetation themselves, though there is not the ghost of a railway line beyond. The fish were after the fly – and something was after the fish, for a heron flapped heavily up from the grass by the river. To the sound of a wood-pigeon clearing its throat and undistinguish-able but suspect comments from a team of boys playing baseball with a strip of rough wood from a packing case, I came to Ottery St Mary.

I found it a quiet, civilised and pretty village – though it does have a rather rumbustious custom of rolling flaming tar barrels through the streets in fine disregard of the fire brigade every Fifth of November: and a local character who took an inflat-able, lifesize and very female doll to the carnival to the outrage of the more respectable villagers who reacted as Victorians are said to have done to piano legs, and made him dress it up. Ottery was also the birthplace of Coleridge – which is delight-ful to Romantic persons, though it would probably not have mattered very much if he had arranged to be born elsewhere; and was the setting for Thackeray's *Pendennis*: but the really remarkable thing about it is that among the many virtues of its Lodge restaurant was the ability to make the only, the *only* good green salad I was able to buy in a month of restaurants in the 610.4 miles between Topsham and Musselburgh. There I and Jenny stayed the night in rooms up a tiny, flowering alley with friendly people in the cottages opposite.

When I got up, there were gleams of sun picking out the petunias in the alley, slanting the grassy shadows of tomb-stones in the hillside churchyard, playing geometries with the planes of the church. Cycling off, dustbins were out early, waiting as stolid as peasants by the roadside; the wind tossed up the undersides of the hazel leaves; once, there was a rider on a piebald horse, flitting, clipping across the road ahead, a ghost of early morning.

I rode back to the A30, which still felt more like the A30 than anything with a Roman ancestry, and headed for Honiton over the river Otter – which is clear and grows mint and green weed, and to which Coleridge wrote one of the most vacuous sonnets that ever sought to romanticise childhood. At Fenny Bridges there was a field of impossibly long pigs and a little, romantic, ancient chapel, which Coleridge could have got really high on: unfortunately, when I passed it, it seemed to have been converted into a pigsty.

At Honiton, the bypass curved north and – having no wish to desecrate with my bicycle wheels the last resting place of whatever prehistoric hippos might still lie beneath it – I crossed under the dual-carriageway to the original course of the road, leading straight through the town. By a line of white, Gothic-windowed almshouses was a chapel in even worse repair than the pigsties, with one entire wall knocked out, the roof teetering on props, and the rest looking very much like one of those building jobs in which, whenever you take one stone out, three others fall down. The chapel was due for a new lease of eternal life, however, under Pastor Norman Gagg of the Assemblies of God, who was keeping the old bell inscribed with 'God will preserve his house', which seemed appropriate to a building which went up in the thirteenth century. He told Jenny that he put little store into bricks and mortar for he would not like people to come to church just because it was a beautiful building: it was just the only place available in Honiton, he said. The mason told me that he didn't know what religion was taking over, but there was going to be a new wooden altar for the old altar stone had been ordered out.

'It was lovely and smooth—a Beer stone, I expect.' (Beer, on the coast, is close to the start of the Fosse Way.) 'It was eight foot by two foot six – we had to saw it in half to get it out. They didn't want it.'

The builder who employed the mason was also building across the road – putting up a new wood ceiling in the sitting-room of his own neat bungalow – for as Derek Perryman told me, he was a compulsive worker with his hands, like his wife Pat who wove endless elaboration with her fingers, making lace.

Honiton lace was once an industry carried on far outside the boundaries of the town: two days earlier, Miss Holman had told me how in her childhood the wives of the Topsham fishermen would add to the family income by knitting Guernsey sweaters in the winter and in summer sitting at their doors with the lace-maker's cushion stuck with pins round which the bobbins would click and toss the thread to form the pattern – but so slowly. In the last century, children would start making lace at the age of five, and by twelve would be expected to earn enough to keep themselves, paid at the rate of one shilling for the amount of lace it would cover, half-a-dozen of them working with a single candle whose light was focused on to the work by a bottle of water before each one. Even in death, there was a considerable difference in prosperity between the lace-makers and the lace-dealers, as the tombs in Honiton churchyard testify.

The lace industry has declined twice: the first time it was rescued by Queen Adelaide who commissioned the finest lace dress in the world from Honiton; the second time by Pat Perryman. By 1970 only eight lace-makers were left: Pat went unwillingly to a class, for she was plump and shy. In three years she was the teacher, in twelve years she was teaching one hundred and thirty-five people, and planning a lecture trip to America.

'It's like a drug, you get hooked,' she told me. 'It's like driving a car – suddenly you can do it. The first little piece you can't believe you've made. This is a piece I did for the Jubilee, with honeysuckle on it, the Honiton flower: there is a saying that the name means Honey Town, but a lot of people don't agree. Derek and I took it to the Palace and went in the side door. We didn't meet anyone important, but we saw the Secretary and got the appropriate letter. It was nice to go inside, I felt proud. These are the Prince of Wales's feathers: the Mayor and I took those, but we didn't see anyone important then. This is the Mayor's jabot – three hundred hours' work by eighteen ladies: still, it wouldn't do for the Mayor of Honiton to walk along in machine-made lace would it?'

I confessed that I had grown to adulthood without ever suspecting the existence of a jabot. It appeared to be the only garment in the world more useless than a tie. Pat's largest project was making a new one for the Speaker of the House of Commons – it had on it a portcullis, the national emblems and an otter (for the River Otter). It was five hundred hours' work, and as a special mark of condescension by the authorities, was unpaid. Pat was perfectly happy about it: I was not happy for Pat but it is the way of the world that anyone who is helpless, simple, agreeable, or can be proved to enjoy what they are doing, can be exploited, and most likely will be.

'I only hope he takes care of it,' I said. 'What programme will he use for it on his washing machine?'

'I hope he does; and he'd better not,' replied Pat. For herself, she was making new designs. 'The traditional flower designs are no flower in particular but this is more positive – you can see this is a daffodil, an arum lily: that frog was traced out of the *Observer Book of Pond Life*, that's the Caterpillar from *Alice*: and in a shop today I saw a beautiful little china toadstool with a butterfly on it – no reason why you couldn't convert that into lace.'

'You could have gnomes, I suppose. But how fast can you do it?' I asked.

Pat took her pillow (barley stuffing is still the best) and clinked her bobbins like a dance of icicles for several minutes, at the end of which there was no discernible progress. 'I admire your patience,' I said. 'I expect they all say that?'

'Yes they do,' said Pat.

Honiton seemed to be a loyal sort of place generally. A removal van was parked in the High Street before an old bits and pieces shop: it had a venerable union jack hanging out of the back.

'Me boss is so patriotic, 'e is,' said the man in the van: 'honest.'

'Is he?' I asked, it being the year of Britain's first colonial war for some time.

'I'll be honest wiv yer: found it in a loft, stuck it out there for a laugh.'

We laughed.

'No mocking, mind,' said the man in the van. 'We are patriotic actually. Yeah.' I cycled off wondering whether I had found the source of British social stability in the capacity to hold at least two totally contradictory attitudes to the same subject at the same time; or whether it is that, since nobody ever says what they mean in conversation, and it is bad form to challenge them on it if they do, it makes it very unlikely in ordinary life that people will ever be offended on matters of principle, which they leave to parsons, politics and the press.

I panted up Honiton Hill which was guarded at the bottom by a little castellated turnpike house, the Copper Castle: the noise of the trunk road was gradually left behind in one of those patchwork views which looks as if it is trying to turn itself into a model of countryside: I began to look down on the birds flying in the vale.

Halfway up, I realised that the road I was on was curving round the hill, whereas on the top there was a line of trees going straight over the crest, obviously marking the original Roman road. Reaching the top, I went back along it to see what I had missed: but even then I had a feeling that what I was on was not the road itself, but a bit of modern metalling running alongside it for there was a kind of ditch between earthen banks, fringed with beech trees. There were ferns in its bed, hartstongue, blackberries, fallen leaves from the year before, holly bushes – even a solitary dog-rose. And a little wicket gate led up to some kind of modern fortress in a field littered with bales of hay, with a tall radio aerial above them. There is good line-of-sight from Honiton Hill: it is crowned by a stone tower motley in the best tradition of follies – Italianate in the main, with a Scottish staircase on the side.

'Built by a bishop, that's all I know,' a man in a Land-Rover told me. 'Probably wanted to get to heaven faster.'

'He was Welsh, you see,' said the next passer-by, a girl in a Jaguar. 'Bishop Coplestone of Llandaff, 18 -oh golly, 18-

something-or-other: he wanted to see the shores of Wales. It's so derelict now, you can't get to the top, so whether or not he did, we never really know.'

The skies were darkening, though it was still afternoon, and it was cold at the top of the hill: I had twenty-five miles to go. Distracted once by a Roman-looking rough track which turned out to lead only to a goat, I decided I would have to keep moving if I was going to arrive before dark, and kept going through a curving landscape of hill and dale, with trees frothing out of it like green fungi, until the open country above Axminster. A train was in the station as I passed: the handful of passengers and a portly railwayman in shiny waist-coat and shiny slicked hair wheeling his baggage cart with monumental deliberation were the only moving things I saw in the town, for the shops were shut, even the long, imperial façade of Frederick Baker, Ladies Wear, and nobody was buying from the old yellow-and-white van of the Hong Kong Hot Food Centre, Chard, parked next to the grey church.

With Axminster, I was off one Roman road and on to another, the Fosse Way, on its way up from Seaton on the long diagonal to the north-east, but I was so preoccupied with the sheer slog of getting up the one-in-ten above the dry leets of Weycroft Mill and with the unfortunate fact that the Tyther-leigh Arms was closed that I missed the old road forking off to the right, and had to go down into Chard – from which I came to Windwhistle Hill and – eventually – to Montacute.

II

DARK GODS
AND TRAVELLING LIGHT

TO BATH via GLASTONBURY

A quiet, grey Saturday was beginning outside my window, with the trees hazy in the hanger above the town, swifts loud and high in the sun above the church tower and a blackbird hopping below among the crumbling gravestones. The Readyveg van was dropping off poly-bags of pallid potatoes white as white. A fountain trickled, the church clock bonged, a distant cock crew and wood-pigeons answered.

There were local sausages for breakfast in a dining-room with a finely-carved fireplace, in which a pair of under-clad ebon ladies were constrained to cross their hands over their breasts, and consequently had to hold up the mantelpiece with their heads – a perpetual reminder that there are times in life when immodesty is the best policy. The other occupant of the dining-room, an Italian tourist, was drinking tea and thinking hard.

'Ah,' I said, 'in this country you won't find coffee like you get in Italy.' A momentary light flashed mournfully in the eyes of the Italian tourist, and he nodded. I finished breakfast, and went out into one of the most harmonious villages of England which was, from Montacute House downwards, as yellow as honey. Ham stone has a gentle colour, and weathers easily to gentle lines: and I later passed under Hamdon Hill, where it is found, the top bumpy with Roman and later quarrying and British camps from ancient times.

There is a quiet presence in Montacute, the place of the pointed hill, *Mons Acutus,* and it is the presence of the past: from the battles of the ancient British when all the land was unsafe, to the dignity and confidence of the Elizabethan family who made their estate there, to the humilities and poverties great and small forced upon generations of people who worked for them and were contented because they had no choice and because it was better to be so.

'The period house which the upper classes pride themselves on knowing how to preserve and appreciate; the shopping centre for the masses – it's even shiny, like caravans at a fair: the British class system is built into the walls,' said Jenny. 'It's in the stones.'

The British class system has been so pervasive throughout recent centuries at least that there has generally been no way to beat it except by joining it with money, in which case – after a suitable novitiate to ensure that self-indoctrination was thorough and that the money was not likely to run out – the parvenu became the gentleman. It was this relative flexibility and the British talents for hypocrisy and being sometimes reasonably decent to social inferiors that allowed our class system to survive where other, more rigid structures, broke. But most common people could not even aspire to be parvenus: they might emigrate to hardship and danger, break the law at home and be hanged, escape to a greater servitude in army or navy and be gloriously maimed: or they might, when they saw the chance, take refuge in obstinacy, dumb insolence and wilful ignorance. This technique, which is enshrined in industrial relations as the 'go-slow', is a particularly British response to a society which distributes its benefits, power and liberties from the top downwards while pretending not to do so, and with us is age-old.

I rode back towards the Fosse Way through the village of Stoke-sub-Hamdon – which is generally sub-Montacute – the estate village itself. Scarcely had I returned to London after my trip than I met at the house of a friend the descendant of generations of village doctors there (one of the good things about Britain is that it is still compact enough to allow such coincidences), and he showed me his ancestor's recollections of the Napoleonic Wars, and the Stoke-sub-Hamdon Volunteers. This gallant body of common people was formed by those anxious to be officers as well as gentlemen in 1798, and disgraced itself in Chard by refusing to quell the mob who – being unreasonably intense on the subject of starvation – were forcing the local bakers to sell loaves at 10d instead of the 20d to which the price had soared, and were exacting promises from farmers that, come harvest-time, their grain would be sold cheaply. Indeed, far from taking this excellent opportunity for target-practice on their own countrymen (even better, because the enemy was a) disorganised and b) unarmed), the Volunteers actually joined them, and had to endure long lectures from their betters about their lack of patriotism as a result. The Volunteers were finally disbanded in 1802 after the Peace of Amiens, got very drunk on cider at the final party, and fought each other with great courage and determination, that being the only action they saw.

Through Stoke-sub-Hamdon I came back to the main road again – the A303 which, on the first Saturday of the school holidays, was howling and whining more than ever. I stopped by a badger on the other side of the road to make sure that it was dead, and it was five minutes before I could cross over to it. There was not a mark on it – gassed or poisoned? I wondered – and I left it stiffening with a tattered crow picking further at its feathers in the branches of a dead tree above, waiting to come down for the eyes. As the cars snarled past me, I felt rather threatened. The wildlife flourishing so close to the crowded, narrow road was a living proof of how cut off from the world people are in cars. A magpie hopped along the side of the road – it would not budge for the traffic, but it flew away from me; when the sound of engines occasionally died into a brief lull, I could hear grasshoppers in the verges, happy, totally unthreatened; Bearley Brook was a mass of green textures with water-plants and rushes that no driver ever saw – I only did because at that point the main road bent to bypass Ilchester, and I had to get off and haul the bicycle and its panniers over a padlocked gate.

I was on something that had obviously been the main road until they built the bypass: the markings were faded and the road was blind, its cats-eyes ripped out and grass clumps growing in the sockets. The verges were haphazard, as if they could not nerve themselves to go wild: the sides were strewn with an archaeology of litter from holiday traffic that had passed years ago. An old woman in a blue overall was walking a small white dog on the end of a lead as if it were still a main road, though there was nothing to run it over – and, indeed, nowhere for it to run to.

'Oh yes, altered it,' said the old lady. 'Been done four or five year: oh yes, we used to have the traffic lined up y'ere at weekends . . . is the old Roman road, yes . . .'

I said what I had been thinking ever since I climbed the gate: 'It's very desolate in a mucky kind of way, isn't it? This crumbling apart, and the grass creeping in: you know, I think it must have been a bit like this fifteen hundred years ago, after the Romans left Britain.'

The old lady shied sharply away from one who was obviously either a dangerous romantic or a lunatic. 'Surprising what they do find when they start digging up,' said the old lady cautiously, with a look that indicated it was probably me. 'You go that way to Ilchester, and you can't make no mistake.'

The Fosse Way then left the ground, attaining Ilchester by means of a footbridge over a dual-carriageway. The houses in the town looked as if they realised that what had been their main road was now a cul-de-sac: the apparent population amounted to two tots in red trousers riding fairy-cycles round in circles.

'Daddy's got a big bike and sometimes *I* ride it,' said one tot, aggressively.

'Big as *yours*,' said the other tot, with an extreme truculence implying that both it and Daddy were in fact much bigger. I rode on before I was mugged.

Once through the town, the main road bent round and I was

back on the unloved and abandoned straight once more. This time, to make it more difficult for the pilgrim, a succession of locked metal gates had been erected across the tired old roadway, at each of which I had to strip the bicycle of its panniers, drop them over and then lift the bike over, holding it at arm's length and lowering it carefully, like some obscure and sadistic piece of army drill. I passed through a dump of pipes of every conceivable kind (marked 'No Admittance' as a firm administrative measure against passing pipe-stealers), over a fence, and up an embankment to four lanes of bypass. The luxuriant yellow grasses of the central reservation hid a deep ditch down the middle, but someone had erected a tiny bridge across, complete with rickety handrail, and I marked it down in my mind as the narrowest bit of the Fosse Way so far, being the width of two railway sleepers. The final stretch of gated track – which included a crossroads used recently enough to have a painted roundabout – had been turned into a rubbish dump, with weeds crawling up from the edges, bits of stone and broken glass scattered among strands of little white convolvulus, but a brave white line still marched down the middle to what looked like an imperial width – for it was not as thick as the white lines they have nowadays.

The road became the A37 to Bath and used once more, but I soon turned off it on to minor roads, heading for Glastonbury past four very clean pigs with a field all to themselves which caused them to actually scamper, as best they could. This was not very well, being pigs, but they tossed up their heads in front and their hooves behind – their tails were already pointing skywards – and grunted in a friendly and encouraging manner as if they wanted me to come and play. I did not, because I am uncertain how one plays with pigs. After the pretty, treed hamlet of Charlton Mackrell and the even smaller, though more pretentious Kingweston, which is mainly a spired church cheek by jowl with a big house, an enormous cricket ground and not a great deal else, I came out on the side of the down above the vale of Glastonbury.

It looked odd: I was seeing it in a kind of compressed perspective, like looking through a telephoto lens, with all its divisions – the trees, the hedgerows – crowding up together. I put it down to my being in a high enough position to be able to look across such low-lying country, but not being high enough to get any kind of vertical perspective. And there was Glastonbury Tor, which you may describe either as the perfect geological blancmange or the perfect geological breast, as it takes your fancy. I prefer the latter, since – having been a young man in that area – my fancy was taken that way on Glastonbury Tor, several times, and has been unable to find its way back to blancmange ever since.

I was nineteen when I came to Mendips, just out of school and examinations, fleeing from a headmaster who had decided that it would be good for me to play at being toughened-up, camping on the tops of mountains and living upon nettle soup: so I took my first job as a guide at Wookey Hole Caves, and discovered wages, beer and girls instead. It was not a decision I have ever regretted, and to this day ghosts of a rather tentative, earthbound character walk that countryside for me, led by a tall, raw-boned creature of what I once thought to be an astonishingly advanced, and now know to be a normal, sexuality, who demanded to be taken on the big wheel at Glastonbury fair. I am petrified by heights so I had to hide my face on her shoulder from about ten feet up to fifty feet down, which did me some good afterwards as evidence of devotion. I remember a curly blonde waitress who laughed, kindly, at a whole summer's worth of desperate romanticism; and a girl with long, dark hair who did not laugh, and remains the most memorable of them all, seriously happy in her purple dress in the bar of the George and Pilgrims.

But I cannot say that – unless we were all engaging in some kind of fertility ritual – the spiritual presence of Glastonbury made as much impact on us locals as it seems to have on some. The Dark Gods of Somerset left us alone. But you cannot pass the Tor without wondering, and there was a roadside sign 'The Isle of Avalon' which chimed in the imagination like those last cadences of the *Morte d'Arthur*, the most statuesque elegy ever written. After that sign, peaceful, pretty, hotch-potch Glastonbury was an anti-climax (although its church tower of golden stone is the essence of Somerset); and its neighbour, Street, which is all sheepskins, decidedly hum-drum. It is all in the mind, Glastonbury, or – some would say – the spirit.

On the outskirts of the town, I stopped for a drink at the Chalice Well which lies below the Tor in a place which was a yew-grove in the time of the Druids, and which has had a mild mysticism about it ever since: its iron colouring gave rise to the legend that the Grail lies at the bottom of the spring and, in more recent times, its waters achieved a slight local celebrity in the matter of boiling new potatoes. I found a garden made round it as a peaceful place, tended by a white-haired lady and a quietly-spoken young man who told me that he had not come to Glastonbury with the intention of looking after a holy spring.

'We have a little herb-tea enterprise, and were thinking of doing something in the whole-food business,' said the peace-fully-spoken young man, with modest commercialism.

The garden was delightful, that summer afternoon, with an air of ordinary beauty and casual tranquillity. There were roses, scented stocks, evening primrose: the stream-bed was bright rust-red where the water ran fast, and settled out to a murky brown in the pools – the single glass at the lion's head fountain, where I filled my water-bottle, was indelibly tinged with yellow. There was cypress, birch and yew, and on a lawn among the trees sat a single meditator, a young man beatific and cross-legged. I waited until he got up, and asked him how his meditation had gone. He said he had a fairly confusing job in a psychiatric hospital, so he had got into Zen Bhuddism and was trying to be at one with things.

'And were you?' I asked, at which he smiled a great big grin that twitched the ends of his flowing moustache.

'There was a really nice family of rabbits playing on the hill there: it was OK,' said the meditator.

As I came into the town on my bike, there were the first Beauty of Bath of the summer for sale at the gate of a little suburban house, and I stopped to buy a pound in honour of the Celtic paradise, the place of apples, which is what Avalon means – whereupon I instantly became a pilgrim, of a sort, like practically everyone else. Glastonbury has been a place of pilgrimage for centuries, with some of the pilgrims mystical, some religious, some hippy, some tourist: and some of the pilgrims staying on. It was described to me as a place that attracts every kind of guru, teacher, prophet, with the result that there are many feuds, jealousies, interests and factions at work along with the legends.

'I remember a learned historian saying to me once, "You

have only to tell some crazy story in Glastonbury, and in ten years' time it's an ancient Somerset legend",' was the comment of Geoffrey Ashe, writer and authority on Glastonbury, but nevertheless drawn there himself. We sat together on a stone in the ruins of the Abbey church, where one of the three perpetual choirs of Britain once sang – two thousand four hundred singers, a hundred for each hour of the day, never letting up on praising God. In its day, the Abbey, like most abbeys, was big business – and the more legends it could muster, the more respectable the abbey was, and therefore the bigger business. In the mystical tourist trade you cannot fail with the burial-place of King Arthur and Guinevere, with Weary-All hill in which Joseph of Arimathaea planted his staff to become the thorn that flowers in winter.

But the pilgrims themselves, and what followed after the legends are no less interesting: the Cromwellian soldier who chopped down the original thorn tree – fifteen hundred years old, they said – and who chopped his own leg off in the process, plainly the just retribution of a merciful God, and serve him right: Rutland Boughton, composer of 'The Immortal Hour', whose own hour was less so but who sought to establish Glastonbury as the British Bayreuth, descending upon the town in the 1920s with hordes of disgustingly artistic people of whom the men sometimes wore no hats and the women no stockings (which was quite shocking), while their leader himself behaved with what Geoffrey Ashe described as 'unbridled sexual licence', and would not elaborate.

Geoffrey Ashe himself lived in a house on the Tor which had belonged to a magician, Dion Fortune, who had been influenced by the more notorious Aleister Crowley. There had once been a magical duel, with spells cast from either side of the Tor, and he would like, he said, to believe that the Great Beast had been in his house.

'Once, I met a magician who knew Crowley,' I said. 'She told me that she was in the next room when he tried out his scheme for penetrating his current Scarlet Woman – which was what he called his girl friends – by climbing on top of the wardrobe and launching himself on to the bed. She said she heard the crash – it was either the wardrobe or the bed breaking, I forget which. As a story I've always had my doubts about it. Have you found any remnants of magic in your wardrobe or anywhere round the place?'

Geoffrey Ashe told me that people who had slept in the chalet in his garden reported having heard a woman's voice in the night saying 'hello, hello, hello', which he had later discovered to be the magician's scarcely original manner of calling up the spirit world. He could not vouch for it himself, but among those who had heard it had been his sons.

Curiously enough, the Glastonbury area had almost no ghost stories associated with it, he said: 'I looked it up, and found the only local ghost was at Butleigh Manor, and all that amounted to was a pair of trousers that walked down the drive by themselves.'

'Still, it would be worth seeing, wouldn't it?' I suggested. He agreed that it would.

A lady tourist came past under the remaining arch of the Abbey: 'Ooooooh,' she said, with her voice going up like a balloon. 'It's *hiiiiiigh*. I wonder why they built such *big places*.'

'I think the English are dreamers,' I said.

'I think they have a very great capacity for faith, though at the moment it's fragmented,' said Geoffrey Ashe. 'There is supposed to be a prophecy by the last of the Glastonbury monks, that the abbey will be rebuilt, and that "peace and plenty shall for a long time abound": I feel that in some way the place will be reborn. But dreams, whatever you call them, are very widespread, and it's just a question of what brings them out into the open. It's often said that the local people who've lived here all their lives care nothing at all for the legends: it's not true, though they are reserved because they've been so beset by cranks, wizards and gurus that they're not willing to open up. It's a curiously intense place: you're constantly being surprised by people who tell you that the Tor does mean something.'

'There's only one thing it can mean, as far as I can see,' I said, and he told me that the Navy pilots flying over it agreed, for they called it 'The Nipple'.

'It's possible that before Christianity the Tor was the centre for the worship of the Earth-Goddess, whose enemy was the Thunder-God. There are the ritual maze paths on the slopes, and the old church had a Mary dedication, which is unusual in England. We have quite an influential women's group here, and one of the feminists organised a ritual maze-threading at the May new moon to reclaim the Tor for the Goddess. They had all threaded it, and were sitting on the top, when there was the most colossal storm of thunder and lightning and hail. . .'

'The Thunder-God?'

'According to Robert Graves . . . so they all ran madly down the hill, and within a few months three of the four principal women in the group were pregnant, and they all produced daughters – so the Goddess was hitting back.'

As we spoke, the Dark Gods of Somerset sent a bat out of the Abbey ruins that lit momentarily upon my hand. I left before they sent something else.

Down the road I came upon a small rally of ancient agricultural machinery. There was no peace there because it was a constant chugging, whirring, thumping, putt-putting, ker-thunnnking and popping of little engines, but the little groups of broad-spoken men and their comfortable wives sitting round their brightly-painted darlings in the golden sun seemed to me not to need any extra contentment from meditation. The group I approached seemed to have a couple of licensed talkers who carried on the conversation in a series of wise-cracks, so that all everybody else had to do was to erupt with laughter at the end of every other line.

'I can get a better ride off the tractor than I can off the missus,' said the Chief Licensed Talker (who wore a bowler hat as a badge of office) at which all the missuses shrieked in delight.

'They don't get away from the women though, do they?' said one missus. 'If you can't beat 'em, join 'em. Bring the teapot and make a cup of tea, bring the dinner – better'n sitting in traffic jams.' She told me that the whole family was involved: what they all did in the winter evenings was to renovate tractor engines – herself, her husband, and the children painting, cleaning, rubbing up the brass – all equally keen, boys and girls alike (which I was glad to hear, though it contradicts my own experience of how little girls and little boys behave towards engines, even without benefit of social pre-conditioning).

We inspected a Powell two-and-a-half horsepower station-ary engine that chugged backwards and forwards on its car-riage as if it would have preferred not to be: it had been found in a pond and soaked in oil for months before it could be taken apart and refurbished.

'That's 1921 and still running,' said the owner proudly. 'You get a 1982 'un, next year he'll be gone and you won't be able to renovate 'un 'cos he's high-speed and made of alloy. That's five hundred revs maximum, that Powell, not two-and-a-half thousand: cast-iron, not alloy: and so simple, any labourer could operate 'un.'

'You've almost got to be a boffin to understand all the knobbs and buttons on a tractor nowadays, with all the European symbols on 'em,' said another enthusiast.

'Do we love our tractors? Course we do,' said the Chief Licensed Talker. 'Ask me wife – a fortnight ago, I tried to take ours to bed.' At which, everybody erupted again. I left Glastonbury with laughter in my ears and a sound like the collected works of Heath Robinson.

Back at the Fosse Way, I pedalled off briskly past some extremely proud white ducks at Sticklebridge Farm, where the road suddenly and very unusually takes a violent kink for no apparent reason round a large field of wheat. After I had come past the Traveller's Rest, which has a Roman legionary painted on its sign, the mystical influence of Glastonbury revived briefly when, at at a tiny stone house called Lea Bridge cottage with Gothic windows, a statue of the Egyptian dog-god Anubis stood guard on the garden wall over a dustbin.

It was a sunny, contented and airborne evening – contentment shining in the taut black back of an after-supper waist-coat heading for its greenhouse next to a roadside cottage: sun on a stubble field being conscientiously gleaned by a solitary crow, also black and shiny, and all the blacker for being alone in a spiky golden waste, while both sun and an infinite repose were reflected from a hot air balloon poised in lofty aimlessness above the fields. As I was trudging up Wraxall Hill, it was joined on the horizon by an airship, scarcely more silver than the haze around it and, shortly after, a buzzing little powered hang-glider took off from a field below the hill and crept around the sky above me like an infant lawnmower which had not yet learned the limitations of its status in life.

On the other side of the crest, the modern road curved round, while the original highway fell straight down the side of Pye Hill in a tiny lane from the middle of which a fox cub got up in a lazy disdain as I approached and then, deciding that I was coming faster than it thought, took to all four heels in a scamper. The fox went faster, I went faster – for the hill was so steep that I had no choice – and until it finally got out of the way by hopping through the hedge with a rude flick of its tail, I was in danger of becoming the first single-handed hunt to bring home a brush as a result of having run down the rest of the animal by bicycle. I barely had time to notice that a roadside house had lined its entire front wall with lines of pottery cats and dogs before I was careering straight out into the main road at the bottom. Fortunately, there was nothing coming and by the time I had made a weary way up to Cannard's Grave on the hill above Shepton Mallet, I had totally forgotten that the force of gravity did anything but make life harder going uphill.

I arrived at the hotel at Shepton, whose grounds appeared to be somewhat smaller than Windsor Great Park. A little red car outside was ferociously scribbled on with aerosol shaving cream, covered with caballistic signs and incantations as if it had once been the property of a demented wizard with a side-line as a barber; in the distance, what was instantly recognisable as a honeymoon couple walked together in perfect step across the grass. I was struck by it because my experience has always been that the requirements of romantic entwining and walking conflict with each other in the same way that one would not attempt to ride a tandem with an octopus. Had they been practising, I wondered? had they got married because their lower limbs were of such perfect ambulatory symmetry? or had the act of getting married synchronised them? If the latter, I thought, there should be an easy way of cutting down the cost of training the Brigade of Guards.

As I removed my computerised mileometer from the bike, the back came off, the batteries fell out, and with them all my carefully accumulated miles.

The hotel had once been the house of some person of taste: as well as the fine grounds, the rooms were beautifully proportioned. In more recent times, however, they had been decorated by a member of the House and Garden Anarchists' Society who loved flowers dearly. In the riot of textures in the dining-room, there was one strong pattern on the central carpet, and another on the carpet round that; there were Regency stripes on the upper part of the walls, quilting on the lower; velvet curtains. There were roses on the tables, flowers on the plates, flowers on the walls, with one particularly cornucopic painting of tulips, hydrangeas, asters, dahlias and marigolds occupying a vase together in defiance of season, the work of someone who had been to classes for many, many years.

People around us were being discriminating about their dinner. 'Oh, it's lovely, dear,' said one elderly lady, brought out for a treat. 'It's lovely and hot.'

Others were being discriminating about politics, and me. 'We don't have any inflation now Margaret's at the helm,' said a pig-faced man with slicked-back hair, in a metaphor possibly drawn from airships. 'Fellow hasn't been introduced to Gillette – haw.' He wrinkled his snout at the sweet trolley with great satisfaction.

Jenny and I turned to our salad: the dressing was loaded with sugar.

The Fosse Way stops being a main road just before the brow of the hill that overlooks Shepton Mallet from the south; passes Cannard's Grave, which I remember as the dourest of inns with the sign of a hanged man, but which the march of progress has changed into 'The Little Blackbirds', with fake bow windows all along its forbidding front; and descends to the Frome road as a lane. There, a toll-house was built square across it, with a roof that overhangs at the front to keep the weather off the turnpike keeper, and you have to detour round it down to the stream and pass the old cider factory, parts of which look as if they go back to the early, angry days of the Industrial Revolution, being over-storeyed stone barns with mean but mullioned windows. There are a number of such buildings along the river Sheppey, and fine houses in Shepton Mallet from the time before that, when the prosperity of the area was woven from wool, though more recently it owed much to the inspired invention of Babycham – that peculiarly English drink for the emergent female. It was in its great days when I was in Shepton – no self-respecting girl-friend would drink anything else since it was innocuous, dangerous, sophisticated, simple, innocent and wicked all at the same time, and in no way offensive to a palate which would have preferred pop. That factory is on the other side of Shepton: in the factory yard, pallets were stacked, there was a brand new bell on the wall, but the gates were shut and the chimneys smokeless; an old red boiler lay drunkenly at the entrance, with rust streaks showing where the cider had got at its rivets.

It is after the factory that the going begins to get difficult for a bicycle. From the stream, the path rises to the top of the Mendips: at first it is metalled, though the only signs of it ever being put to use are the splatterings of some long-passed cow. Then, all of a sudden, it changes.

'Like a river-bed,' said the couple out for a Sunday morning walk I met on their way down from the top as I was going up: 'lot of water been down here.'

I agreed, having been bumping the bike over six-inch boulders for the past several hundred yards, though in places even these had been washed away by winter rains to reveal great slabs of stone in the bed. It was very hot going up the hill, and the flies had come out to welcome me. When I stopped for breath by a fence-electrifier ticking away in the grass like a most unstrategically-placed time-bomb, my mileometer barely showed a mile, which was humiliating after the proud 95 it had borne before the batteries fell out. I began to hate it.

Though progress was slow, there were compensations: dog rose, ragged robin, cornflowers of intense blue, utter remoteness, with wood-pigeons flapping out of the branches of the tall bushes at either side within yards of my approach, smaller birds flitting up from the grass within a few feet. The day was blue and white and perfect – apart from the mileometer and a certain amount of difficulty with the tape recorder as a result of petals having fallen into its works, which is not something even the most professional of machines is designed to cope with.

Approaching the top, I could ride again, with my pedals swishing alternately through the grass: there were tumbledown drystone walls in the light Mendip stone, golden corn, a hayfield of motley greens and yellows and purple grass-flowers. And rubbish. It seemed especially perverse for someone to come all the way up here to dump an old red cart. And a doorless red and yellow motor-lorry from the 1930s, with a silver cockerel on its radiator, upright even in retirement beneath an alder tree. And a coach – bulging with the fashionable trim of yesteryear – *Duple*, a *Vega Major*.

It was difficult to believe, but it seemed that someone loved this congeries of junk: for an unhappy-looking mongrel with a dirty black-and-white coat was chained to the coach. It was shivering, either with illness or an excess of responsibility in actually being confronted with a passer-by to guard the coach from. It growled deep in its throat like a jammed electric motor which is burning out, but it submitted to having its head patted – though, for form's sake, it kept growling all the while. There was nobody around – indeed, no room for anybody in the coach, it was so full of bits and pieces. Oddly, beside it there was a freshly-painted oil-drum – bright red, with a fantastic pattern of stars, curves and zig-zags in green: it was not unlike the bridal car of the night before, except that here the effect was permanent, and done with some artistry. However, the wizard appeared to be out.

I carried on up the track but I had not gone a few hundred yards before I came upon a second coach called 'Station Road Coaches': just after it a tinkers' caravan explained everything, but the tinkers had gone off with the wizard. The trees ended and I came out into the sun on the top of the Mendips, with humpy fields and the rock showing through at the side of the track. Over a road there was barbed wire across the Fosse Way on the far side, and I could go no further: I dog-legged round the lanes towards Beacon Farm, and came upon the Fosse once more, a cart-track with bushes encroaching upon it and large stones in its bed which did not prevent a lot of it being a bog, even in the height of summer. This was all right if the bog was not too wide since I could stand on one edge and wheel the bike across the other: the danger was that if I and the bike had to lean too much, we would both go flop in the middle of the mud, as expressed in the equation:

If the base length of a triangle be in excess of the coefficient of friction of two bicycle wheels, the angle obtaining beneath two sandals be excessively acute, and the wearer of those sandals be sufficiently obtuse: then, SCHMUCK! (*Vernon's Theorem* from *Principia Mathemudica*)

The grass was dappled with the shade of the unkempt hedges that reached high above my head: there were trees down across the way. Soon there was hardly even a track, no more than a clearish sort of space between the bushes, but the way began to rise, and got drier. Still I could not cycle, but there was a fresh wind and I came up between a field of ripe wheat and a hayfield that was more yellow and mauve than green into a little plantation with a patch of delicious wild raspberries growing along its edge. I realised that I had come to Beacon Hill, a hill fort before the Romans came, and afterwards the crossroads of the Fosse Way with the west–east road from the lead mines of Hinton Charterhouse to Salisbury and Winchester.

I stopped and – between raspberries – listened to Beacon Hill: it was quiet as quiet, except for the flies and the wind in the leaves. It felt old. But then it had to be ancient since only an exceedingly primitive people would go over a hill like the one ahead when they could just as easily go round it: there was no path going off to the side that I could see. It was ridiculous, but there it was: I had no choice but to attack the ramparts of Beacon Hill fort with a bicycle. Not even the Roman legions had that sort of handicap, although the only defenders there to attack me were the flies.

Though the rampart was not particularly high in comparison with, say, Ben Nevis or Mount Fujyama, it was precipitous, and the earth crumbled from the surface of the path worn up it by people without bicycles, especially bicycles without heavy panniers.

In the first assault upon Beacon Hill, the attacking force took The Roman Philosopher by the nose, and pulled it up like a donkey: half-way up, The Roman Philosopher, resenting such treatment, fell over to one side. The panniers showed their independence by rolling to the bottom of the hill. More flies came out to watch.

In the second assault upon Beacon Hill, the siege party advanced upon hands and knees, and succeeded in establishing a base camp of two panniers on the top of the rampart.

In the third assault upon Beacon Hill, the army began by advancing backwards, with The Roman Philosopher held by the nose as before, but a detour was taken in the direction of a small tree growing out of the bank, in which first the attacking

force and then The Roman Philosopher roosted. Turning its
rearguard to its van, and its van to its rear, the attacking force
then pushed The Roman Philosopher from behind, with its
feet against the tree. After a while, *Vernon's Theorem* operating, the attacking force fell on its face, and completed the
onslaught on its stomach, grunting. The defenders were
routed, and a guard of honour in the shape of a small family of
toadstools (which were, of course, at eye level) welcomed the
victors to the top.

Beacon Hill was beech-crowned, fine-grassed, brown leaf-
and black leaf-mould strewn (in the wet patches you could see
that the blackness went right down for centuries) and was
vaguely concentric, full of mysterious ditches and bumps.
There was a flat stone placed at its centre, a gratifyingly
dramatic touch, though it was short on sacrificial bloodstains:
apparently the human sacrifice involved in scaling the ramparts was considered adequate. There was no path across it, so
I went round in its circles until I discovered wheel-marks
which led to a forest track and then came out on to a road: there
were no ramparts at all on this side of the fort, it seemed.

There was the Fosse Way again, a track across the road. A
little way down, there was a bus pulled in under the hedge,
with pots of tomatoes growing against the protection of its
front bumper, also an ancient but respected Morris lorry and a
little old Austin car. Two men, one cheerful and swarthy in a
sailor's pullover, the other fair-haired and pale-skinned, were
taking the Sunday afternoon outside the bus: a pretty, open-
faced woman was doing something domestic within, and two
middle-sized and two little girls in bathing suits were playing
nearby. There was a board advertising 'kittens' pinned to a
tree.

Having had enough of climbing ramparts, I stopped at the
group and asked whether the Fosse went straight through:
they said it did, though it had a bend in it, for the original
course had run diagonally across the field next to them. I was
rather surprised that they knew for they seemed to be travelling people – although stationary enough to have tomatoes. I
rode off along an easier track, with hay-making in the field
next door although, after the bend, the Fosse decided to share
its path with a spring so that I had to bump and skid downhill
with my legs out at the nearest I could get to right-angles to

stop them getting covered with mud. I came to tarmac once more and, after a slight kink at Oakhill, rejoined the Roman straight as a main road well before I caught sign of Downside Abbey at Stratton-on-the-Fosse, where Jenny and I were to meet for lunch in the King's Arms.

'We stop serving at 1.15,' said the barmaid, with great politeness and evident satisfaction.

Jenny and I sat under the flower-baskets outside the pub, eating peanuts.

'They didn't have gypsies' teeth,' I said, 'and they didn't speak like gypsies.'

'Let's go back and talk to them,' said Jenny. So I locked up the bike to the drainpipe of the King's Arms as a reprisal against the barmaid, and we took the car back to meet the travellers in their old motor-coach parked in the green verge of the Fosse Way: I have seldom been so glad of a second thought.

There were three grown-ups, four little girls and an indeterminate number of kittens, most of the time: and the general tendency was to belong to the Faa family. There was a very white, tall man who had come visiting from another caravan down the road in a pair of very revealing corduroy shorts which made his legs look like the inter-marriage of a pair of muscular bean sprouts. He was, he said, a Hogan and related to one of the two great tinker families of southern Ireland, though his father was a farmer and his mother a teacher – neither anxious to acknowledge the family connection. He was working in a local quarry, he said: he had been made redundant from the technical department of a large multinational company after many years, and was glad to be out of the rat-race and into open-air work for he had spent twelve years travelling up and down motorways to the tune of sixty thousand miles a year and had all but ruined his health permanently with the strain. The other visitor was Sarah, a grubby nymph in a shiny green bathing suit anxious to assert all the authority available to a four-year-old with the phrase 'I'm a little teapot' which she repeated so often that it seemed as if she must have had great success with it as a statement of philosophical position in the past.

It was not difficult to tell the visitors from the Faas. Jerry
Hogan might have been relaxed that sunny Sunday afternoon
but he was lined with old anxieties, whereas the Faas' faces had
something of the roundness and the glow of contented apples.
Sarah was charming and knew it, whereas Lorna Faa (who was
nearly twelve), Katie (ten) and Fanny Faa (just turned seven)
were charming, not as an end in itself, but as a by-product of
being already confident and peaceful people. The atmosphere
was so close that it felt like stepping into the family in a
children's book – before children's books were influenced by
social realism, that is; and the voices of the Faa children were
those of the days in which people thought it a good thing to be
well-spoken. Like any other story-book family, the Faas
welcomed us in, were friendly, and made tea on a little
gas-cooker. It being summer, their prize possession – an
antique stove enamelled with dog-roses that had come from
the Low Countries and had probably once stood in a barge or
showman's caravan – was not lit.

'You can bake cooking apples in it, and chickens, and
potatoes,' said Katie.

'Daddy cuts out the core and fills them with syrup,' said
Fanny.

The bus had been partitioned across the middle: the sleeping
quarters were at the back, and there was a living-room with
bench-seats centred round the antique stove. There had been
great Do-It-Yourself: every nook was no longer a nook, but a
cupboard. There was an imposing brown tea-kettle of battalion size in which to keep fresh water (the smaller girls lifted it
with difficulty, but lifted it all the same). And there was
grandmother's paraffin lamp that came out of a horse-drawn
wagon: its round brass base allowed it to swing and swivel in
its rolling home, and it had a cut-out fitted, so that if it tipped
too far it shut itself off like a ship's lamp.

The Faas came from Romany and showman families themselves, they said, but apart from that fitted into no pigeon-
holes. Mary Faa's family were Scottish: her grandmother did
palmistry in the fairgrounds and had a place on Bognor Pier
before she died. Mary herself had been brought up on the road.
Conrad Faa had early memories of travelling but the family
had moved into a house early on, before emigrating en bloc to
Australia.

'So I had schooling: mind you, being a Romany, my father never stayed in one place too long,' he said. 'I think we saw every county in England, and every state in Australia.'

As soon as he was an adult, and had the chance, he went back on the road again. He told me that the hardships of the life included hauling their own water in ten-gallon milk-churns weighing just over a hundred-weight when filled, and which had to be carted about on the principal family heirloom – a nineteen-thirties Morris Commercial lorry, never to be sold but to be cherished and coddled and have new bits made for it, for ever and ever, amen. He echoed what the tractor enthusiasts at Glastonbury had said to me: that you could go on and on repairing such a vehicle, while a newer model just wore out.

'That's a bit of old England that old lorry,' said Conrad, 'and as stubborn as old England as well – it's refusing to die.'

He was a good mechanic, engaged in building a twelve-volt generator to run the television set and charge the batteries for the bus lighting: he repaired and dealt in motor lawn-mowers and grass cutters for in the recession there was little money to be made out of scrap. They were finding it difficult to make ends meet: In the past, he had always been able to push himself to earn something to put by, but recently he had had to work eight to ten hours, five to seven days a week to do no more than keep going.

'I could be in a nice warm factory all day earning double for half the hours, but that's the price you pay for independence,' he told me. 'We never entertain money from the State because once you've taken that, you're trapped in one spot. Schools pin you down as well, if you can't educate the children yourselves, but the biggest problem is if one of us has to go into hospital. What we've done in the past is to get somewhere to stay on a farm or try to rent a piece of farmland for the period. Fortunately, we're all healthy. But if you do see a Romany in hospital, the place is crowded till he's out or buried. All of his family and the families who know him descend, whereas the unfortunate invalids and old people from the sedentary way of life in the bed next door hardly ever have a visitor.'

The family ties were evident. Conrad had lost both his

parents six months before: he still showed the hurt. That was the disadvantage of being close-knit, he said: it took a long time to get back to some semblance of normality.

'You can never get back to normal, can you?' asked Mary. 'You just learn to cope with it, but at least it's not like putting them in an old people's home, never going to visit them, and always talking bad of them after they struggled to bring you up.'

We all disliked the coldness and rigidity of society and its fondness for making rules. Control was the reason for bringing in gypsy sites, said Conrad. 'Once they've got all the travellers, gypsies and whatever else there is on the road in camps under lock and key, they're trapped – one lorry will block the entrance to a gypsy site. I think Council estates are built a bit along those lines as well – they seem to have one way in and one way out, almost as if the government was expecting a lot more riots and trouble in the future. I can feel for the people on those estates – they're really trapped.'

I suggested that he did not seem to be doing much travelling himself.

'We've been here a long time simply to finish converting the bus,' Conrad told me: 'The Council have been very good, but if they slapped a twenty-eight-day notice on us we'd have a hell of a job to move.'

'It would ruin the tomato crop,' I said.

'If the police have asked us to go in a certain time, we've always done our best – if possible. We get on well with the police, us having an honest reputation.'

'Somerset is one of the better counties, I think. If you go to Dorset it's another matter,' said Jerry.

Conrad went on: 'We've found that if we're on a green lane they usually leave us alone – their responsibility ends on the highway, I think. On the tarmac road which is the Queen's highway, you wouldn't stop for more than a week, if that. You can't blame the police – it's the law. But these old Roman roads, green lanes and droves are the only places you can stop without being moved on very quickly.'

Conrad certainly had reason to fear a twenty-eight-day notice: apart from the tomatoes and the semi-converted bus, which so far travelled occasionally into Glastonbury to pick up petrol and the shopping, there were two caravans – the one the family used to live in and which was due to be broken up, and an old trailer, which the children said was to keep all the muddles in.

'We've had the old caravan quite a long while now, so it's done its job,' said Lorna in her gymkhana voice. 'The sides are bowing: this one's fun, 'cos it's high off the ground: but Sarah, she has trouble getting up the stairs.'

'We're just getting it done *up*,' said Fanny, confused by the preposition.

There was a knocking on the door of the caravan. A middle-class couple had seen the notice on the tree and stopped to ask about a kitten. They were sporting a slight air of bravado at a) buying anything on impulse, and b) approaching anyone so eccentric as to live in the wrong sort of dwelling. We all went outside to demonstrate the selection, but the kittens were determined to keep their number indeterminate. They were playing by the wheels, and as soon as one was grabbed, another wriggled out from underneath the coach. The children were sent to scout the nearby hedges, on behalf of 'the lady', as the middle-class woman was called as a matter of careful routine.

'Perhaps the old entourage is a bit larger than it might be,' admitted Conrad, surveying the car, the lorry, the two trailers, the tomatoes, and a hedgeful of rusty bicycles beside his workshop (the boot of the bus) which was full of generator parts and old lawn-mower carburettors.

'I have a fine collection of old gaspipes myself,' I said. 'You never know when they might come in useful. And five bicycles.'

'There's three there: that's a lady's Elswick, that old nineteen-thirties one – an old lady's, and old gent's Hercules – I ride that one myself. Pre the diamond safety-frame era, the Elswick – look at the top of the forks.'

It was certainly good solid stuff. The Elswick, the Rudge and the Hercules lay in harmony in the hedge, united by a convolvulus tendril which curled round their spokes. Conrad told me that he likes to keep the place as tidy as possible, even when processing scrap because he had no wish to live in a sty. It was very different from the chaos I had seen on the other side of Beacon Hill, I said. He told me that the coach I had seen was occupied by a couple of ex-art college students and that the dog I had patted on the head had a reputation for extreme ferocity, though he himself thought it just a reputation. It explained all the caballistic symbols on the old oil-drums I had seen.

Jerry said, 'When you travel along this Roman road, practically everyone on it is some sort of character: they're not normal people, like.'

I remarked that a caravan – or even a bus – must be cramped and uncomfortable.

'What people don't appreciate is that the old horse and wagon was hardly ever lived in – it was a mobile bedroom while you lived outside. That's why Romanies of those days were that nut-brown colour because they were out in whatever weather: sometimes they'd throw up a bit of a tarpaulin shelter open in the ends where you could keep an open fire going and cook in the rain but they still virtually lived outside,' said Conrad.

'What are the pleasures of the life?' I asked.

'Freedom first,' said Mary: and Conrad added, 'Total awareness. You feel the changes instantly: the weather, the seasons, buds in the hedgerows coming out.'

Mary said, 'You're living life as it should be lived – there's nothing false about it at all, it's just natural. Hard work, but it doesn't kill anybody, does it, hard work?'

Nor did living in a caravan turn people into villains, said Conrad. 'There's a lot of superstition talked about Romanies. They're supposed to be thieves, drag children off with them but I find that today's murderers and child-molesters are all from houses. The Yorkshire Ripper was house-bred for generations, I shouldn't wonder.'

I stared round, Jerry seemed to have disappeared. I looked to the ground, and there were two long white legs sticking out from under the bus with kittens playing round them.

'What's your friend doing under there?'

'Trying to catch kittens,' said a muffled voice. There was a pause, a grunt, and a slight sound of scrabbling. 'You'll have to make do with this one,' said the voice from under the bus, a shade brusquely.

'You're lucky to get anybody to take them,' I said.

'Ah,' said Conrad, 'we breed beautiful kittens up here, sir. My wife is very fussy about animals and wouldn't dream of dumping or drowning them. It's all part of the nomad instinct.'

He told me that animals were not only an economic resource to the gypsy but part of the family: it was an article of Romany pride that the children would be safe with the 'vanner' – the big horse that pulled the living van – walking under his belly and between his legs without being trodden on, or kicked or bitten.

'It might look cruel to an outsider walking past to see a dog chained up to a caravan chassis, or living in a forty-five gallon drum,' said Conrad, 'but that animal is regularly exercised and has a much happier and more content life than some pampered creature that's overweight and being killed by kindness.' I felt a shade guilty as he said it, as if he was talking about me. 'A Romany would never allow a dog in his living quarters – not because the dog is germ-ridden, but just because he wouldn't. The favourite Romany animal is the lurcher who brings back food for his master. A well-trained lurcher is a beautiful thing to watch – it will actually drop a hare or rabbit at its master's feet. It wouldn't dream of sampling any of it himself – though of course he does get quite a bit of it.'

At our feet, a pair of legs wriggled, the kittens scattered back under the coach, and Jerry emerged, holding up a squirming animal in triumph. Both the triumph and the whiteness of the legs were slightly diminished by ambient mud. Impressed, the middle-class couple accepted the kitten immediately.

'They took Sarah's one, thank goodness,' said Katie to Lorna, with practical satisfaction.

There might be more bicycles and kittens in the hedgerows, but Conrad told me that whole species of butterflies were disappearing from them. There were a lot of Red Admirals about, he said, but very little else: even the Cabbage White had hardly been seen that year in that part of the country. Jerry said there were butterflies at Milton Hill, near his quarry at Wells, and a host of different wild plants. 'But go anywhere else,' he added, 'and nature has been farmed out of existence with pesticides. Nowadays, people look on animals as a piece of technology, pumping them full of antibiotics. It's dreadful. And as for gassing the badgers, when you don't know how many are going to be trapped down there in agony . . .!'

'Equal to the gas-chambers of Hitler and his boys,' said Conrad.

Jerry agreed: 'People seem to judge the horror of something by the size of it sometimes. If it's an ant, you can pour a kettle of boiling water over it with equanimity: if it's a horse – as in the IRA bombing raid in London – people talk about their deaths more than the actual people being killed. But the size of something has no bearing on its value in the eyes of whatever you like to call the being up there – He must look on that just the same as we are.'

Jerry brought out his camera, a massive ancient Polaroid and took a picture of us all so that afternoon would go down to posterity but the film had been in the camera too long and refused to develop. The coach was scattered with photographs as one of its few concessions to permanence: Mary said that she had had none as a child, and didn't want her children to miss out. So I fetched my camera, and was required to take innumerable snaps of the smaller girls being thrown up in the air by their father.

At other times, the children were flitting about the countryside like sprites: one moment you were talking to them, the next they were behind a tree, the next jumping over a gate, the next chatting to you again.

Back at the bus, we spoke of books. Jerry admired H. G. Wells' *Outline of History*: Conrad said he was an avid reader and liked anything from Biggles onwards.

'I think any book has a message or portent in it, however you interpret it. I like Neville Shute. I'm a bit of a fan of pre-war Britain, when things were so much simpler – there was a code laid out for you and you followed that (or didn't at your peril). A better time to live than now I would have thought. I've got a tremendous respect for Ezra Pound. D. H. Lawrence I like, and Louis McNiece – but Dylan Thomas says everything for me.'

His recollection of Romany tales or poems was hazy. From his childhood he recalled:

> *Eeny meeny mackeracker,*
> *Rare eye dominacker.*
> *Chickeracker lollipopper,*
> *Rum pum poo.*

Mary remembered:

> *Mary went to poff the grise,*
> *All among the diddicoys:*
> *Up jumped the muskro*
> *To lay on Mandy's grise.*

It all sounded extremely immodest behaviour but appeared to be equally incomprehensible to everybody.

'It's a different form of language,' said Lorna authoritatively: 'like "shooshi" is a rabbit and "itchywotchy" is a hedgehog. Do you want a kitten?'

'It would be nice,' said Jenny hypocritically, 'but I haven't got room in the car,'

Katie said, 'Sometimes if you have a big sort of gathering of gypsies, you can make a big fire and sing round it.'

'What do you sing?'

' "The Rover", "My Bonny": my mum knows a lot of songs, like "John Riley" and the one we sing when we go to Glastonbury Hill.'

'That's at Easter,' said Katie, 'and we sing it as we're rolling the eggs down the hill.' It was amazing: here was a piece of folklore, perhaps sung at fertility rituals over thousands of years, to be heard from the mouths of babes and sucklings in a country lane. Jenny lined up the babes and sucklings: readied the tape recorder: they opened their mouths, they sang: 'You are my sunshine . . .'

'That's a made-up song,' said Jenny, rather severely.

'You sing it when the sun rises . . .'

'Yes, through the clouds . . .'

' 'Cos you need to get up at five o'clock . . .'

'Through the door at Glastonbury Tor . . .'

'We see the sunrise through the little door, and it's really nice. I think Glastonbury Tor is one of my favourite places to visit, such a big high hill to climb up. You really think it's something that you've conquered, to climb up Glastonbury hill. For about two weeks after you keep telling your friends.'

'People believe that witches live in the Tor . . .' said Lorna doubtfully.

'Spirits,' said Katie. 'But I just think it's a nice place.'

Mary brought out her guitar and sang. She had a beautiful clear voice that would have impressed on a concert platform, let alone on a bus by the side of a rutty lane. Then we all sang. Her songs were gypsy, Jerry's Irish, the children's Welsh, and mine English. Sarah contributed a wail, having just found out that her kitten had gone.

In the cramped quarters of the old bus, the afternoon had an openness I never find in other people's houses. It was as if a small patch of the world had suddenly broken out in an infectious peacefulness and sanity.

'We're quite happy with the simple truths, I think,' said Conrad. 'We're not trying to pretend to be anything other than what we are. Most people have an ambition of some sort – ours is just to keep travelling and remain free. I want to take this bus across the Channel, and travel down to the travellers' festival in the Camargue and meet all the other Romanies. You can get a twelve-month visitor's passport now: it used to be only three months and that was too short.' I wondered why he needed a visitor's passport until I suddenly realised that it was all part of the freedom of having your name in the records as little as possible.

'Over the hills and Faa away,' I said.

We said goodbye and I left, thinking that Britain would be a poorer country when the last traveller was cleared from the green lanes and the verges on to a neatly regulated official site, where he could be made to fill in the proper forms.

Having passed most of the afternoon in talk of music, books, plants and freedom with the Travellers (which is how I always think of them – as a group like the Wombles, or Roo's family), the rest continued in a similar vein. Jenny and I drove to Kilmersdon where they were ringing the bells of the yellow-towered church, and among lawns and herbs was the house of a gardener. This gardener would never need to repair lawnmowers for a living. He had room on his shelves for a great number of books. He could afford to put contemporary art on his walls and his garden was much more than a few pots of tomatoes sitting on the front bumper of a bus, but he and the Travellers talked a similar language of civilisation – and it was not a tongue I found commonly spoken on my trip.

Gordon Taylor was a director of the Herb Society: on the sunny slope behind his house, which was secluded beyond the edge of the village, he had four thousand herb plants: lovage for the casserole, evening primrose for medicine, lemon balm for summer drinks, green and bronze fennel ('both excellent for slimming,' he said, pointing the remark in my direction), angelica for confectionery, grey furry marshmallow, sorrell for soup, mint for tea and virility, as the Arabs think – which is ridiculous of course, but I nibbled a leaf, just in case, and wondered whether mint sauce preserved the effect; purple lavender and pink, salad burnet, golden thyme which is not too fussy about growing in heavy soils, herbo barono, used in Elizabethan times to flavour barons of beef, a run of lad's love along the hedge, artemesias, sage – narrow-leaved for cooking, broad-leaved for appearance.

'And another thing about fennel . . .' said Gordon Taylor, 'the Spaniards keep a little bottle of liquid concentrate of the seeds in the fridge as being good for the eyes. And there are very few spectacles sold in Spain.'

'Full of people who can't afford them,' I speculated to myself.

The herbs that so fascinate the gardening middle-classes have acquired a scent of romance from the associations of the cottage gardens and the gardens of great houses in which they have been grown for so many centuries. They occupy an intermediate status between vegetables and flowers: it is difficult to feel romantic at the thought of a fourteenth-century cabbage, but herbs are a symbol of power and mystery in literature from the nursery fairytale to *A Midsummer Night's Dream*. But, Gordon Taylor said, everyone from ordinary folk to duchesses had been to see his herb garden before publishing took up so much of his time. The duchesses he referred to as 'titled critturs', for he was a Californian 'time-warped' to this country twenty years since, he told me.

It was difficult to draw out his opinion of Britain, for he was diffident about criticising his adopted country. Under pursuasion, he said that when he came from California, he found the British to be 'sustained, decent, and incredibly polite'. Maybe the flip side of the servility was hypocrisy, which he admitted could be absolutely staggering in Britain, and he found too much of a 'mañana, mañana attitude' he said.

'It's not that I think England is a slightly dozy and dreamy place, but in the early sixties when I first lived here, it was high journalism to say that there was some crumbling of the highly-structured class system – as shown by various working-class actors making a break-through on stage and film. But I hear class in people's voices all the time, and when a supposedly informed politician or sociologist says the class system has broken down, I know that it ain't.'

At least he, as an outsider, could not be typed by his accent, I suggested. He agreed: it had made him a free agent.

A theatre enthusiast himself, he was aghast at Britain's neglect of such a traditional and profitable industry (in terms of tourism). The only reason he could see for the poverty of government support was that theatre was intellectual, intelligent and artistic – and therefore anathema to many Britons: he found education impoverished and under-regarded generally, he said. Britain was lacking in terms of giving more people a chance to learn more and have more, he added.

I left him in what in every sense was an oasis of taste: the long stone house with the bells of Kilmersdon ringing over it, books and pictures within: outside, the sun was shining through the leaves of his herbs, and a silver-tabby cat was stretched out on the path in the warm.

When we got back to the King's Arms, the bicycle was still locked to the drainpipe, and was soaking wet: I could not work out whether it was the result of the flowers having been watered, or a successful reprisal to my reprisal on the part of the King's Arms. Jenny drove to Bath: but I pedalled off with a damp behind.

The next town, Radstock, was a grey town, though since it sits on top of a coalfield, the least it could have done would be to make an effort towards black occasionally. The old terraces were grey, the new housing estates, the Railway pub, A. S. P. L. Higgins General Stores and Westfield Methodist Church were all grey: the only splashes of independent colour were a car wash twirling its bright frills like a ballerina, and a hairy man dressed from head to toe in brilliant red, trying to hitch a lift in company with a large number of multi-coloured bags and a golden retriever which, as I passed, he was kissing on the nose.

Being late, I did not try to trace the original road which the map showed as running at least partway through the town as a footpath, and twisted up the hill above a factory chimney which said it was 'To Let' in a large notice on the side: it made me sad to think of all the people in the world desperate to rent factory chimneys. Here I had discovered their opportunity, but either they were in the wrong place, or the chimney was in the wrong place, or I was in the wrong place: it seemed insoluble.

Past Peasedown St John post-Roman generations had bent the road in and out of the valley of Cam Brook, but I plunged straight downhill on a footpath: screened from the new road by the hedges, it felt quite remote with its ferns and nut-trees until, half-way down, I came without warning to an encampment – several caravans and a well-established garden with rose-bushes, slap in the middle of the Fosse. A strangely thin-faced man, his chin pointed like the Queen of Hearts (if the Queen of Hearts had suffered from anorexia), was sawing something on a little table with the ineffectual precision of the elderly: his big bush-baby eyes made him look Martian. A severe-looking woman, grey-haired and grey-faced, was at the doorway of the nearest caravan to see me past, but the dogs came out at me – an old black mongrel with few teeth left, but what there were looking to be sharp, and with a mad roll in its eye, lurched up, snarling, and an extremely small creature with a curly tail came and chattered angrily at my shins. I wished the Martian-like man good evening, to which he replied in Martian. I said that he had a couple of good house-dogs there, whereupon the Martian-like man said yes, they were all right, and without malice knocked the little one over the head with his piece of timber to prove it. The path broadened, and I came to the bottom of the hill behind a hay-waggon, so large it filled the lane entirely, leaving wisps of grass on the trees above and the hedges at either side.

Winding up the other side above Dunkerton, it was difficult to connect the peaceful valley below me with anything but the pastoral. There had been pits – and they were gone; a railway – and that was gone; a canal – that, they had never even finished building. What I saw, in the soft gilding of the evening sun, was a very little farm far down in the hollow, the farmer standing at his garden gate with a brown dog and two sheepdogs playing round him – I could see the white on the tips of their tails frisking backwards and forwards in their enthusiasm – and the bent figure of an old woman making her way into the house from the scrubby orchard like an animated mezzotint. In between cars, tricklings of a stream came up from the valley, whose hillside pastures were eaten away in brown splodges by the stumblings and scamperings of generations of cows.

At the top of the hill, I turned back along the Roman track to see what I had missed, and came upon a wheezy man tending a bonfire beneath his apple trees.

'What they do call Four Winds up y'ere,' said the wheezy man, who was tanned, with peaceful blue country eyes: 'bloody wind do blow all round. But, as I say, in the winter it's cold, in the summer yer can breathe, can't yer? I went down to Bournemouth last year – go up and down, the hills down there – and I had a job to breathe, dirty stinkin' diesel. That's the humdrum of the city, ain't it? Going to Bath, are you now?'

'Edinburgh.' The bonfire flamed, cracked its timbers, and sent clouds of smoke up into the apple boughs.

'Bloody hell, rather you than me. What's yer got on the side, then?' I showed him my digital mileometer. 'I seen somethin' on tele, I don't 'spect you've heard of: new cash register thing at Tescos, passes through this computer and comes out with the name of the goods yer bought, the price and all, and it's like bloody lightning – marvellous, ain't it? I seen that tonight and I thought, pretty soon yer won't need bikes, you'll be just wobbling your hands before long and yer'll be going along, won't yer?'

I retraced my steps, and continued my journey along a farm track, whose tall thorn hedges had grown over into a tunnel at the top, so that when the birds came out of them, they flew away before me like bats in a cave passage. I bumped over exposed tree-roots past Fosse Farm, with its stones turned almost red in the evening light and voices floating from it across the fields, past a cottage that looked as if it had been derelict since this part of the road declined into a track, but there was an old ladder still at rest against a tree in its orchard. The track became a path, then a prolonged bed of nettles: I slashed my way through to the top of the hill, much stung.

I arrived at Bath with the wind tickling up my nettle-rash, and stopped to take a photograph of The Bear, which has a full-size polar bear for a sign, in the presence of an old man in a stiff white collar, who spoke like a pair of bellows – in puffs.

'Turns round when 'e 'ears the church bells ring,' said the old man, at first pant. 'Yes 'e does, mind,' (pant): 'when 'e 'ears 'em.' He went on his way much satisfied.

'It's an extremely fine animal,' I remarked to another by-stander in the pub doorway.

'Oh yes,' said the bystander, with great confidence: 'fibre-glass.'

I rode on in the dusk to the hotel beside the weir at Batheaston. One of Britain's few privately-owned toll bridges crosses the river here. Its 'secretary-cum-banker-cum-general dogsbody' – which is how its custodian described himself to me – was collecting the new pence at the front porch of a little Victorian cottage beneath a sign-board in gothic lettering advertising the going rate in old pence for: horses walking; carts drawn by one, two, three and four horses; cycles, and cycles for two; wheel-barrows, perambulators and motor-cycles; persons riding on horse-back, cattle (per head), sheep and pigs (per score); donkey and cart, wheel-chair drawn by hand, and wheel-chair drawn by donkey.

'And persons walking weekly,' I said to the custodian in wonderment.

'They didn't miss much in the old days,' said the custodian.

'You won't be getting the animals nowadays,' I suggested.

'Oh yes: in the cars they are,' said the custodian.

'I don't particularly mind motorists myself,' I said.

'No, animals in the cars – all sorts,' said the custodian. 'Dogs, cats, parrots, goats, monkeys – you name it, it's in them. We've even had a llama walk across here.'

'A what?'

'A llama. There was two chaps going down to the West Country walking: they pitched tent in the field over there for the night and came back this way in the morning with their packs on the llama.'

'Extraordinary,' I said, and made my way into the hotel, wondering how you worked out an equitable toll on a llama.

Later, Jenny and I sat on the terrace above the river. Every now and again an engine would purr up the toll bridge, stop, and purr off again. The rush of the weir grew softer in the evening: you could almost hear the fish rising in the pool. A half-moon leaned elegantly to one side as if it were auditioning for the part of a Madonna in a fresco, and reflected in bright freckles in the moving water below the weir, where two swans gleamed duskily and left a twin wake of light. For a while there was still colour in the marigolds by the lawns: mist blued the far hills. Then the damp of dew about to fall chilled the air, the sky went mauve and the quiet stone arches of the old bridge went mauve to match.

'If you don't want the light on out there, sir, I'll turn it off,' suggested the barman helpfully. 'It's more romantic.'

'I suppose he's entitled to be male chauvinist,' said Jenny. 'I've done everything Andy Capp's wife does today: I bashed the car, and I did the washing.'

'You needn't have done the washing.'

'It was penance. I did it very well: I was a good martyr.'

Mist began to rise from the river, a wraith-version of the bonfire smoke from the garden of a house beyond the trees. The fire flickered weakly in the eaves, the moon grew luminous, there was the momentary waterfall of the sound of a late train across the valley. In the field opposite, the grass got deeper in the dusk.

III

BEYOND THE BUN

TO CIRENCESTER via GRITTLETON

To me, Bath is the town in which an elderly maiden aunt sat very stiff and straight in a big Regency house on Richmond Hill – and nobody ever talked of a possibly scandalous and certainly unfruitful something-or-other that might have occurred with some gentleman of the Indian Army two generations before, beneath the punkahs of the British Raj. Like the rest of my paternal aunts, she was a tough, starchy old creature (there being a great difference between the two sides of my family, only my mother's relatives being prone to allow spiders to occupy their teapots out of sheer compassion). When workmen came to the Regency house, my paternal aunt would always refuse the use of her kitchen for them to make tea with their own provisions, on the grounds that they were impertinent to ask: she kept her good head for stocks and shares, died symbolically golden when she was seventy, though I often used to see the old, filmy eyes peering out as from a mist, looking for some communication not concerned with money and social standing that she had missed somewhere along the way. From the fine windows of the Regency house, over the lawn with the cedar and the medlar tree, I used to see the lights of Bath twinkle like spots of synthetic gold down in the valleys, over the hills.

Returning to Bath for the first time for many years, I met no one who is not normally to be found there, viz: immigrants and visitors. It may be that Bath has its own population, but it is not easy to discover: it has been keeping away from more temporary folk for about two thousand years now, and has grown very good at it. If there is such a native society, I imagine it headed by a reincarnation of Sul Minerva, the romanized Celtic deity who bears much the same relationship to the waters of Bath as Britannia does to the oceans. I see her as leading a coterie of ferocious old ladies resembling my aunt in a procession of Morris Minors – of which there are many in Bath because of the presence of a well-known Morris Thousand restoration centre in the city. There is nothing like the Morris Thousand for demonstrating the extremity of British engineering probity and uprightness: it has most of the spiritual qualities of a sedan chair apart from the presence of four wheels and an internal combustion engine: and the fact that the front two wheels have been known to rust off at awkward moments only adds to the resemblance.

Whatever really enduring population there is in Bath, however, is probably the servant class who may be assumed to have been around heating hypercausts and carrying sedan chairs since the very first Celtic chieftain dabbled his toes in the warm mud and decided that hot running water was something special. Nowadays, the servant class has become the service industry, and serve what Ron Deamer, an enthusiastic city guide, described to me as 'the new élite' – the tourist off the coach for an hour between Stonehenge and Stratford-upon-Avon.

'Every pillow-case that's slept on has to be laundered,' he

said. 'Every soggy tomato sandwich has to be cut. That is, every tomato sandwich.'

I thought that it was surprising how little things had changed in two thousand years. Today the city has the Ministry of Defence Navy Dept: then it had Roman soldiers on furlough. The guide waxed lyrical on the psychological effect of the warm springs on people longing for their sunny homeland.

'The local Celts lived on the hill tops, but the Romans came here and found treasure.'

'Hot water.'

'Yes. They created a leisure centre in the style of Italy.'

'You mean a bath,' I suggested.

'Exactly. In which they screamed with delight as the strigil scraped across their back, or the hairs were plucked from under their arms.'

'I never really thought of the Romans as being such an out-going sort of people,' I said. 'Alas, that in these days of detergents, no one gets dirty enough to have their skin attacked with a wooden scraper to any noticeable effect.'

I admired his ingenuity in finding anything at all interesting to say about the Roman mania for bathing: for me, when you know that the Romans built public baths, you know enough. Similarly, Beau Nash and his beau monde are a yawn – only good for the encouragement of fine architecture and as furniture for the duller chapters of novels: it is significant that when Dickens sent Mr Pickwick to Bath, he made the most interesting milieu not Society but Mr Weller in the company of servants.

It is the building and maintaining of Bath that is interesting – not the people who come there: centuries of maintainers great and small, from the Morris Thousand Centre to Ralph Allen – the original of the beneficent Squire Allworthy in Fielding's *Tom Jones* – who used his franchise as post-master to such good effect that within a few years he had developed the 'cross-post' (which put an end to the cross-country mail having to go up to London and then out again), and discovered a Jacobite uprising through reading other people's letters. He then bought land on the south side of the city where Bath stone lies, and was even more successful with quarrying.

There is no city in the British Isles to compare with Bath for elegance: parts of Edinburgh may compete, but are colder in stone and climate. Bath is a warm city, even if there were no hot springs to make the office people hang out of their windows for air on a still summer afternoon: it welcomes. One of the great good fortunes that can come to a town is that it should flower and fade – and spas, which are suddenly fashionable and suddenly passé, exhale a distant elegance in their declining years like the elegiac fragrance of pot pourri. Bath is too bustling to be melancholy, but the fact that there is no longer much money to be made out of prescribing water has preserved it from the chic hardness that glazes a sophisticated resort like Vichy. Bath has had its edges rubbed by two thousand years of visitors, from the Celts who threw coins into the bottom of the original spring as offerings, to the Romans, to the fashionable eighteenth century, to the coach parties today, so that tourism, which is normally such a fleeting, insubstantial activity, has a certain permanence and a certain ancestry.

I did what all tourists do, and went to the Pump Room, which was all tall windows and chandeliers and brighter than I had remembered it from my visit there with my elderly aunt when I was a child. Then it had had a sallow gloom about it, like the tired skin of an old lady: now I found it grand but not aloof.

There was a tremendous tinnitus of tea-spoons and coffee cups as a perpetual percussion to the Gilbert and Sullivan coming from the Pump Room Trio. It was like a decorous improvisation of tambourines at a dance of jokey tomb-stones. I came to the conclusion that the skeletal air was not the Trio's fault, but the natural consequence of eliminating Mr Gilbert entirely, and reducing the work of Mr Sullivan, a full orchestra, opera chorus and soloists to a piano, cello and violin. As a juvenile musician, I noticed something of the same effect in a piece of music which I picked up second-hand, a transcription of the overture to 'Tanhauser' for violin and piano. It was made by a Mr Edgar Haddock, and – since I had no accompanist – when I played it on my violin, the effect was even thinner than he had intended.

There was something immensely British and endearing about the Trio: there was none of this continental showing-off about them – they got on with the Gilbert and Sullivan, and no mucking about. Such transcriptions always remind me irresistibly of the nursery: by the time you have lost the horns, the oboes, clarinets and flutes (with the little bit extra for the piccolo, not to mention the split part for the violas in bar twenty-five), the subtleties of the original picture are so reduced that you are left with something with the bold colours and simple outlines of a child's picture book. The violin carries the tune as nobly as Peter Pan, staggering slightly from time to time under the weight of a world of cares borne by childish shoulders: or it is as sweet as Snow White, or as frilly and ornamental as Cinderella's ball dress. The piano keeps everyone in order as conscientiously as Christopher Robin, thumps its chords in the marches like Edward Bear going thump down the stairs, and tinkles at the top like a Walt Disney blue-bird. The cello wallows around in the depths like Puss in his Boots, or a couple of bright red bunnies tumbling over themselves in oversized galloshes. I am convinced that the no-nonsense, gallumphing quality of string trio arrangements is why the form appeals to the British as a type of social music which stirs ritual pleasure (but not too deeply) and does not interpose intellect between you and your Bath Bun (which, as one might hope in the Pump Room, is worth eating – though Bath Buns as a class have a design fault involving insufficient sugar and an inadequate number of currants).

Where Glastonbury has had its perpetual choir, the Pump Room has enjoyed almost perpetual chamber music. Music has been heard there almost every day for two hundred and seventy years or so. Initially, there was a chamber orchestra: the Trio dates from the nineteen-forties, and plays every day except Christmas and Boxing days.

The Pump Room Trio were less mature than I had expected: the young beard and glasses at the piano and the slinky blond lady cellist had forty years to go before they were beaten into insensitivity by a Chinese torture of tum-te-tums in common time falling repeatedly upon the eardrums. The violinist was deputising for the regular leader, who was on holiday: he had recently retired from being a chemistry teacher, but had always kept up the violin, he said. He had a chamber violinist's face – gentle, a little weary and worried. When he played, his bow-tie was knocked sideways, much to the interest of a small Japanese boy, who came up and stood respectfully gawping by the platform. The violinist winked and nodded at him over his semi-quavers: the little Japanese boy, Suzuki-trained, remained static in inscrutable wonderment.

I clambered round the Trio with my tape-recorder and hung the microphones over them from the little balcony above their semi-circular stage: during bar-rests they assured me it was safe, even for one of my weight. The music generated an effect of familiar jollity – like laughing at an old joke, and not caring that you had laughed at it before. Afterwards, I invited them to coffee: the lady cellist had taken off her conventional lady-cellist's dress, and somehow insinuated herself into black velvet trousers and a tee-shirt so that she looked even more feline than before, and introduced herself as Shena. She took out a tobacco tin and started to roll her own on the moderately-spotless table-cloth: the melancholy-featured violinist said that music had always been his first love and addressed himself to a Bath Bun and cream: the bearded pianist told me that the tradition in the Trio had been never to rehearse. The present trio, however, apart from adding most of the classical trio repertoire to the library of some three thousand pieces bequeathed by a former violinist, had got tired of walking the eternal knife edge of sight-reading in public: now they had brief rehearsals and almost sight-read in public. They did it very well, as I heard when they gave up substituting for a whole opera house and played music written for a Trio in the first place: Shena Power, the pianist Alistair Hinton and the violinist Peter Schrecker were all highly professional musicians.

They had to be careful not to repeat the same pieces too often, they told me. They would dodge from a Mozart trio to Eric Coates and from there to Cole Porter and Gilbert and Sullivan: it was all in a day's work (whichever one of the three-hundred and sixty-three working days in the year it happened to be). The lady cellist said it was a fun job, but a bit of a panic working seven days a week: she sang in folk clubs, and had to zoom off from the afternoon concert, and be back in time for the one the next morning.

'I would have thought this was all very irritating,' I said, listening to the noise of the tea-spoons around me, like the sound of a thousand silver bells.

'You only notice the clatter for the first day or two,' said the pianist, 'after that it's just an every-day thing – you play knowing that for some people its background music and that some others have come to listen.'

'In fact, it's worse when they suddenly go silent and you wonder what you've done,' said the lady cellist.

They did candle-lit chamber music concerts in the evening, when the coffee cups were replaced with glasses of wine, which were quieter. Looking around at the fluted columns, the elegant pediments and fireplaces and ornamental mouldings, it struck me that modern lighting, and even the light of day, was unkind to eighteenth-century interiors – it needed something subdued like candle-light to soften the edges of its formality.

The lady-cellist caught me glancing at the soft edges of her formality and said that she was just about to cycle off home and do the cooking: she normally went round in dungarees, and when she had come to be interviewed for the job, had turned up in jeans.

'Very un-Pump Room I would have thought,' I said.

'I'd been teaching in a Comprehensive School – class music – and wanted to do more cello. So I gave up, and signed on at the Job Centre for something temporary. A couple of days later, I got a letter saying, 'Temporary cellist required' – I couldn't believe it. I'd just been swimming, and my contact lenses were feeling a bit insecure, but I jumped on my bike and rushed up here. I had no cello, I remember: the chap who was retiring allowed me to use his. They threw a couple of pieces in front of me to sight-read, listened to me for five minutes, and said, 'You start on Monday.' I said, 'When do we rehearse?' They said, 'Well, we don't really.' I said, 'What day off a week do I get?' They said, 'Well, you don't.' That was two and half years ago: I've been here ever since, and love every moment. Well, possibly every other moment,' said the lady cellist, more critically. 'It's smashing, but you just have to organise your life round the inevitability of coming here.'

'You might expect Bath to be the hub of snobbery, but it isn't,' said the pianist.

'Cosmopolitan, that's what it is,' said the violinist, abstracting himself from his Bath Bun and cream. The pianist went on: 'Of course, there are still the old ladies who come and crook their little fingers and sip their coffee, but on a Saturday morning you'll find all the local people with the kids and the shopping. They dump them both down on the floor: the shopping doesn't scream, but the kids do sometimes.'

'The music stands are very high,' said the melancholy violinist. 'I have to use cushions.'

'There are so many people passing through,' said the lady cellist: 'they all take our photo, and you get this image of us being put up on somebody's wall along with the family photos and the other snaps. We don't know them but they've taken back an image of us – it's rather a strange thought.'

'It's like that with me,' I said. 'I talk to you for a morning, but then I go home and live with you for months.'

'You have to concentrate on what you're playing,' said the lady cellist, 'but because I'm facing the audience, I sometimes wonder what certain people are doing here – and how many con-men or murderers we've played to. The old fiddle player has a lovely story about a couple who came in every day for a week: he would read his newspaper, she would read her book. Every one assumed they were newly-marrieds. Then, about the seventh day, the door at the back burst open and a furious lady stormed up to the table and started breaking crockery over the other woman's head. It was the injured wife. The old fiddle player said, "We went on playing, but in the end the sound of breaking crockery got so bad, we had to stop." It's the going down of the *Titanic* really: whatever happens here, we're not supposed to stop playing.'

'I used to sing to eating people,' I said, 'It was an Elizabethan restaurant. I used to put "Minstrel" on my income tax form. Unlimited plonk. That too was making music while things were going down all round me, I suppose.'

'We like playing palm-court stuff best of all, 'cos the setting's so marvellous, people come in and get the feel of it straight away. They come up and say, "I've never been this close to live music before".'

'You're a bit like court musicians,' I said: 'like something out of eighteenth-century Brandenburg–Prussia. But music patronage isn't what it was – you can tell that by the number of buskers. It's not only a sign that the British are a musical nation – it's also an indication that the British are a musical nation who don't like to pay their musicians money.'

'The café orchestra tradition has more or less died – there used to be one in every corner caf.'

The pianist said: 'No self-respecting restaurant would be without one – our previous violinist played in most of them in Bristol. Even Woolworth's used to have a sextet – seems inconceivable now, doesn't it?'

After I left the Pump Room Trio, I tagged on behind a guide who was telling his party at considerable length about the Great Drain, and descended to the mouth of the Roman outflow, from which the waters gush in a barbaric torrent, with a splash and rush and a roar in a miasma of warm, moist air; the stream of history flowing at the rate of a third of a million gallons a day, and a temperature of forty-six point five degrees centigrade. In the King's Bath, where the great carp swim to eat up the algae, there is Roman, medieval, seventeenth-century, eighteenth-century and nineteenth-century architecture, all together.

Here I met Stephen Bird, a resident archaeologist, who told me that the Baths were even more impressive when they were lonely at night. 'I come in here to work late sometimes. When the floodlights are on, the sky is dark and there's nobody around, you can hear the water far more clearly then, and the flapping of the pigeons as they go past. It's quite a mysterious place.'

In the afternoon, I went back to the Pump Room to take the waters. Though they were dispensed by two pretty students in mob caps, they were not the same waters that the eighteenth-century failed to enjoy. The National Health Service ceased to regard Bath water as something it could officially pay out for in 1973, but it was the discovery, a few years later, that the waters could actually kill people that really damaged their image as health-giving. The virus could be fatal only in an infinitesimally small proportion of cases – but one of the cases occurred. So the waters that I took came from a bore-hole in another part of the city.

The process of serving the water seemed to be like drawing beer, except that giving change was easier.

'How much do I get for tenpence?' I asked of the Bathmaids. They giggled, and said that it was usually two-thirds of a glass but, if I would drink it, they would give me a whole one.

'If people only sip it, it's a waste really,' said the first Bathmaid.

'It's not that pleasant,' said the second: 'Epsom Salts' taste, dentist's mouth-wash, TCP, Milk of Magnesia – that's the sort of thing people say about it.'

'Some just think it's tap-water,' said the first Bathmaid.

'But our doorman drinks it every day,' added the second.

'On principle?' I asked.

'No, he likes it.'

Connoisseurs of the element were all around me.

'It's very dry,' said a passing infant with authority. 'If it was chilled it would be quite nice.'

'They used to drink three pints of it a day when they were on the cure,' I told him.

'Did they?' said his mother. 'I would have thought it would have rusted their insides out.'

'Couldn't call it refreshing though, could you?' said the infant with the palate, belabouring his point. A German lady tourist sipped, and made a noise which was either a prolonged clearing of the throat or an extremely critical comment. An American suggested that it would be better with bourbon. The Trio came in for the afternoon session, settled themselves, tuned their instruments and began the Boccherini Minuet in A.

'Good Lord, what a strain on the bladder!' said a country gentleman with a glass in his hand.

On my way out I ran into the archaeologist again. 'I've tried the water,' I said.

'How was it?'

'Not too good.'

'That's a milder version, that stuff from across the city: the older stuff was stronger, and tepid. Like the medicines one had as a child, it tastes so awful that you feel it's bound to be doing you some good. There are forty-one minerals in it, and if they don't kill you they probably cure you: it's enough to soften any stiff upper lip, this water. Good luck,' he added as we parted, leaving me in some doubt as to whether the wishes were for my journey or the well-being of my insides.

Outside the Baths there was an enormous hole in the road. Looking down it, I saw arched passages, through which men were trundling rubbish in wheel-barrows.

'What's going on down there?' I asked the man in charge of the hole.

'Trying to get our way into the bank over there,' said the

hole-minder. 'Got our three worst chaps on the job, mind.' At which a prolonged rhubarbing noise arose from the depths, with cries of 'oi oi' and 'yer yer'.

'Is there anything Roman down there?'

'Only them three and they don't go far.'

I returned to the hotel to treat my interior generously with alcohol, lest any kind of encrustation from one or more of the forty-one minerals should form therein.

The next morning, when I went to the cellar where The Roman Philosopher was stabled, passing draymen were making free with the horn. 'Parp!' went The Roman Philosopher.

' 'E's 'appy neow.' 'Parp!'

'Ooh dear, that's 'is. Ooh 'ell.' 'Parp!'

'You dropped a clanger this time.' 'Parp!'

'Let's 'ave another go.' 'Parp! Parp!'

Rescuing the profaned bulb from beery fingers, I wheeled The Roman Philosopher out into the morning where a man in a green overall who was sometimes a waiter and sometimes a gardener was scraping minutely at the herbage growing up between the asphalt. This was obviously a pleasure to him, since his own herbage had been shaved extremely small along his upper lip so that his moustache was hardly more than a line of single hairs. I asked him how to get to the Fosse Way: he replied in the British Rococo School of Giving Directions, in which the teller ornaments every turn, and then repeats the ornament at least four times, with variations.

'The sort of directions that make it superfluous to actually go there,' Jenny said afterwards.

The gardener was courteous and softly-spoken: his voice undulated gently like an incantation in which, from time to time, fragments of local mythology rose to the surface and sank again, like yeasty bubbles in a beer-vat.

'Of course, of course, sir – Colerne,' (he rolled the 'r' to three or four times its normal size): 'Colerrrne, that was the old way, wasn't it? The old Fosse road at Colerrrne – don't quote me, I'm rather ignorant about these things, but I think the Old Fosse road at Colerrrne used to go up the top of the hill you see there. There's a finger post – 'scuse my dirty nails, won't you –

Colerrrne, Colerrrne, up the hill to the left and there's a little road that brings you out to Colerrrne – that used to be the old Fosse Road, and you go through Colerrrne, and then as you go into Colerrrne you'll see what we call the Three Shire Stones (if you're interested, sir) – three huge great stones with one on the top, and one foot is in Wiltshire, one in Somerset and one in Gloucestershire, and then you go direct through the airfield: you don't veer off to the village of Colerne.'

'I see,' I said: 'I don't go to Colerne.'

'But you'll see a large house that's been renovated – that's what we call Hunter's Hall, and in the very old days (my father is a native of Colerrrne, and he tells me that half that house is in Somerset and half in Wiltshire, or half in Gloucestershire and Wilts), in the very old days when they used to have the cockfighting (father, of course, is dead and gone many years ago) – that was in the old days when the police would only go that far, they wouldn't encroach on others, so they used to do the cockfighting in the Wiltshire half of the house and when the beadles were coming, they'd move over to the other side.'

Fearing that the introduction of a new topic might be precipitate, the gardener retreated to familiar ground, and talked more about the Fosse Way as it related to Colerne '. . . I haven't been up (what d'you call it?) the Fosse road, what we've called the old Fosse for many, many years, but I know that brings you on to the top of Bannerdown and runs you through into Colerne that way, but what I would do – naturally, you have a map, you would know the way – you'd go on into the Shoe at Marshfield and through what we call Mountain Bower, and drop down by Castle Combe, and you'd get to Cirencester, if you knew your way. I don't know how far the Fosse road goes now – it used to go right up, and then naturally once you get to the top of Bannerdown, you'd have to veer to the right to pick up the main Colerne-Marshfield road. Start looking on the left, 'cos that's where you'll find the Three Shires: as you get further you'll see Hunter's Hall, then you have to veer off to the right for Colerrrne, but if you want picturesque, you'll keep straight on.'

'Yes, I will.'

'Through the back end of Colerne airfield, right up, Shoe Inn's looking at you – straaaaaaaight over, and that's the old

Fosse road. I'm very interested in these old things, but I'm afraid I neglected them when I had time. I'm retired now, live at a little place called Kingsdown, we look straight across to Colerrrne, but up round our way is so full of history, people say "You ought to have been born donkey's years ago".'

'Sorry?'

'Donkey's years ago. The old turnpikes where the stage coach used to run, Hazelbury Manor, one of the smallest chapels in England, highwaymen used to hide his spoils in there, had to have it reconsecrated and all: beautiful old Tudor manor, and they used to have secret passages coming down where the kitchen is now on to the main A4 road, and the other one comes out in the chapel. We had a customer used to come in, a millionaire I think, ever such a nice gentleman and he said, "Where do you come from?" I said, "As the crow flies, sir, about two minutes from you." "D'you know the Manor?" "Indeed I do, sir, and have you still got that big Aga cooker in the kitchen?" "No, we've had that out, I've built it up level, there's about two foot of concrete under there now." "Well, under that Aga cooker there's some big flagstones, and there's a couple of passages going under there." "*Where*?" he said: and he had plenty of money, couple of Rolls-Royces, Bentleys, Mercedes – he would have digged it up you see – fantastic man.'

'Fantastic.'

I left in the general direction of Colerne.

When you have turned left at the White Lion in Batheaston (which is cheek by jowl in the same terrace with the Viking Wine Bar and the George and Dragon (Free House) in what, even for the enthusiast, seems an overkill of alcohol, you go up a Truly Awful Hill, and only on the top of Bannerdown does the road straighten out to go past the Shire Stones (whose feet & etc. etc. and have FG and MV written on them in an undignified manner) under their dark beeches, and Hunter's Hall (where, in the days when & etc. etc. they used to & etc. etc.).

There were larks on Bannerdown, and I had the great feeling of being on top that comes from riding along a ridge where one can see the country for miles on either side.

It was one of those fine, windy days that intensifies colours, the dark blue of vetch, the paleness of cornflowers, the red of

poppies, convolvulus white: they were making hay on the
airfield, and the scent blew in gusts over the road. They were
also playing soldiers, with a group of lads very serious about
hiding themselves beneath a millinery of waving vegetation
on their tin helmets, though there appeared to be not a lot that
could be done for the rest of them in the way of camouflage. A
sign on the airfield said it was 'a prohibited place within the
meaning of the Official Secrets Act', for the benefit of the
innumerable passers-by conversant with that meaning –
hedgers and ditchers, housewives, hairdressers, ten-year-
olds, vagrants, itinerant fortune-tellers and all: it made me
blush for my own education that I had no idea whatever what
it was talking about. Plainly the airfield was not prohibited to
males between the ages of sixteen and twenty-five wearing
plants on their head, nor to haymakers, but I could not work
out where cyclists came in relation to either.

Past the airfield, the road headed straight down below
overhanging ash trees, to wind gently along the side of a little
valley whose stream flows from Fuddlebrook Hill. There was
a gentle, uncommercial wildness to its random wooding and
rough pastures: wild marjoram waved tall, mauve flowers
against a drystone wall; under a sycamore tree, a dappled mare
fidgeted in the shade by an old wooden manger making a great
fuss about the flies, switching her tail and nodding her head
furiously, and opening her mouth to snap as if she were going
to bite flies the size of hedgehodgs. Her whinnyings and
stampings were ignored by a line of more patient horses,
maintaining stiff upper lips in the yard of a hillside riding
school as they waited in the heat for the mistress, a blonde with
tight administrative curls, to finish lecturing a fence-full of
little girls, perched like sparrows, itching to be up and off.

The road smelt of the passage of many horses as I came up
out of the valley to the crossroads at the Shoe Inn, whose
garden was bordered with those stone mushrooms they say
used to hold up barns in order to keep out non-
mountaineering mice and rats who couldn't cope with the
overhang. As I looked at them, I meditated that it is no wonder
one only ever sees the mushrooms, and never the barn on top,
since this peculiar architectural practice must rank in terms of
stability with building the Eiffel Tower upside down: and how
did they get rid of the rodents when they stopped building

barns on stone mushrooms? I rolled gently over the rolling landscape between drystone walls which were capped by a vertical stacking of slabs: where this had fallen, I noticed that the stones flaked and weathered where they lay flat. Although it does not have the richness of the Ham stone I had left behind me or the Cotswold stone I was coming to, the rough limestone of the Mendips, used for walling and building alike – even up to tiling the roof with it – gives a rugged unity that feels right in hill country. After a while, the road became conscious that there was no one but me to observe it keeping the straight and narrow, and began to indulge itself in discreet but friendly windings between rough meadows, a hayfield with a buzzing tractor: it crossed a watercress stream. There were harebells in the verges, and other flowers in ranks of purples, blues and pinks.

At the Salutation Inn which stands with its double mounting-block by a grove of beeches, at one stroke I changed country (for it advertised Cotswold Beers) and also came upon the explanation of the name that had puzzled me since Topsham: there was the salutation on the sign – an eighteenth-century gentleman down on one knee before an eighteenth-century lady, each pledging the other in a glass of wine. It was an old sign, its silhouette figures weathered through in patches to the undercoat, so that the lady and gentleman looked as stylised as Javanese shadow-puppets and as frail as if they had been toasting each other since the days of the peruke and the full-bottomed wig.

The Fosse became a cart-track just after it passed under the M4 motorway, but I detoured in a triangle to see Grittleton House, built for the nineteenth-century MP Joseph Neeld by two quarrelling and remarkably obstinate architects, so that it has Dutch gables, Italian medieval windows, English Tudor chimneys and a lodge with a French gothic turret ('not kept up like it used to be years ago,' said the postman). The influence of the estate pervaded the village and the countryside – from the parkland trees, now with grain rather than pasture beneath them, to Grittleton pump (a magnificent creature of Victorian solidity called 'Patent – The Safety Water Elevator Co. Ltd. Dunstable', which made me wonder what was the hidden peril I had failed to observe in water-pumps), to Fosse Lodge. This was rather on the small side, considering it had to provide an excuse for the existence of diamond chimneys, a tower flying both a tattered union jack and a fox weather-vane, with a snooty dove sitting surly in the turret itself, and a nearby barn with a belfry.

But by now I was late for lunch, so I didn't dally on the Way: and when it turned to cart-track once more I spun off to the village of Easton Grey, where Jenny and I had arranged to meet at the pub or, if there was no pub, at the church. Further delayed by having to offer assistance to an extremely small boy trying to cross a cattle grid far too big for him and in mortal terror of his leg slipping between and losing a gumboot, I came to Easton Grey and, to save time, briskly demanded the whereabouts of the nearest hostelry of a resident out walking her small dog.

'Pup?' queried that lady, in what sounded the purest near-Lithuanian.

'You know – King's Head, George and Dragon, White Horse, Black Horse, King's Arms, Merry Tadpole, Spotted Dog, Princess and Artichoke.'

'Ha!' said the lady, thinking. 'Heidi!'

'Hiding?'

'Heidi!' (severely): looking down I saw my sandals in danger of flood. 'Iss natty, darlink. Perrhappps if you go furrderr.'

'In which direction?' I asked.

'I do not know. I haf not been that farr.'

I went in all directions: rushing down to the infant Avon, and panting up the hill again, with the gears popping out in my hurry with a sound like the collapse of a saucepan factory.

'Oh dear,' said the near-Lithuanian, wincing, as I passed her again: 'be carr-ful.'

Easton Grey was very pretty, and not only had no pub, but no church either: the nearest thing to it was a tiny chapel in the grounds of a Very Big House: I reached it just as Jenny was in the act of pinning a message on the door. 'Dumbotnik!' said the paper: 'I was here: where were you? You are here: I am not.'

'Now is that a message to stick on a church door?' I asked. 'You might have started a heresy.' We picnicked on the lawn beside the drive. A man who might have been the Owner of the Very Big House drove by and scowled at us: it was most gratifying to be noticed by the landed gentry, unless he was the butler, or the under-gardener, or somebody else entirely.

We returned to the Fosse Way, which at that point was a layby at the start of a cart-track, in which a cheerful gentleman in a van was enjoying a peaceful cup of tea from a thermos. 'I shall take my shorts off,' I told Jenny.

'Can I take the money, or is it by invitation only?'

'It's track now, most of the way to Cirencester. I need my jeans: there'll be nettles and things.' I unpacked the jeans and retreated behind the car.

'Great big rats,' volunteered the man in the van. 'Be careful.'

'Really?' I paused with my shorts round my knees: in my exposed position I felt vulnerable.

'Foot across. Foot deep. Goin' along and they jump up at you, like . . . like . . .'

'Tigers?' Jenny supplied what seemed an appropriate word.

The man thought about it. 'Well, er, I suppose so. Fanciful-like. Yes. Like tigers.'

I decided it was too hot for jeans, repacked them, and set off up the track in my shorts. I had not gone far before I appreciated the truth of the man's warning. The wheel-ruts were indeed extremely deep and, in midsummer, as solid as the North Face of the Eiger. If I rode along the bottom, the pedals caught at either side and bashed me back and forth like a pinball: if I rode along the top, I fell into them. The fact that I was also going downhill, and had both hands full of crab-apples picked from a wayside tree thus preventing me from using the brakes, made my progress even more interesting. At the bottom of the slope, I came to a boggy patch, and stopped in a foot of mud. Fortunately, there was a way round the mud: it led through a tall clump of fierce stinging-nettles, and a thornbush.

Sometimes it was track, sometimes footpath; there were stretches of grass with stone not far beneath it; loose stone (put down by the water-board for access to a lonely, whirring sub-station and on which the bike slipped and slid until I had to get off); short sections of real, tiny road; bits of gravel drive to private houses; a muddy stream-bed with a single stepping-stone. Briefly, I sped down a white, dusty road such as cyclists must have ridden a century ago, with tall grasses and rich flowers alongside (and a plump girl jiggling interestingly on top of a load of hay taking its time behind a tractor, but no room to pass and no point in passing).

Though it was often impossible to decide whether I was walking down the road or its ditch, the way was a wilderness of the pleasures of being remote in the country: gleams of gold from the cornfields glimpsed through the tangled coppice, shrubs, bushes at either side; stepping carefully to avoid bright butterflies taking the afternoon sun on the path; and, in a little valley with a winding of alders between its meadows, an ancient packhorse bridge across a river that goes down to Malmesbury to swell the Avon, but which here is a quick, clear stream between massed banks of textured green – feather-flowering rushes, flat and finicky pondweed, froths of water-elder. That was the feel of this road, not of marching legions – though, I was told later, a Roman ford lies beside the bridge – but of a slow world of ordinary legs, of a pedlar with his burden, a gentleman with his horse, a youth heading out into the wide world, a countrywoman with her basket of eggs, a labourer in search of work, an old man returning home – single travellers through centuries of summer days.

But most of the way was ruts, and most of the way I dragged the bike – my hands and arms aching, my bare legs cut and stung to pieces, for one of the side-effects of wheeling a bicycle through thick grass is that as it goes it drags out nettles which flip round and hit the backs of your legs: a minor discomfort, but one which it is impossible to ignore, so strong is the conditioning of years of tearful childhood. Just past a wartime pillbox grown far too old to defend itself and now guarded by thistles, I was dive-bombed by a squadron of horse-flies. I came to the conclusion that at the next main road, I would leave the Fosse: cycling to Cirencester was one thing, walking to it another. But at the next main road the Fosse was tarmac once more anyway. Doubtfully, I went straight on.

The tarmac did not last for long, but curved away from the original track into what had been an airfield, with a 'Private – Keep Out' notice, and a bull chained by the nose to emphasise the point. There was a farmyard at the end of the airstrip, with a queue of cows waiting instead of bombers, and a whirr of milking machines where there had once been the roar of engines. There are few things more derelict than a dead airfield: the ground so open, the buildings so casually scattered, jerry-built beside roads that go nowhere. Hut No. 1, Hut No. 2 with the glass out of their windows, the asbestos roofs crumbling, crazy stove-pipes rusting, trees growing out of the walls – but the same wind blowing across that filled the windsock when I was in bootees, forty years ago.

Through the farmyard gate, and I was on the Fosse again, a grass track through a wilderness of hedge, with the wind rustling sloe bushes, ash trees, shaking the Old Man's Beard. It was hard pedalling through the grass, and I was just about to get off again, when in the distance I saw another cyclist wheeling a bicycle. I came up with him at a hundred yards of real road before the track began again. It looked awful.

'Going along to Ciren on the Fosse? – probably just as well you met me,' said the cyclist, an open-faced young man in an old, cracked waterproof. 'See that plane going up there in the distance? That's Kemble aerodrome – the Fosse goes across it, but I don't think you can. You used to be able to ring up on the edge of the airfield and they'd come and take you across, but last time I was there, it was all derelict.'

I bravely concealed my disappointment: 'Perhaps I'll go round then.'

'You could go . . . no, it's not really cyclable down there either.'

'Never mind.'

'You could push it,' suggested the young man, helpfully, 'there are paths. It's just rather thick scrub, that's all.'

'I think I'll go round. Are you?'

'Oh yes I am. I just use that bit of the Fosse: cuts off a hill for me.'

We cycled off together along the road to Chedglow. He was James, he told me – had been at Oxford, but had dropped out, opting for a quiet life.

'Bit early for a quiet life at your age.'

'Well, this cottage sort of came upon me,' said James, vaguely. He was returning from a day wrestling with huge blocks of limestone, rebuilding the mill-pond at Shipton, filling in time before taking a course in the autumn.

'Glass-blowing.'

'You'd need a peaceful sort of temperament for that, I should imagine.'

We reached his cottage: I refused his offer of tea, and cycled on because it was getting towards evening, going cross-country to the main road which would rejoin the Fosse Way at Jackaments Bottom. It was a curly lane past fields of sheep and with bars of sunlight descending between the clouds on the horizon. I became aware of a prosperous solidity to the houses and the countryside alike: it began to feel like the Cotswolds.

At Jackaments Bottom, I found prosperous solidity at a standstill, with a gentleman with a military moustache scrutinising the internal works of a Daimler, stuck on an awkward corner with a country bus slewed across the road behind, and the bottom part of a bus-driver's uniform protruding from the car bonnet.

'I can see the bloody engine, but I casn't see the starter motor,' said an entombed sort of voice somewhere ahead of the bus-driver's uniform: 'bloody marvellous, 'en it?'

'Plenty of battery there, and everything,' said the military moustache. 'I've left the wireless on so you can hear.'

'I am a nursing auxiliary in a geriatric hospital,' said the wireless.

'That's the trouble with a car this size,' I said sympathetically to the military moustache. 'You're helpless when it stops going: marvellous until then.'

'I know,' replied the man with the military moustache, as if he believed me.

'Still casn't find the starter motor,' complained an area associated with the busman's legs.

'Want a push?' I offered. The military moustache quivered slightly, but said nothing. The busman's legs wriggled backwards, pulling the rest of the busman after them.

'You don't want a push?' I was anxious to get on. There was a pause.

' 'Ave to give 'ee a little push,' suggested the busman: 'clear 'un off.'

We cleared her off: she was extremely heavy. I went on my way feeling superior, with Kemble aerodrome on the opposite hillside. It did not *look* deserted. I passed Thames Head, but there was no sign of the Thames: in a richly golden evening, I arrived at Cirencester.

At the hotel, I discovered that Kemble aerodrome had in fact been very much alive: Jenny had been to a flying display by its resident squadron.

'Why didn't you go across the aerodrome?' asked Jenny. 'We could have had you ringing up the control tower, and a row when they wouldn't come and get you, and then you could have climbed over the fence – we might have got some sound effects of guard dogs – and you could have cycled across the runway with lots of sound effects of jet fighters at Mach 1, or whatever it is they fly at. You might even have got arrested, which would have been good for publicity.'

'I see that the proximity of men in uniform over-excites you,' I said. 'Did you enjoy the display?'

'It was marvellous. You missed the Red Arrows.'

'I'm just happy they missed me,' I said.

The Cotswolds are the virtues of the English-made stone and land: they are a unity, they are kindly, modest, well-sized, they make good neighbours more easily than they make acquaintances or friends (which is as it should be, since friends are few, and acquaintances neither here nor there). In the Cotswolds, two thousand years of English history have turned out more or less right in the end, or at least true to themselves. They are peaceful, beautiful and not much spoiled, and if you set down William Cobbett to ride them today, he would know that this was a country that changes little in centuries before he got to the end of one wold and on to another – though this is something you are never conscious of doing. Wolds are vague and mysteriously ancient – the word means 'cleared land' – but the fact that they are uplands is a link with the time when farmland and trackways were on the hilltops, and all the world below was forest.

Georgina Attwood, Superintendent Registrar at Moreton-in-Marsh, further along my way, described the Cotswolds as 'tranquillity in a gentle landscape'. Vaughan Williams, most pastoral of composers, was a child in the vicarage of Down Ampney – I saw the name on the map along my route, and decided it was an essential place of pilgrimage – and his music says the same.

'The essence of country living is people,' Georgina Attwood continued. 'You are a person, you know your neighbours, you worry about them. I had some young nieces to stay with me from the town: they walked into the village to do my shopping with me, watching all the car drivers greeting me as they went past, and they said, "You know absolutely everyone in the whole world, don't you? We never see anyone to wave to." I thought that summed it up.

'A lot of people wouldn't agree with me, but I think that part of our country attitude is that we *like* to acknowledge the squire – we like to feel he's there, and that he will be the President of our society. He brings something to us, and we hope we bring something to him in asking him to do these little things for us. If you do away with that imbalance, you lessen the richness of village life.'

In the Cotswolds, like anywhere else, people shift round more nowadays, both physically and socially. There are outsiders and holiday homes in the villages: the pub often remains, but those other two community centres without which a village cannot thrive as a village – the Post Office-cum-shop, and the primary school – are usually threatened, if they have not already gone, while the parson has to dash round to several churches on Sunday. But the heritage is hale and prosperous.

Much of the land is still privately owned, with many of the traditional divisions between land-owner, tenant farmer and labourer still there under the surface. Medieval England does not live only in the great, mellow wool-churches; the pulse of the feudal system beats gently in the houses of the squirearchy and the cottages of those who are content to polish the antiques rather than have the worry of insuring them.

Jenny and I had an introduction to a beautiful house, but the lady gardener we had hoped to see was away, so we met her daily instead. Rene Hart, who was shelling peas when we arrived, was a softly-spoken woman with grey hair drawn back into a bun, nervous hands, and a manner as domestic and modest as the smallest creature in Beatrix Potter. I could hear the girl in her still: she had a gentle giggle, grown mature, which she used to express her incredulity at the very idea that, in a different world, she might have lived in the beautiful house herself, rather than polished it in.

'I should be scared!' said Mrs Hart. 'If you're with other people it's all right, but I wouldn't like to stay here on my own. There's such burglars going on nowadays: I'd rather have my own little cottage.'

She led us into the drawing-room whose antiques and books spoke of a civilisation bred over centuries, and sat very upright on the edge of an armchair, as if it would be improper to lean back in it.

'I think you feel safer in your own house,' said Mrs Hart almost firmly, and told us how she was taught as a child to touch her hat to the parson, and drop a curtsy to the people from the Hall when they passed in the road; and how there were only three staff in the garden now, since the lady gardener did so much herself.

In the garden was a yew walk, a water garden, a marble bench supported by the most patient stone lions, lawns, trees and the most decorative kitchen garden that ever was. There were artichokes, sweet peas, alpine strawberries, thick-stemmed chard, white and green and ruby; tight cabbages, ornamental kales, mint in flower, purple peas, beans grown in pyramids, onions and beetroot popping their bulbs up out of the ground like babies throwing off the blankets; yellow-flowered marrows, cages of raspberries, flowering lavender with bees; and an arbour in which vines and peas twisted among each other in a harmony of fruit and vegetable.

It was the vegetable expression of an ancient order, in which everything had a place, and that place was peaceful, and people cared for excellence, each after their social station. I left the house and garden hurriedly, before I should start to think that I might like to live there myself: and Jenny and I returned to Cirencester.

Cirencester, which is quiet as a carved stone now, has not yet got over having been the second most important town in Britain, which it was a millennium and a half ago. In those days, Cotswold stone meant tesserae: and there is no telling how much fine pavement remains underground in the foundations of the houses that lined the grid pattern of the Roman streets. That was often the best place for it, too, I was told by David Viner, the director of the local museum.

'It's preserved for other people to care for with greater resources: the next generation, the next century even.'

They were in the process of lifting a Venus mosaic about fourteen feet by ten at that moment, he said. The owner of the land at Kingscote was giving the mosaic, but the cost of restoration and installation would be well over £5000.

'We rattled the tin in the usual way. I well remember finding it with a group of others in 1971. We were amazed at how shallow the buildings were, and we couldn't believe our luck. That's not the point of archaeology, of course – that's to recover information and preserve it – but it's nice to find nice things. You can imagine the sense of joy: we went off to the pub and had a pint.'

'Does your sense of the past go with you into ordinary life?'

'A lot. I can walk from here to my house in Tower Street and know where I am in relation to the Roman town which is beneath my feet. The front window looks out on to what was until recently a garden centre: it used to be part of the Roman centre – possibly the baths – and I see it in my mind's eye.'

He showed me his favourite exhibit: the Mosaic of the Hare, which was part of a floor from a town house of fourth-century Corinium, and now hangs on the museum wall with the animal itself sitting in the middle looking lifelike enough to be just on the point of wrinkling its nose. The hare is the symbol of the museum less because it is beautiful than because it is typical and frail – made so long ago by local craftsmen in local stone using expertise which has never been lost in all the fifteen centuries since: and the surrounds are damaged and left unrestored.

'The land was being used as allotment ground, and the mosaic was so close to the surface that it was possible to dig your spuds, and come up with a handful of tessera. It's accidental vandalism I suppose: a reminder that it's easy to destroy something and very hard to preserve it.'

Cirencester does not only preserve its past in the bright and cheerful museum: there were Roman dishes on the menu at the King's Head: '*Patina de Piscis Fricta* – herring dipped in beaten egg, fried in oil with vegetable juice and wine, and sprinkled with ground pepper'; a stew of lamb and oinion with lovage, cumin, vegetable juice and wine – to be accompanied by '*Pisa Simplici*, peas baked with origano, lovage and wine' (it seemed to be an odd way to treat peas, and unlikely to work well with the *Pisa Gelata* we get nowadays); and '*Dulcia Domestica* – salted dates fried in honey with chopped nuts'.

The Roman recipes come from Apicius, a first-century gourmet, via Marian Woodman, who was asked to write a booklet for the museum, and ended up experimenting on her family.

'Were they happy experiments?' I asked her, over tea and cakes. She said that they were, on account of the fact that she had been careful to avoid things like stuffed dormice, and boiled ostrich with feathers intact. It occurred to me that the one thing worse than boiled ostrich with its feathers on was probably the process of plucking an ostrich.

'And I don't have the heart to fatten snails in milk until they can't get back into their shells. But I did try things like asparagus patina, which is a sort of baked custard of asparagus liquidised with various herbs and spices, and which is really rather good.'

'The stuff which always made me shudder just to think of it was liquamen,' I said. 'Barrels of salted anchovies left to rot in the sun and the juice poured out and added to everything.' Mrs Woodman told me that I was allowed to use ordinary anchovies or Gentlemen's Relish as a substitute.

'Of course the Romans introduced to this country not only the stinging nettle, but most of the herbs we use today, plus dandelion, apples, pears, quinces, turnips, carrots, peas, beans of all kinds, nuts and dried fruits, smoked ham, smoked cheese. If there was anything available, the Romans had it.'

'Sounds as if the natives had a pretty thin time before the Romans got here,' I said.

'Awful diet: just a porridgey type of thing and the odd hare and things thrown into the pot – which of course they went back to after the Romans left.'

'They're still serving it in a good many places today,' I said.

Cirencester has a Cotswold-stone Tesco's and a Cotswold-stone 'Burger Castle': it has largely escaped the plague of universal shop-fitting which has ruined so many an English town. I went and sat on a seat between the church and the war memorial, looking out on to the market square, and a very small part of the world went by extremely peacefully.

A plump, red woman was very severe with a little girl for being so disrespectful as to sit on the steps of the memorial, which was crowded with containers of flowers for the Falklands' dead, including one posy in an old boot. I could not work out whether it was an unusually pathetic offering, or some kind of pacifist satire, and the group of punks hanging round the square could not enlighten me. They did say, however, that sitting on the memorial was a matter of great local controversy, and they were always being told to get off under threat of being fined £50, whereas older people were left alone. As punks, the youngsters seemed to be total failures, being just about as inoffensive and agreeable as is possible for a self-styled social outcast to be: the best protest they could manage was for one of them to drop his trousers and 'moon' at me when I took their photograph, which he did with a smile so broad that it would have soothed away any sense of shock from an elderly nun.

Returning to my bench, I found my seat taken by the shopping bag of a man with fierce white hair, bow tie and intellectual spectacle-frames. Ormiston was his name, he said: he was a Yorkshireman, he said, come to Cirencester as an engineer almost thirty years before: and what he said summed up the feeling of the town for me.

'The past is your compass, guiding you in a society in which there's too many things alike. To hold in your hand something that's got tangible links with the past makes us feel there is purpose in our existence. No amount of talking in the books does that – ten thousand words, what does it mean? Some years ago, they were excavating in the middle of the town to build the police station, and they came upon the actual pavement of the Roman road. I knew a fellow helping in the dig, and when he told me about the find, I said I'd like to have a look at it after tea. So I did and there he was, digging and sifting. I asked if I could come down and he wanted to know why I was so keen. I said, "Because I want to be able to say that once in my life I did actually stand all square on a real Roman road."

'And I did actually stand on that pavement: real physical contact,' he continued. 'And I saw the grooves that were cut in the road where the carts ran up and down.'

IV

A SIMPLE ENGLISH NOSE

TO MORETON-IN-MARSH via BOURTON-ON-THE-WATER

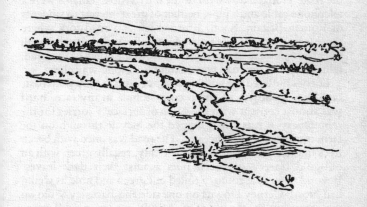

I went to unlock my bicycle from its drainpipe in the courtyard
of the hotel to discover that a nestful of fledglings had decanted
themselves nearby. Infant sparrows were hopping between
the spokes, attempting to fly the impossible height to the
pedals and – as is often the way with the young out in the
world for the first time – flapping a great deal all over the place
to very little effect. Carefully I trod between them and contorted myself round the front forks to replace the digital
mileometer. The back came off and the batteries fell out again,
among the fledglings who seemed unperturbed that they were
hopping all over my hard-cycled miles. Patiently, I put everything back together – as is often the way with the mature

107

citizen going out into the world for the umpteenth time, & etc. & etc.

It was bright blue, light gold and breezy as I rode out from Cirencester. The sun made angular rooftop shadows down the middle of Blackjack Street: the wind blew smells of early morning baking on to the streets and flipped at the empty shopping bags of a small battalion of white-haired ladies off, very firmly, to make a surprise attack on the early morning shops. The determination of the elderly ladies was often distracted by babies in prams and supermarket trolleys but the babies were not at all distracted by the elderly ladies: it seemed a very one-way sort of relationship. As I left the town, I came upon an archaeological excavation, or hole, in the middle of the road: I looked down it but the only visible remains were a telephone cable and a pipe, neither of great interest to students of Roman Britain. Soon, I turned left at a road fork where there were more definite signs of antiquity: yellow hatchings all over the new road to warn drivers from the north of the bend: telling me that the road was straight for a long way ahead.

Lorries buffeted me with their slipstreams as they went past, one blew a shower of sharp corn-stubble in my face, but I was almost content with the swop of surface + lorries for the remoteness + ruts I had lugged the bicycle through on the farm tracks before Cirencester. The road was lined with beech trees in their midsummer prime: richly, regally green with an old-gold tracery of beech nuts against their dark leaves. Beyond them, the country rolled out green and gold as well: I had North Cerney Downs on one side and Barnsley Wold on the other, but for the life of me I could not see any difference between the two geographical features.

It was Down I was looking for: Down Ampney, which my book said was the birthplace of the man I think of as the most pastoral of English composers (since he was often pastoral, and wrote, if not the most, a lot). I never quite know why it is that Vaughan Williams, along with other English composers of his period, evokes the countryside so unfailingly: whether I am conditioned by years of television background music, whether open, modal harmonies suggest wide open spaces, or whether some breath of the fields actually did weave itself in among the melodies of folk-song, and thence into the orchestra? Most likely, it is a conspiracy between Vaughan Williams and me: he says he is going to be pastoral, and I believe him; then when I hear something else of his, I still believe him; and, possibly, what we both call pastoral is not pastoral at all, but the English Romantic Soul which we have to de-personalise by sticking trees and fields all over it.

In my search for the vicarage of Vaughan Williams's father, I had not been able to find Down Ampney on the map, but ahead of me was Ampney Down, which might be the same thing upside Down. I turned across the fuzzy-bushed course of the old railway beside the road. The birthplace of the composer was revealed as a large corrugated iron shed with a weathercock on the top. Notwithstanding the precedents for persons of a religious tendency giving birth in barns, it did not seem like a vicarage. I approached the only music critic in sight who was driving a tractor backwards and forwards in some inscrutable agricultural task, and offered the opinion that the surroundings did not look like the birthplace of a Great Composer. The man on the tractor looked around, thought about it, looked around him again to make sure he was not being precipitate, and came to a decision.

'No,' said the man on the tractor, with some caution. Pause. 'Any particular Great Composer you had in mind?'

'Vaughan Williams.' The man on the tractor looked as if he would have been rather happier if I had said Johann Strauss. 'My book on the Fosse Way says he was born at Down Ampney.'

'Ampney Down Farm, this.' (The man on the tractor looked relieved at being able to place me at last – not a tramp, intellectual, stray concert violinist or bassoon virtuoso fleeing from public acclaim, chicken-stealer or VAT-man: here was a simple grockle.) 'Down Ampney down there.'

I hauled out my Ordnance Survey, discovering – in alphabetical order – Ampney Crucis, Ampneyfield, Ampney Knowle, Ampney Park, Ampney Riding, Ampney St Mary, Ampney St Peter, and Ampney Sheephouse. At last, several miles away to the south, on Ermin Way, I found it.

'Never mind,' I said, giving up on the Great Composer, 'I must have got the Way wrong.' The man on the tractor bade me farewell, suffused with contentment at having come upon an idiot relatively early in the day, with time ahead of him to relish the encounter.

Some miles further down the road, I came to a bungalow set back from the road above the slope of a hill: the home of Bob Cook, builder and enthusiast for Cotswold stone. I came upon a half-completed garden wall of it as I came up to the front door, but I wanted to know more about something so influential in forming the character of that country.

Originally, Bob told me, people would dig a hole in the ground and build a house with what they'd taken out of it – whitish-grey in the south of the Cotswolds around Cirencester, a yellow-orange past Stow-on-the-Wold and up towards Chipping Camden. It is a soft limestone and was once mined rather than quarried, for usable stone is about eight to ten feet down – no distance for a modern excavator, but a long way for a pick and shovel. At Faringdon, they had broken into old mine galleries and found candles and clay pipes from three hundred years before.

'The old cottages would be thrown up out of random walling: all shapes and sizes with jumpers – massive big stones plonked in the wall to make it go up quicker. Then you'd get coursed Cotswold stone six and four inches thick with just the occasional jumper; and finally, in your manor houses, ashlar, a stone that's cut into blocks with a saw. But some of the old cottages are precious antiques, especially when you get the mullioned windows and all the bits and pieces that go with them. Double walls with the best stone outside – warm in winter, cool in summer – twenty-one inches thick (I don't know what that is in metres).'

'Who does, who does?' I asked, remembering cottages of my childhood in which the condensation shone on the bedroom walls on a winter night, and fungus flourished in the hall, sometimes openly, sometimes in secret behind prematurely-doomed panels of plywood and other inexpensive building materials. My recollection of the romance of cottage life was the romance of damp and other inconveniences that required substantial applications of middle-class prosperity before they would go away even temporarily. How the original cottagers had managed, I shivered to think.

Bob was into repair techniques by now. For stonework he would always use a rather weak mortar with lime in it, he told me: cement was too hard, had no give in it.

'Up to the late 30s, our fellows would dig drift from the side of the road – you'd get a certain amount of throw-up from a stone surface. Back at the yard, they'd knock it up into a huge heap of mortar with water and lump lime which would all bubble and melt. This would be done weeks before you needed it: it would go semi-hard, but the labourers would knock it up again before you used it. We built some houses with that in Northleach in 1939, and they're as good as ever. Tudor fronts on them: I'm afraid I don't like everything too symmetrical – I like angles and apexes, lots of gables, returns, porches, entrances, everything going round the corner a bit. It always looks attractive. Mind you, the fellows I employ, it gets on their nerves if they have to build too many angles.'

'I can see it might,' I said, thinking that a similar problem might have afflicted the constructional demons called in to build the house in the wood for the wicked witch who insisted on a fabric of reinforced toffee and barley-sugar, and an adequate supply of gables to catch the attention of wandering children.

Bob told me that he was busy with a fantasy at that moment – a summer-house: 'Rather luxurious – circular with a conical stone slate roof with a glass lantern and a stone ball on top.'

'It sounds more like a lighthouse than a summer-house.'

'The great thing is to get the old stone – from a farmer pulling a barn down, say. Stone slates are very precious: you really look after them. They start big at the eaves, diminishing as they go up the roof, and as they've been re-used over the centuries, the big ones have been chopped down and down in size so that they're very scarce now. They all had their different names in different places in years gone by – round Northleach it was "Long Levens" at the bottom going up through "Short Levens" and "Crowsfoots" to "Muffeties".'

'Like blue slates,' I said: ' "Ladies", "Small Ladies" and "Duchesses".'

He told me that one village had had its telephone box built in Cotswold stone with a stone roof so as to chime with the surroundings.

'Hell of a job to find the phone if you're a stranger, mind you, but it certainly blends.'

What he really liked to see in Cotswold houses were mullioned windows: I could see his manner warming up at the very thought. The quarries made them now, he said, instead of there being a mason on site and a metal casement from he local blacksmith, but his men still knew how to repair and titivate them.

'It takes a good fellow to put 'em together: sill, jambs, transom, mullions, label mould (that keeps the water off the windows), kneelers (little return angles on the end of the mould), but when you've got lead lights in them, you can't go better.' He looked out upon the world through mullions, even though he lived in a bungalow.

'With your affection for Cotswold stone cottages, what are you doing living in a house like this?' I asked him.

'Well, I didn't build it: I bought it for privacy. Inside, it's all right: outside, it looks ghastly – imitation stone roof on it, "Yuk!" I thought when I saw it, not my cup of tea at all. But the position is second to none and you can never have a superb house in the correct spot unless you're Lord Vestey, just over the valley there: he has it, he really has.' He pondered the good fortune of the aristocracy for a moment, then brightened up, and chuckled. 'But, you know, from up here we actually look down on him a little bit. It's a pretty view, just over the ridge: trees and a valley. I'd like to see that when I die.'

'Well, when you do, you'll have a good undertaker, from all accounts,' I said, for Cyril Sly of Northleach is known the country round.

'Mr Sly? He is *so* nice. I've known him all my life, and the Sly farm and the Cook farm go back to my great-grandfather's time. We've always been in building: but he is a natural undertaker. He makes it so easy, he really does.'

'You can't ask more of an undertaker than that,' I said: and went to see him.

Cyril Sly lived in the main street of Northleach, which is a cross-roads with old stone houses and the Cotswold Country-side Collection; this is a rural museum housed in the former House of Correction which looks like a lowish sort of castle and was the brainchild of a progressive magistrate, Sir George Onesiphorus Paul, who deserves to be remembered, if only for his name.

The undertaker's front door was more in the way of a portal:

heavy, black and low, set into Tudor stone. The undertaker himself was on the telephone when I arrived, and since there was no telling whether it might be tactful to disturb him, his sister took me off to the old barn at the bottom of the garden where she was working on a model of the local church, which is a fine one for a small village, built by wool-staplers in the fifteenth century as the sister church to Chipping Camden. There was to be a floral festival and the model was designed at the head of her floral carpet, and was made of seeds and grasses.

'It's inside me and I've got to get it out,' said Miss Sly. 'The panes of glass are the seeds from the hogweed, there are sycamore wings here in the tops of the windows, and Timothy Grass round the edge of the door. The doors themselves are laurel leaves, with goose-grass nail-studs, and all the spars in the windows are made from the stems of cow parsley. I'm not sure which grass this other one is on the tower – it's the one we used to go "tinker tailor soldier sailor" to – but it's plantain for the pinnacles, and I've got a sunflower seed for the handle of the door.'

Looking at the church, it struck me that someone only had to sprinkle water over it for the whole thing to sprout.

Mr Sly had finished his phone call. He came up the garden path in his shirt-sleeves, and took me back to the house past the old carpenter's workshop, all dusty skylight, hand tools and a pair of trestles waiting in patient certainty in the middle of the floor for something to come and sit on them. His living room was plain and solemn with a great stone mantelpiece, on which stood a large clock; and as we sat either side of the fireplace, I could hear it ticking.

The Slys took up their trade in 1916 when the previous undertaker, the much-respected Mr George Bee, took his last journey up the church path he had trodden so often before – for the first time for years in an unprofessional capacity. Mr Bee had combined his business with being a house-carpenter: Cyril Sly's father began as a wheelwright, and continued the craft until the 1930s.

'It usually went together – there was a wheelwright/carpenter/undertaker in every village, but eventually they all died out. Father died in 1976,' added Mr Sly, absentmindedly. 'He was ninety-five.'

'Good lord!'

'Yes, he was a great age wasn't he?' said Mr Sly with great satisfaction, and went on to tell me that it was all horse-drawn funerals when he was a lad, though the splendours of black horses and plumes went out before his time.

'As a little boy, it was difficult to understand. People would come to order the funerals and pay their bills. They used to get upset more than they do now and cry a lot more. It was at Northleach hospital that I saw my first body. When Father took a coffin up to the little local chapel of rest, I remember seeing it through the door – just at the door, I didn't go in.' He laughed a diffident half-laugh, as if it was not quite proper to let it out. The clock on the mantelpiece chimed gently but firmly, and made me start.

'I've been into most of the big homes and every little one for miles around. We try to treat all of them the same, and if I dare say so, people treat me almost as a member of the family. I think they feel relieved after I've gone, but when I arrive, they say, "Leave it to Cyril – he'll look after it." Sometimes a young husband has lost a young wife, or a child has died – you rather wish you weren't doing it then: there's many occasions like that when you feel it's been a real sad funeral.'

The doorbell rang: I wondered whether we would be disturbed and why, but nobody came in. Mr Sly went on to say that he didn't think of himself as particularly mournful by nature. Though most of his clothes were dark, he had a brown suit and a grey one to wear for his principal relaxation, which was going to church on Sunday morning. It sounded a bit of a busman's holiday, but if it is true for most people to say that 'In the midst of life we are in death', it is ten times more relevant to an undertaker, whose potential customers are apt to open the most convivial conversation with a leg-pull about him going round sizing them up. Many times repeated, it would be enough to make anyone lugubrious, I thought, but Cyril Sly seemed content. 'I like gardening when I get the chance,' he went on, 'but I don't have much time.'

The clock ticked, endorsing the sentiment for all of us.

'We don't have any "sign on the dotted line" or anything like that and we hardly ever mention money. We never ask if they want it like so and so's for each funeral is an individual one: most people want it done nice and plain, according to their circumstances. I know the families and remember previous occasions, and our books go back to Father's time. Some people will follow tradition and have a certain style of coffin – English oak, perhaps, which will cost more than an elm one. It's possible to buy ready-made coffins, but we stack our own timber to dry and our best coffins are handmade. Elm is difficult to buy locally now, but it's still in reasonable supply in the north.

'We've had military funerals where the coffin's been draped with the Union Jack and soldiers for pallbearers; we've had Scotchmen with bagpipes. There was a chief-constable of police who died at Bourton-on-the-Water and I should think every chief-constable in the British Isles was there.'

Cyril Sly told me he never used cosmetics on a corpse: he thought they might possibly make up bodies in towns where the firms might be more business-like, but he was a country undertaker.

'They say that if you don't go to London, you die a fool,' said Mr Sly, somehow managing to convey that the truth of the matter was quite the contrary. 'Well I hope not, because I didn't go to London till quite late in life. I went to the Wembley exhibition. Then, we went to collect a coffin at Heathrow but the plane was late so we toured London in the middle of the night to fill in the time – round Nelson's Column and Trafalgar Square, Horse Guards' Parade, the Mall, Buckingham Palace.'

I learned that hearses lasted very well, having low gearing to accommodate all the slow driving: that a proper speed for the open road was thirty miles an hour, and that if the journey was difficult to time, the thing to do was to leave early and find "a decent layby" in which you might lay by decently until the mourners' cars caught up: that Mr Sly's no-claim bonus was in a glorious state of shining purity and always had been.

However, there remained one question I particularly wanted to ask, though it was difficult to know how to put it. I said: 'Death is an incredibly important event in anyone's life, I suppose, but all the same, mixed in with the sadness and misery there must be some humour, unconscious or not . . . er . . . er . . . Have you got any recollections of particularly unusual incidents in the past – strange reactions to death? Strange events?' (This was an elaborated version of the question which is traditional among radio interviewers and in its briefest form is: 'Have you got any funny stories?')

'I don't think I could think of one, not at the moment,' said Mr Sly. On the mantelpiece the clock struck once more.

'Doesn't it affect your own personality, being associated with death so much of the time?' I asked.

'I'm probably slightly light-hearted in the week but during the service in church, I'm calm. I think at the bottom of my heart, I enjoy my work – I always have. I feel very happy at it. I like people, I'm prepared to help people. I have a responsibility, and I feel it.'

The clock was still striking. 'But it can't be much fun, can it?' I asked.

'I'm not really interested in anything else. Perhaps I dare say, it's your life.'

Mr Sly chuckled: and ushered me to his front portal, with the chimes still ringing in my ears.

As I rode from Northleach and the day drew on, the sun drained the colour from the landscape of cropped fields dotted with hay-bales like primitive dwellings, rolling stubble, darker wheat in wait for the combine, charred fields where, like wheat, the fire had grown in straight lines. The grain was so dry that the light hit it and stopped dead, glistening all over the ears. In the lulls between the cars, I could hear the dry clatter of wheat ears, one against the other, in the breeze that picked the heat up off the road and threw it at me.

The yellow of the tiny toadflax in the verge was an echo of spreading fields of flowers as bright as mustard. Great purple thistles flowered in a dip of the road with old shrub roses someone must have planted on the banks, their flowers looking impossibly large in their wild setting.

I passed a couple who had parked their car a little way up a farm track and were engaged in offering and experiencing what I took to be The Traditional Milkmaid's Temptation (as defined in our folksong heritage) by the side of a field of long hay: the girl in a dress of cornflower blue, the young man holding out to her a flower of the same colour, a harebell, possibly. It was either extremely romantic or rather calculating of him, I thought, or possibly both: the distinction is often blurred in such circumstances.

The decline of The Traditional Milkmaid's Temptation in the twentieth century is not to be attributed to the rise of the milking machine and any consequent shortage of milkmaids. Formerly conducted in the highly salubrious English Pastoral Setting, the Temptation depended on the countryside being regularly and intensively patrolled by persons of a variety of occupations brimming over with lust: it only needed an itinerant sailor / gentleman / ploughman / grenadier to encounter a milkmaid / fine lady / shepherdess / female haymaker to provoke outbursts of sexuality usually certified as exceptional by the parties concerned.

Looking back on this apparently golden age of travelling relationships, the lone cyclist cannot but ask the question: 'Where are these persons now?': to which the answer is 'On wheels'. Mobility has killed The Temptation which was one of the relatively few sexual activities known to begin with the feet ('As I walked out . . . & etc &etc). If you are walking, it is difficult to ignore other people on foot and to avoid a period of enforced proximity if you are both travelling in the same direction. The phenomenon is very similar to that defined in *Vernon's Second Principle of Social and Physical Geography (Theory of Lifts)*, viz:

> If, in any given lift, sex + sex = two, then the reaction cannot be indifferent, and the moment of coincidence may be acutely interesting. There is no communication between the first and seventh floors, but a power failure may be a different matter.

Today, the car is hopeless for chance encounters because all the people behind hoot at you if you stop for an instant: the only way the GT young man can get to meet the convertible young lady is by bashing into her bumper, but then they have a row. Bicycles are better for meeting people, but it is often risky to ride abreast; trains, buses and aircraft are insufficiently solitary; cruise liners are too obvious; dodgems are too transitory. The only thing for young persons to do nowadays is to make a prior arrangement to get in the car together in the first place, and get out of the car together in the second, which should preferably be more secluded than that chosen by the couple I had just seen. But where is the happenstance in that? Having meditated, I glanced back: it seemed that the girl had accepted the flower.

Not many miles had passed before I was subjected to temptation myself. As Fossebridge hill (which, from the cycling point of view is a kind of gentle journey-to-the-centre-of-the-earth and back again) I came upon a seductive branch of bright red apples hanging over a garden wall. I turned round once, slowly, in the road beneath them meditating like a character in Aesop, but then two streams of traffic were upon me, and I was driven onward by a hundred accusing eyes, doubtless the keener for what they may have observed by the hayfield. Fortunately, there was another garden wall, and another apple tree a little further on.

I had just passed the garage of 'Eric Loving – put new heart in your car' when Jenny drew up alongside.

'Did you see Loving?' I asked.

'Oh, they really were, were they?' said Jenny: 'Yes, I thought they were.'

We made our separate ways to Bourton-on-the-Water.

Bourton is an exceptionally pretty village, with Cotswold houses and spreading greens; and its water is the Windrush, which flows clear and gently over gravel through the centre of everything and has to be crossed and re-crossed on rustic foot-bridges to get from one tourist attraction to another. Some people find that a model village, an extended aviary called Birdland, a model railway lay-out and a trout farm in which you can 'feed the trout and watch the water boil' add to the attractions. Most of those people appeared to be already there by the time I arrived: certainly there was little room for any more. They sat on the grass, they ate ice-creams, they paddled in the brook, they walked over the rustic bridges, and when they had done that they walked back again: most of them were enjoying themselves with such decorum and solemnity that it was difficult to be sure that they were enjoying themselves at all.

A surly-looking girl scowled darkly into her ice-lolly; a

stout old woman with a bandaged leg looked funerals down the path, waiting for it to be time to go back to her comfortable seat in the coach; a baby footballer, all of three years old, kicked a windfall apple seriously round the pub lawn, obviously wishing he was back home in his garden with a proper ball.

'That little boy's spastic all up to here,' said a pig-tailed nymphet to her mother with great satisfaction.

'Surely they could do a tracheotomy or something?' said the chairman of a self-constituted working party set up to consider what you should do in the event of swallowing a wasp with your ploughman's lunch or lager. By a lobster-coloured man peeling uncomfortably in the shade of a tree, a more recently reddened lady carried on the family administration from behind her sun-glasses.

'Don't drink with that: it's someone's straw, isn't it?'

'No it isn't,' replied her son. 'I found it in the river.'

There is a specially aimless walk for enjoying yourself; it is supposed to help the holiday-makers convince themselves that they can go anywhere, and ends up by giving the impression that they have nowhere to go. I could see people who never wanted to go to Birdland going to Birdland; women who had spent their lives hating model railways, going to the model railways out of sheer boredom. Families loitered outside the trout farm discussing the price structure of a fifteen-pence bag of fish food and the notice warning that they would visit the trout farm 'AT YOUR OWN RISK', as if the trout were some kind of freshwater Jaws.

Taken over by the general lassitude, Jenny and I followed a dog paddling wet dog-foot patterns down the pavement to the Victoria Hall whose lawn was set with tea-tables (folding, so as to be equally adaptable to bingo). Ministering to the tables were ladies with tea, ladies with scones, ladies with craft, ladies with jumble, and generally-assistant ladies.

'You at least must belong to Bourton,' I said to the ladies with the tea-pot and the scones.

'We are Bourton,' replied the lady with the tea. 'We are the WI.'

'I'm surprised you can stand this lot,' I said.

The ladies were tolerant: 'They've as much right to come as we've got to go to the sea-side, haven't they? A lot of people say it's a bit commercialised, but you've got to boost trade, so you mustn't grumble, must you?' asked one lady, as if she was far from sure of the answer.

'Come on a Bank Holiday, you won't see an inch of grass,' said another.

'Gives a bit of life,' said another.

I said that I had noticed as I came along that even the Baptist church had a sign which was larger than usual, as if it were infected by the general desire to advertise its attractions. The ladies gave a little flutter of weakish laughter. I was just concluding that I had come upon a society of people who had been turning the other cheek for so long that there was no cheek at all left in them, when there was a small voice from the back:

'If they came for the beauty, I wouldn't mind,' said the small voice, 'but just look at them! They could do what they're doing in their own back yard: they don't even look at the trees and the gardens – they make straight for the ice-cream place and the fish and chip shop.' The tolerant ladies issued a succession of high and nervous laughs.

The small voice went on: 'It's not for us that live here, but I feel for the village itself – I think of it as a separate entity. It's been absolutely desecrated, it's like a poor old lady that's been mugged, it really is. The grass is worn down, it's dog-eared, it's tired – and we haven't got a village to show one of our own visitors, it's all taken over. I would hate it if no one came at all, but I'd like the right people to come and appreciate its beauty – take care of it and not abuse it. We're just a Cinderella for the rest of the Cotswold villages.'

I took tea and scones with the ladies, both of which were priced at about half of what they should have been, and were being ignored by the tourists in favour of the more expensive official attractions. The small voice, which turned out to be quite forthright when I got closer to it, told me that where there were now summer attractions there had been shops – a drapers, a furniture shop, a wool shop, two grocers, a tailor, a blacksmith, a small department store.

'It was a delightful little convenient village which everyone visited because it was in the vale, with the river and little industrial things around it. It is a beautiful village, and it *is* sad to see it so desecrated.'

There is one shop in Bourton which is both a tourist attraction and small industry – the Cotswold Perfumery. The tourists come and mill around in the shop dipping glass samplers into ink-wells of fragrance, and getting their noses thoroughly confused before they buy anything – if they do. However, a principal part of the business of John Stephen, perfumer (he refuses to call himself a perfumier) is supplying perfumes for toiletries and other industrial products. He is a professional nose – or, as I soon began to think of him, Nose.

His laboratory was neat, white and cool, with blinds over the roof-lights to keep out the sun: fluorescent tubes lit his empire of bottles – brown chemical bottles, row upon row on the shelves, plebian essences that came in such quantity that they had to sit upon the floor, tiny phials of coloured liquids of aristocratic clarity.

'Every single perfume material is subject to damage by light – especially sunlight,' the perfumer told me, 'that's why all the windows are blacked out. Most of the sensitive materials are in amber bottles, to protect them even from the fluorescent, and the very sensitive materials are in the dark, in the fridge. If you buy a perfume, the fridge is the place to make it last longest – and the worst possible position is on the dressing-table in full sunlight, because that will damage a perfume within an hour. In a fridge, perfume will last for years.'

'Cheese may not taste so good though,' said Jenny.

'It's not so much that perfumes don't like high temperatures (though they don't),' the perfumer went on, ignoring her: 'it's changes in temperature – up during the day, down at night.'

'So another good place to keep perfume would be a wine cellar?' I suggested.

'Yes, as long as you don't mix the bottles up.' From what he told me, it seemed that he had as much to remember as a patent lawyer: and he had to remember it all with his nose. He had begun to experiment with fragrances and blending when he was still at school.

'No one in this trade will tell you anything: they're very coy about trends and what they do. When I meet other perfumers, I tend to talk about the weather. I was self-taught, and I think that if I'd known what I was letting myself in for, I would never have started. It's not easy to make a nice smell, especially one that a lot of people like, but it's very, very easy to make an unpleasant one.'

It is difficult for anyone to learn about perfumes. There are few books on the subject: the old ones are rare, the modern tend to be very technical. In shops, people feel diffident about asking questions and, when they do, they often get ignorant answers from the people behind the counter. The packaging, the price, the name on the box, all add to the confusion.

'Describing a smell is a real problem because people aren't educated about it as they are about taste, sound and sight. Most people say things are "sweet" or "strong", but sweet-ness and strength are nothing to do with an odour type: they ought to describe things as floral, herbaceous or woody.'

'So I need a course in Nostril Linguistics?'

'To describe fragrances yourself, you need an olfactory memory and you can only get one by smelling things every day and trying to remember them. You can't make perfume if all you know is that the smell is too "something" – you have to be able to pick out the woody or herbaceous note in order to be able to change it.'

In spite of this, the Public Nose shows a certain sharpness of instinct. It often picks out as a favourite perfume one contain-ing particularly expensive fragrances like jasmine or tuberose. Having bought it regularly, the Nose becomes extraordinarily sensitive to any alteration: it is impossible to alter a best-selling perfume with impunity, for perfumes are not like wine, where someone will prefer the 1976 Chanel No 5 to the 1983, a fruitier year. (Buying samples of the ingredients are kept all year in a dark refrigerator, so that the next season's intake of supplies can be compared and adjusted.)

People's tastes vary with age: the composition of their skin changes, so that a perfume may suddenly react with it dif-ferently, or others in their thirties may suddenly lose their liking for a perfume they wore in their twenties. Some people get hooked on a fragrance, like a tune that runs around the brain: they demand it in everything – the bath, the car, the talcum powder and the soap.

The problem of being a perfumer is how to talk to your nose, and remember what it says. I soon began to feel that our language is simply not subtle enough to say much about scents: our conversation became more and more like the process of attempting to play Mozart on a steak and kidney pudding. Since there is no language for the nose, it has made its own out of colours and sounds.

'You can split perfumes up into as many groups as you like,' the perfumer explained to me, 'but if you begin a spectrum with light green notes – floral notes – you can get spicy florals, herbaceous florals, sweet florals, and so on. There are aldehydic-type notes – aldehydes are a group of chemicals discovered about the turn of the century and which became famous because of their use in Chanel No 5. Then there is a sheep-type classification.'

'I've smelt sheep in my time,' I said, 'but I didn't know they made perfume out of them.'

'Not sheep, *Chypre* – French for Cyprus. When the Crusaders invaded the island, they found a sticky substance that adhered to sheep's wool as they walked through the bushes, and which they had to boil out before they could use the wool. That was labdanum – very thick, sweet and gooey, and highly aromatic.'

'Chypre and sheep both, in a way?'

'I suppose so. Cabochard is a typical chypre-type note – such perfumes have got heavy bases – things like oakmoss, patchouli, vetivert and sandalwood – usually with a floral middle-note and an orange or bergamot top-note.'

The expensive boxes on the chemists' shelves account for only about a fifth of the perfume industry; the rest is industrial. Nor are French perfumes necessarily French: many of the most famous names have no perfume departments of their own, and the contents of the bottle may well come from America, Switzerland or Japan. The perfumer said he might be briefed to create a perfume for anything, from toothpaste, to boot polish, to car freshener.

'So there are experts who buy from you, you are an expert buying from other experts – and throughout British industry, a great chain of noses?' I asked.

'That's right, but it's shrinking: as companies get bigger, the number of noses gets smaller.'

'We had a go at scent when I was a little boy,' I said. 'Layers of wallflowers and rose petals in jamjars in the sun: cotton-wool came into it somewhere, and we filled them up with oil. I can't remember what sort of oil we used: we were a bit hazy

about the distinction between vegetable and mineral oil, I
think, so I wouldn't be surprised if it was diesel.'

The perfumer hardly blenched, but I think I saw his Nose
twitch. He told me that the roses should have been picked
before they opened, to get the best of the fragrance. I wondered if the same technique could be applied to the making of
rose-petal jam.

Perfumes such as those that were in the mind's nose of
Shakespeare when he described the scented sails of Cleopatra's
barge were quite unsophisticated. Four centuries ago, perfumers only had a limited range of natural materials – because
many florals were burnt by the heat of the steam distillation
used then. Today's techniques are cold, using hydrocarbon
solvents to produce a much wider and more natural range – at a
price. The perfumer quoted me £9000 or £10,000 a kilo – about
£1 a drop – for tuberose absolute: jasmine was only half the
price. Both are unique in being the only flowers that continue
to create essential oils after they have been cut, and are laid
individually on greased trays in a process called *enflorage*. New
flowers are put on the trays every day for a season of four to
five weeks: every day, the grease absorbs more of the essential
oils, which are eventually solvent-extracted and washed with
alcohol to become an 'absolute' – ounces of which are the
product of tonnes of flowers. Hence the price differential with
something like humble orange oil which is excellent value at
£1.50 a kilo for anyone who wants to go round smelling like
marmalade, and with chemicals which may not sound romantic but which are universally used.

'Every major success since 1880 has marked the discovery of
a new chemical. It began with Houbigant's Fougere Royale,
which was a soap. Paul Parquet, the perfumier, used a material
called coumarin which smells slightly – coconutty,' said the
perfumer, momentarily lost for words.

John Stephen had some eight hundred essences in his bottles, and a pair of electronic scales weighing to a hundredth of a
gramme. With these, his refrigerator, some laboratory glass, a
bench, little test-strips with a texture in between blotting
paper and filter paper, an extractor to clear out unwanted
odours, and a pipette, he was equipped for work: all he needed
after that was the Nose which, he admitted, was not insured. It
seemed reckless.

Perfumes are analysed by a process which is grandly known as 'selective olfactory fatigue', but the principle is simple – it is the same as diagnosing which illness is most likely to be dangerous to you by observing which is the one you die of.

'The Nose becomes numbed by exposure to certain fragrances: so you take a dip of perfume, maybe pick out one of the top-notes first – say, bergamot – then smell bergamot to exhaustion. When you go back to the tester strip, you'll be able to smell everything but bergamot, and perhaps notice patchouli, or rose: exhaust your sense of smell to those, and other things will come forward.'

I was getting curious about the contents of the enigmatic brown bottles: the perfumer told me I might find them difficult to recognise.

'Smells are very rarely experienced on their own: they usually have a back-up of other senses – you see a bunch of roses, and your nose knows what to expect. People can remember smells – a particular odour can take them back years: to school for instance.'

I thought of my schooldays – socks in changing rooms; liver and bacon, boiled potatoes, tapioca pudding in the canteen; pervasive disinfectant in the corridors – and wished that I could forget. Perhaps it was because of those associations that I recognised amyl acetate instantly as pear-drops: but the second bottle was more difficult.

'A bit like the dentist? Smells like – some sort of food (usually is food, in my case) – acid-ripe? Not a very high note, somewhere about the C above Middle C, I should say: a two-octave perfume.'

'It's iso-eugenol, found in clove-oil and carnation, which is one of the spiciest of the florals. It reminds people simultaneously of flowers and the dentist – that's the clove – and they can't equate the two.'

He brought out lemon grass, which I failed to recognise; and sandalwood oil, from the bottom of the spectrum of fragrance and too low for me to smell at all. Then another well-used bottle.

'It's another treble clef: quite delightful, but . . .'

'Take your time smelling, always.'

'A perfume with plenty of body, enticingly clothed.'

'How about citrus?'

'Of course – candied lemon.'

'Well . . .'

'Or orange? Except that it's not orange. Grapefruit?'

'It's a peppery note.'

'That's what I meant – lemon with black pepper on it.'

'It's bergamot. Like citrus but not too harsh – very popular.' A lot of people like this sort of fresh note to liven them up in the morning, and a perfume with deep musky notes to make them seductive at night.'

'Oh, is that how you do it?' I asked, interested.

'No, that's a cliché.'

'So what *do* you do to be attractive at night?'

'What do *I* do?' replied the perfumer, uneasily.

'No, what does one do?'

'I think you should choose a perfume to go with your character.'

'What would that be? Bearing in mind the attraction at night.'

'Well, I don't know you personally,' said the perfumer, as if this were a particularly desirable state of affairs. 'A Fougère type? I don't know whether you like Fougère perfumes?'

'Nor do I.'

'Say, fresh mossy with a hint of lavender. Old gentleman's cologne – that sort of range.'

'Really?' I said. 'I wouldn't have thought those sorts of notes would have suited me at all. At night.'

As we left the laboratory, a dog was nosing the dustbins.

'Has your dog a good nose?' I asked.

'Not my dog, but they smell molecules where we smell drops. Must be getting a complete overdose – I can't imagine what must be happening in its little mind.'

'What do you do when your nose gets fatigued?'

'You just leave it, because otherwise you make so many mistakes. There are some materials that are very, very fatiguing. Ionone, which is used for violets – you can't extract any fragrance from violets, you see, any more than from carnation or lily-of-the-valley: I'm afraid Devon violets have never seen a violet, least of all from Devon. So you have to make it synthetically, and ionone is a group of chemicals that are extremely exhausting so if you're going to do any work on violets, you always do it at the end of the day. Zonks your nose out completely.'

The dog and I looked at each other as if we both understood what it was to be zonked – the dog because its nose was superior, mine for the other reason. I headed for Moreton-in-Marsh with a scent of cloves in my plebeian nostrils. (I think it was cloves.) The road led across a wide green vale to a round hill on the top of which was Stow-on-the-Wold. A signpost at the top said Cirencester was nineteen miles behind, so I stopped to check the mileometer, only to discover that I had forgotten to clip it back when I started off from Bourton.

'How have you done?' demanded the cheerful young land-lord of the Redesdale Arms in Moreton-in-Marsh, after he had first offered me a drink and then recommended the local crayfish on his menu (for Moreton has the wide streets of a coaching town, and the Redesdale Arms at least has not forgotten that the words 'hostelry' and 'hospitality' begin in the same way).

'I'm not quite sure,' I replied. 'I've got a computer fault.'

'So have we all, sometimes,' said the landlord, tapping his head in an understanding manner.

V

OF PEDIGREE AND PIES

TO NEWARK via LEICESTER and MELTON MOWBRAY

'You're mad,' said the breakfast waitress at the Redesdale Arms when she heard I was pedalling off to Leicester that day.

I took it as a compliment: it was a very English thing to say, partly because it was one of those tentative overtures at friendliness that come out somewhere between joke and insult because our society is so awkward at casual intimacy but for which we make allowances, and partly because it showed how important eccentricity is to us. In some countries the madman, the possessed, the dervish is god-given: England is like that too, in a calm, everyday sort of way. We value the one who stands apart from the crowd as a seer whose world is askew from our own (but may very well be the right way up – who knows, or cares?), even if his vision may only extend to keeping a houseful of stray cats, or cycling to Leicester when he could go in a car. Indeed, we prefer minor eccentricities to major ones – we like our lunatics to be social. Listen to a group of young girls and hear how often they say 'You're mad,' to their friends, just as the waitress did to me.

'All the same,' Jenny said, 'it goes across two whole maps. Are you sure . . .?'

'Think of Scott,' I replied nobly, 'Marco Polo, Vasco da Gama, Hannibal and his elephants.'

'But his elephants weren't on bicycles.'

'I was thinking of myself in the context of Hannibal,' I pointed out.

I was off before nine, up the wide, warm-stoned coaching street, and past Spook Erectors (which is not something that goes bump in the night, but a strangely-named market-stall company on the fringe of the town, by the verdant-banked single-track railway) out on to the main road with the early-morning cars and farm lorries. It was a grey morning to the north-west, but the strong headwind whistling about my ears was already chasing sunspots of white gold over the cornfields from the east. I felt myself leaving the borders of the South and West, and coming to the Midlands.

It was extraordinary how abruptly the change occurred: a patina of yeoman style and confidence settled throughout centuries of prosperity seemed to fall away: even the road that at Cirencester had marched across the wold had begun to amble among lowlands and fidgety hills. There was a daub of a sign advertising wayside onions, and a plain farm whose bright flowerbeds in front could not tidy the tumbledown outbuildings and sheds at the back: things no longer felt quite kempt as I came over the crest of a sheep-spread hill down to the tufty willows lining Paddle Brook, the boundary of Warwickshire.

The difference began with the trees. I had seen occasional dead elms ever since Devon, but now they advanced over the landscape in ranks, in files along the hedgerows. They were spectral, with all vestige of elmness leached back to the soil by the winter rains: twigs and bark gone from each one, leaving only a pale and spiky skeleton.

Our comfortable country in our comfortable century is not

much used to '*memento mori*', but that is what the dead elm says to us, as desolately as the human husk dangling in chains at the crossroads spoke to former ages. Worse, the elm is the pattern of our very own twentieth-century brand of disaster – no longer the personal mishap but the general plague bred out of an over-crowded, over-stimulated world that strikes without reason, and strikes everywhere. The general disaster is nothing new of course, but we can see it coming, and we are so near controlling such things that we fear the one we may not be able to control even more. The dead elm is the gibbet on which hangs the spectre of our destruction of nature, of the aftermath of nuclear war, of incurable disease and the fear of cancer, of the unfortunate genetic twist that turns a virus into an unstoppable murderer. The elms are a warning as well as being so sad in themselves to those who loved them when they were green: and they take on a despairing air as their extremities decay and break off at random, leaving twigs going all ways, as if blown by many contrary winds.

Where there were buildings, it was the sudden loss of Cotswold stone that made the difference. Though there was a brief revival of stone at Halford, Cotswold architecture vanished from my route with the county boundary. The mullions went, to be replaced by wooden window frames: the stone became paler and soon there was nothing but brick – and it is strange that yellow stone should be warmer than red brick, but it is so, nevertheless.

Indeed, after Halford, where the main route bends away towards Warwick, practically everything but simple countryside vanished from the Fosse. The road was suddenly quiet, and with the quietness – and the insistence of the road on going very straight over the top of every possible rise – my pace slowed as well. I passed an old iron gate in the hedge, twined with convolvulus and sagging happily, indifferent to the fact that it would never open usefully again. For me too it was a carefree sort of day.

I smelt a dry smell to the corn, as if tiny particles were trying to lodge in the back of my throat. A flight of thistledown went past and I realised that I could hear the wind again, blustering into my ears, carrying the fretful bleating of sheep. The white cloud was breaking up, the grey cloud a memory on the horizon. The wind was strong enough for the birds to plane on it: I stopped to record its rustles in the branches of an oak tree, and an oak-apple toppled through them with all the impetuosity and uncertain aim of youthfulness, and bounced along the road with misplaced confidence, as if it were off on a journey of its own.

There is the most tremendous sense of continuity of feeling about this part of the Fosse Way: going so straight over everything in its path, it brings you forcibly into contact with the contours of the land. There is no skirting or evading: you have no choice but to revel in its downs and wrestle with its ups – and as you toil to the brow of the hill, you can see nothing beyond, but you *feel* it going on and on in the same way, for so many miles as centuries. Even the imagination of the highways department seemed to have been touched, for the road was now signposted as the Fosse Way for the first time.

Past verges of tall grasses waving rich heads of what, since my toga lesson, I knew to be Tyrian purple, I came to the Hole in the Road. It was not a very big Hole, but it had two men to shovel in it, and a third to stand by it wearing yellow oil-skins as a badge of high office, and swing the Stop-Go sign. He swung it for me. I have always wondered why some roadmenders get to swing the sign and other roadmenders get to dig, but I did not like to ask in the hearing of his companions for fear of disturbing the even tenor of their digging.

'Got down to the Roman bit yet?' I asked.

'Har. Ee arr ee aar ee,' said the man with the sign, swivelling it.

'Eeeeeeeee-awr-ee,' went the sign.

'Sorry?'

' 'E are'e, 'e are,' confirmed the man with the sign: 'an' 'ee are on 'er. 'Aven't seen 'er yet though.' A car approached, stopped, and waited: but the man with the sign had turned round to talk to me. 'We dig trenches across 'er: couldn't tell no difference. So, dunno.' Within the Hole, the diggers were becoming restive: they could see the car, but were they both to have to do all the hard work and watch out for cars as well? 'But they make-believe a bit, don't they?'

'Yes, they do.'

The younger and more impetuous of the diggers compromised on a strangled grunt, and another one when the man with the sign turned round with an inadequate display of embarrassment.

'Eeeeeeeee-awr-ee.' The car went past. 'Eeeeeeeee-awr-ee.'

'The Roman road could've went somewhere up 'ere.' The man with the sign turned back to me. Immediately he had done so, the only other car within five miles came over the brow of the hill, stopped, and waited patiently. 'But it were only a track, weren' it? 'Oss 'n cart effect.' The diggers seethed. 'You goin' up towards Lincoln?'

'Edinburgh.'

'Doin' well, then: nice weather for it.' There was a furious double bellow from the hole.

'Oops!' I said, 'there's another one.'

'Eeeeeeeee-awr-ee. Eeeeeeeee-awr-ee.'

'Sorry about that,' said the man with the sign, turning back with more frivolity than contrition. Over his shoulder I saw the top of a slow cattle-truck clear the brow of a hill, a procession of cars and vans behind it.

'I think I'd better be getting along,' I said.

'Cheerio,' said the man with the sign amiably, gazing after me.

It was some while before I was passed by the procession of vehicles. When they had gone by, I looked back down the long straight to see that the diggers had given up digging, had got out of the Hole, and were waving their arms and shouting at the man with the sign: there seemed to be in progress some attempt to divest him of his yellow oilskins.

It was no-frills farmland, with the newly ploughed fields as rich as milk chocolate: once there was a brown farmhouse with arches to its barns, as if William Morris had been at them: 'Lower Fosse Farm' said the map: 'Fodden's Farm' said the farm. Considering it was obviously this century, I have seldom seen such unity in house and outbuildings. A number of very straight miles further on – over the Warwick and Napton Canal, where the narrow-boats *Cocky* and *Pioneer* rode between the locks in that half-tidy, humdrum way that narrow-boats have – I came upon Jenny in the garden of the Plough at Eathorpe, the first pub on the road since Halford.

Jenny was keeping company with a Superploughman, which was a gargantuan garnish entirely surrounding a vast bread, cheese and pickle.

'I've met you once already today,' she said. 'I passed a turning, looked down it, and there was a cyclist. I said, "There's Tom, that's definitely Tom, 'cos he's wearing blue shorts and a white top." I couldn't imagine why you'd gone off the Fosse, so I turned round and went to have a look. And there was no cyclist there at all: there wasn't even a different cyclist. It was strange . . .'

'You weren't confusing me with a very fast man with a handlebar moustache and an orange sweater down to his knees, going south?' (That was the only cyclist and practically all the traffic I had seen recently apart from a funeral cortége, a rude green lorry called Mitchell's For Potatoes which had come near to qualifying me to join the corpse, and a London taxi weighed down with luggage and Mum and a sleepy little girl queening it in the back.)

'I wasn't confusing you with anyone very fast. Nor anyone very fat . . .'

'Very well,' I said, 'I'll go and get a Superploughman.'

'It's not a Superploughman, it's a Superploughman's.'

'A Superploughman's what?' There was no reply. 'I think it's extremely indecent of him,' I said, 'to leave his apostrophe "s" dangling in that manner. There might be children about: I saw one only this morning. Do you suppose, by the way, that when taxi-drivers' families go on holiday, they have to have those awful conversations where you have to huddle up against the front window and still can't hear, or are they sometimes allowed to sit back in their seats for safety and comfort?'

'I haven't the remotest idea.'

I went to the bar. 'Could I have a Superploughman's, please?' I asked.

Apart from a garnish more or less on the same scale as *Paradise Lost*, the Superploughman's appeared to derive its prefix from the addition of onion. There were rings of raw onion, golfballs of pickled onions, slivers of spring onion and a pot of very sweet pickle (which of course contained onion).

'Does this tell us about any peculiarity of English taste?' I wondered.

As we sat in the sunny garden at the crankiest of tables, the Other Cyclist arrived on a well-used bicycle with a weather-beaten saddlebag, and leaned it next to mine in the summer-house, momentarily quietening the loud fledglings in its ivy. He took a check shirt from his saddlebag – for he had been sunning himself on the bike – and as he approached I remarked on his tan. He had been cycling round the countryside a lot, he said, having been made redundant from an engineering firm that winter.

'It doesn't affect me as much as some. I live with my elderly mother – who's quite healthy, actually – and I've decorated the house inside and out, and I help people. I never was a work-aholic: I'm a more philosophical type, and I've got a fairly strong sense of humour. So I haven't been depressed, like a lot of unemployed people – but I must say that its made me pretty bitter that one can be summarily dismissed after thirty years' service.'

After lunch, we pedalled off together: the headwind was stronger still, and we laboured against it.

'Does it affect you, being stout like that?' said the Other Cyclist, puffing.

'Well, you have to pedal it about.'

'You've got courage,' said the Other Cyclist, with what seemed to me to be unnecessary awe. 'It must be *rather* difficult. Of course your weight, you know, will increase your speed downhill.'

'I know.'

We came to a hill going up. He had five gears to my ten, so we got off and walked.

'I'm sure English gradients are worse than continental ones,' I remarked. 'Even with my low gearing, I've been on and off several times since Exeter. But in France, I only had to get off once in a thousand miles – and that was going up a rampart to a castle: and Italy was pretty well the same, in spite of all the mountains.' We passed a dead pheasant by the roadside: there was a brief hiatus in our pedalling before we decided it was over-hung.

'It's one of the great things about cycling,' said the Other Cyclist, 'picking up oddments. I've found two Paisley scarves, one quite nice bowler hat, and half a crate of tomatoes. It's amazing what people lose. I turn off here: 'byee.'

The road took a minor kink through Princethorpe where a little girl was sitting on the grass at the roadside very seriously feeding her puppy on lemonade from a paper cup, and went straight into the wind again which went wild in the top branches of the hedge, whipping it into a frenzy, making the leaves dance like dervishes, and the twigs sway. Where the verges were mown, it ran through the short grass like a shiver over the back of a green dog: where they were long, it tossed the feathery tops like a platinum blonde shaking her head. It whipped off the edges from hay bales on a farm-trailer in front of me, rolled them up, and whistled them off down the road in curls, wriggled the curls into a golden serpent, until a passing car sent them flying apart again.

At the next farm, I passed a wayside shrine to the Fosse Hill Herd of British Friesians. On the Roman Catholic continent, you find little icons to the Virgin Mary along the roads: the British prefer to put up notices reverencing cows. On the pasture in the valley, their accredited ladyships seemed unconscious of their celebrity – unless the fact that most of them were lying down doing nothing was a sign of social status, as it is among human beings.

There is a cosmic lumpishness about cows: a cow lying down is the original Immovable Object; a cow falling against you is an Irresistible Force (and the thought of one cow falling against another cow is too dreadful to contemplate). Cows are the only exception to the physical law that 'Every action has an equal and opposite reaction': for every cow has an equal and obstinate inaction, which is what makes it almost as boring as menhirs.

At Bretford I crossed the infant Avon by a tiny bridge guarded by a short-tempered traffic light: there were no swans, but a family of moorhens was so surprised by anyone actually stopping to look over the grimy parapet at their weedy water that they scattered in all directions going 'wheep, wheep, wheep' in alarm as if they had electronic insides. The road twisted into the village, and more violently so round the Motte and Bailey at Brinklow, which was cottagey-smart along its green, the Crescent. I bought milk there, with a comfortable feeling of being broad-minded about cows, and drank it by a field of sheep overlooking the M6 motorway. Comparing the flock of sheep with the flocks of cars, it seemed that the sheep were rather the more independent of the two. Having just crossed the main line from Rugby and the Oxford Canal, I wondered why the people on the motorway should seem so regimented when there were actually far stricter constraints on travellers on both the water and the railway: I came to the conclusion that there is a difference between a lot of people agreeing to be bound within one large module of control, and a lot of little individual modules behaving identically, as if they were ants. It illuminated a distinction in society as a whole, I thought – that restrictions ought to be of a general character, and freedoms individual.

There was a perceptible difference in the countryside: it was flatter, duller, with fewer hedgerows. Somebody had been improving the efficiency of agriculture, and there were no longer the wild flowers in the verges that there had been as I left the Cotswolds. I passed a tractor much too big to be a tractor at work in a stubble field – creeping over the ground like a big green beetle: with double tyres, a cab like an airport control tower, and a harrow, a plough and a whole barnfull of agricultural machinery on the back, it bobbed over the ground like a ship over a choppy sea, a wake of seagulls heightening the illusion. With the more exposed country, the wind was so strong that I did not even pick up speed going downhill. It was a confusing wind, a battering wind – as if I was being constantly pursued by a flock of birds hitting me round the head with balloons. For the five miles after the motorway, the road ran as straight as if it had been ruled – until, past one field of redcurrants attended by numbers of interested sparrows and another with a crop of broad beans, I came ponderously and painfully to High Cross.

High Cross, the intersection of the Fosse Way (south-west to north-east) with Watling Street (south-east to north-west), turned out to be neither particularly high, nor a cross – since somebody had built a house there and, though one could probably have followed the Fosse Way through the front door, hall, back scullery and down the garden path, it was more convenient to go round. This meant I missed the monument to the 'centre of Roman England' erected by the Earl of Denbigh and friends in 1712, but since that had been struck by lightning in 1791 and now consisted of re-erected remnants, I bore with the disappointment – the more easily since the Fosse now became a track among the fields, with a sometimes rough but rideable surface, and trees to shield me from the wind which rustled pleasantly as they did so. A notice told the public to use the kissing gates rather than the field gates, which I thought unusually complaisant of local Authority. Red Admirals snoozed on the path, and there was sometimes a carpet of green-gold groundsel, which is everything one could wish for in a weed since it looks pretty, pulls up easily, and grows back quickly so that people who don't like gardening can pull it up again, rather than having to go on to the nasty stuff like couch-grass.

I had not gone far, however – down the wooded track, along a footpath and over the tiniest of brooks to skirt the edge of a pasture – before I realised the truth of Authority's advice about the kissing gates, which I was debarred from using on two grounds, viz: having no one to kiss; and being accompanied by a bicycle. Using the field-gates instead presents a problem.

The first part of the problem centres on the lack of hands, the necessity being to hold the gate up with one hand, pull back the catch with the other (releasing any safety-catch with a third). With your fourth hand, you hold the bicycle upright, leaving the fifth standing by in case it starts to fall over (it being too heavy to support single-handed when heavily laden).

The second part of the problem can be conquered with the aid of little more than an out-of-the-ordinary stoicism and patience. The initial ergonomic difficulties having been overcome, the gate will generally be found to open towards you. Dodging in a spritely fashion to one side (which had better be the appropriate one, or you will certainly regret it), you swing the gate open as hard as you can, and rush forward in a series of small circles. Do not attempt to go straight by holding the handlebars steady since you need the other hand to take the shock of the rebounding gate hitting your bicycle hard on the back mudguard. All you have to do then is to repeat the procedure until you have advanced beyond the gateway, when the Five-Handed Method may be used to close the gate as you opened it.

In the absence of five hands, the knees may be used to pinion the front wheel if there is danger of collapse, and the stomach may influence the handlebars. A camera (the more expensive, the better) may be lodged beneath the crossbar to allow you to provide additional support with your windpipe.

The way became a metalled lane, and then a small road. At the point when it did so, a rather large and expensive car was drawn up behind a workman's van in a secluded spot beneath ash trees. The car was empty, but as I approached, I saw the workman and a lady sitting bolt upright in the front of the van, looking extremely correct, and extremely surprised to see a cyclist in such a deserted spot. It occurred to me that they were most probably representatives of Authority out to check on the correct use of the gates, verges and other natural attributes, and also – since this was the second time in two days that I had come upon such a thing – that, given half the chance and a bit of convenient herbage, the English are probably as randy as stoats, or randier.

The lane turned into a layby, and became a main road once more, with lorries flinging grit in my eye. But it was a golden evening, and I travelled some way in the company of a meandering river with banks of red earth steep-cut down to swiftly-flowing water.

Indeed, I was to come closer to it than I realised. Soon, there were many houses and a dual-carriageway. I wanted to go round to the south-east of Leicester and derived an ingenious route of minor roads from the map. But no sooner was I leaving Blaby and heading for Oadby (both of which sounded as if they had been christened after something that came out of a pond), than I came down a road in the dusk to find my way barred by water – not the Soar itself, fortunately, but a tributary. A large motorcycle was parked by the water, with a girl on the pillion. The bike was rather potent and the girl rather young, but she was doing her best to preen herself up to look 500 ccs rather than the 45 or so she actually rated. I had certain qualms about the river, mainly because I seemed to remember passing a sewage disposal works a little while before, and was unsure whether it was upstream or downstream. I stood and looked at the river, and the girl looked at both of us.

'It's a ford,' said the girl. 'It's not very deep that side.'

'Left or right?'

'That one.'

I hoisted the bicycle on my shoulder to keep the panniers

from getting soaked, and compromised by splashing through the middle. The water was pleasantly cool, and did not seem like the outflow from a sewage farm. I hoped. There were still a few minutes of twilight to spare when I squelched into the hotel, where a wedding reception was in progress.

'The young lady's gone looking for you,' said the receptionist. 'I knew where to send her 'cos I know the Fosse Way quite well. Not the field bit,' she added, over-emphatically.

'Does the field bit have a reputation then?' I asked.

'I wouldn't know – didn't even know there was a field bit, actually,' said the receptionist. 'Breakfast is at eight.'

I went upstairs with a squat man in morning dress, whose dangling tails made it seem like sharing the lift with a celebratory frog.

'You're a bit wet,' he said, encouraging the sensation.

'I discovered your ford. The party seems to be going very well down there.'

'There's another 150 coming in a moment.'

'When I see a wedding that size, I always think . . .' I began.

'. . . if someone said to me, "Go through that lot again", I'd never do it,' he continued.

'Nor me.'

'If anyone asked me to get married again . . .' he meditated.

'Whose wedding is it?' I asked.

'Mine.'

Leicester is tied together with wool. Knitting on the hand-frame was a cottage industry in the Midlands from the sixteenth century, and the 'stockingers' were first organised into a factory in the early 1800s by Nathaniel Corah, whose family firm remains the largest employer in the city, producing socks and knitwear for chain-stores. The firm's motto, 'Profit, not without honour' seemed to me to exclude a rather large and attractive area of human existence from consideration, though I suppose it is something for a firm to have a motto at all. I did not feel that I would have got on with the astute Nathaniel who was obviously far too sharp for me with such phrases as 'A nimble ninepence is better than a slow shilling', but craftsmanship is always impressive, and Leicester hosiers cover the world in every sense. I went to Corah's, parked my bike next to the Chairman's yellow Rolls-Royce standing authoritatively at the front door, exchanged a brief ribaldry with a rather oily bunch of hands taking the sun nearby, and was taken to see the socks. (I myself was barefoot, since I prefer sandals.)

Machines grow dull these days when control-functions disappear inside micro-chips, but not sock-machines: they have all the complicated glory of the nineteenth century still in them. They stand in lines, like guardsmen, each within a web of moving, coloured wool, and go through an intricate stationary drill with clicking cog-wheels, running chains, nodding escapements, tapping cams, until a string of toeless socks winds endlessly and rapidly round a revolving drum. The socks are finished by ranks of ladies, each of whom has a machine whose business end is a long silver snout, like an elephant's trunk: the lady covers the snout with a sock, and the metal elephant is so irritated by this that he instantly sniffs the sock into his insides: but finding that, after all, it is only a sock, he blows it out again with a huff like the sound of an enormous pea-shooter – with the sock mysteriously changed.

Tony Mayes, the man in charge of the sock-machines, told me he had been doing the job for forty-two years with never a dull moment. There are so many different types of socks – fifty styles in the department at that moment, he said. The main skill of the job is changing over from one pattern of knitting to another, which involves scores of minute adjustments.

'I've got friends in all the factories in Leicester on the sock side. There's a nice feeling in the trade: we share each other's tips. Work will crop up even when we're playing bowls on a Saturday afternoon, or in the evening when we're in the pub, and the two wives will have to take a back seat. "How's trade?" we'll say. "Oooh," they'll say, "we're up to our necks in it." '

'In socks?'

'Yes, "Changing," they'll say. "I know your problems," I'll say, "we have the same." '

'So do I,' I said, 'that's why I never wear them.' I failed to shake his confidence.

'I went to Hong Kong for a holiday at Christmas: all the children there were wearing our socks – it makes you feel something a little bit on the proud side.' He was proud of his

town, too. 'A lot of people say Leicester's drab, but I won't
have that: I find it very pleasing. It's not a seaside place – far
from it – it's a real working place, very, very busy.'

The motto of the City of Leicester is *Semper Eadem* –
'Always the Same' – but a more accurate one would be
'Changed for the Worse'. The ancient, half-timbered Guildhall breathes a comfortably burgerish civic pride, but the
thing that struck upon my eye as the expression of municipal-
ity in more recent times was the exceptionally unpleasant
road-building, and the environmental mess surrounding it,
for which the standard new shopping-centre was an inadequate compensation, being not a lot less heartless than such
places usually are (and, being devoted to the making of money
on the large scale, it is hard to see how they can be anything
else).

Since people obviously have had taste in Leicester in the
past, it is puzzling that there is so little evidence of it in the
present: and it is even more remarkable that the food should be
so unremittingly ghastly in a town that has the only market I
have ever seen in Britain that bears any comparison with a
French equivalent.

'Chef, you know those two tossed salads you did? There
wasn't any dressing on them,' was the cry at my hotel as I sent
back the bowls of despairingly nude lettuce to wilt further in
the atmosphere of indistinct remonstrance that emerged from
the kitchen whenever the doors swung, like gusts of sultry air.

'He's some sort of juggler, that chef,' I said to Jenny: 'tosses
things up in the air, catches them again, and that's cuisine.'
Then I sent back the wine, which was so thick I could not see a
spotlight through a glassful held up before it. Then I wished
the chef *had* been a juggler, for the main course came, and he
had tried his hand at cooking that.

Leaving aside the question of dressing, the fate of the British
lettuce is an area of some mystery. Mathematicians and experts in semantics concur that where there is an outer part,
there must necessarily be an inner; biologists and sentimental-
ists suggest that every lettuce has a heart; domestic economists
have made extensive observations of greengrocers, and have
concluded that the lettuce sold therein is more or less what one
might expect, i.e. lettuce. So why is it that the British salad so
frequently consists of the leathery green outside? What is the

black hole in the British restaurant kitchen that swallows all the crisp bits? And why does no restaurant ever, ever use cos lettuce – which is the only variety commonly available in this country which combines texture and flavour?

I went to the market to check that there was such a thing as cos lettuce left in the world. There was. Leicester market lived under a plastic roof shaped like egg-boxes, and about as watertight, as the plastic buckets hanging above the stalls testified. It was very big, very cheap, very varied, and many of the stalls that sold fruit and vegetables set them out with some artistry.

Markets have their own language, which is designed not so much for communication as for marking out your territory, which you do by bawling louder than the stallholder next door. The tongue has a primeval quality, by reason of impairment of the vocal cords, and escapes any possibility of accidentally becoming comprehensible by not only being indistinguishable, but also in code. Hence:

'POUND TWENTY–FIVE GRANNIES.' (An incitement to violence against the older generation.)

'ROYAL SWEET AIREDALES.' (Unguessable.)

'THIRTY PENCE A WALLOON.' (Melon.)

'GREEK HOLIDAY TODAY.' (Great cauli day today.)

Morris Neal, whom I found trimming cauliflowers with a gigantic knife with the air of a platoon of Ghurkas penetrating a difficult patch of jungle, told me that Leicester people were 'cauliflower mad': they didn't want to know another vegetable, only peas and beans in mid-season, and then they were glad to go back to cauli: he could sell four or five hundred crates a day. He was a grower himself, from Boston in Lincolnshire. Sometimes he sold 'markory', which I could not identify, but guessed that it was something like Good King Henry from its resemblance to spinach, and sometimes samphire, gathered from the salt-marsh. He was going to plot a couple of acres with strips of vegetables he knew nothing about, to see how they sold. He never ate cauliflower himself, he said: he preferred greens and meat, especially meat.

A richness of variety has come into Leicester with the Indian immigrant population – although the Indian population seemed very anxious to disguise this virtue under a mask of platitudes. I asked one stallholder how he found Leicester when he first came there, and he said it was just like his home town, which seemed unlikely. Only the beefs surprised him, he said: beefs, lambs and porks in the butchers' windows, the porks with an orange in the mouth. He found British food very, very nice; British people very, very nice: and we went on from there, in ever-decreasing circles. Something was wrong somewhere: me, for asking the question; he for not answering it; or somebody else, for making him afraid to answer it – more than that, for refusing even to consider the possibility that different races might admit to being different, and yet live happily together in the same country. (A couple of old Poles I met were hardly less sycophantic, rhapsodising in broken English on the subject of fish and chips, but at least with them there was a moment of honesty when the broad smiles faded, a Slav look came into the eyes, and they said: 'Of course, it can never be the same as your own country, can it?')

It was only when I met the Indian Kids that I began to find out what it is like to be an immigrant in Leicester. They were hanging round outside a gaudy ice-cream parlour that offered a kind of fluorescent, plastic, self-service café society: there were four or five of them with nothing to do, and in consequence plenty to talk about. In fact, they were young men – Sixth Form age – but balanced so precariously on the line between child and adult that they seemed much younger than they were. They talked in bursts of hopeless energy, and what they said was that they had no place, because they were caught between two cultures.

'We don't know how it is to live in a society where you're not hounded all the time, not always looked at as different. You get to the stage where you segregate yourself.'

'Melton Road.'

'It's a sanctuary.'

'I was born when Indian people started moving there – it's Indian shops, Indian cinemas, the lot.'

'We call it "Our Bombay".'

'We hate going there.'

'It's wrong: they're not mixing. We should all mix.'

'I met this Indian gentleman last night, bewildered because he didn't know which bus to catch. How long had he been waiting there for another Indian? He kept on saying, "Melton,

Melton", but I couldn't tell him, because I didn't know his dialect.'

'We're caught between: we can't fit into white society, and we can't fit into our own. The older generation say, "Just look at the way they dress! They just want to be white." But we don't – we just want to be us.'

'To walk in the street and not be looked at, not to be something different: no hassle, no skinheads.'

'Where I live is mostly white. We were the first Indians there: got bricks through our window, our wall knocked over, two thousand pounds' worth of damage. It makes you bitter – and scared – but you have to keep it inside you, otherwise it progresses until it's gang warfare – there's a gang to every area in Leicester, almost every street. At the end of many evenings' we've had to run out quickly because there's trouble brewing, or we've got hit, or chased down alleys and cornered, and beaten up.'

'My mum comes home crying sometimes: both my parents are ordinary day labourers in factories and my mum gets all the shitty jobs. I say, "Why can't you complain to the foremen?" and she says, "They're white as well." '

'A friend of ours is a trainee manager in a hotel. They were having a brochure done, and they said he mustn't appear in any of the pictures – and he's the best worker there.'

'The work ethic is more in the Indian people than anyone else: they're so scared they'll get dis-established or something.'

'That's why Indian people like to work for themselves, 'cos they know that if they work for white people, they'll get rejected, or they'll get all the scum jobs. Work in a factory with fat chance of becoming a foreman, or own your own shop, work hard and reap the profits – which would you choose? It's the only way out for them. It's all family, of course.'

'The family is so close, it's unbelievable: therefore they won't let the children break out of it.'

'I speak English to my parents, and they answer me in Indian: they speak Indian to me, and I answer them in English. We're being heavily influenced to believe in their gods, have arranged marriages. I'm not supposed to marry anyone outside my caste. It's stupid.'

'Nor me. It's pathetic.'

'Nor me: they've got to be Patel.'

'We say we'll leave home, but we can't.'

'We're working on it,' said one youth, bravely.

'There'll be a time when I'm independent,' said another. 'I've made a conscious decision to leave home . . . and then I'll just say "goodbye" to my mum,' he added forlornly.

'All of us have gone through the stage of thinking: "If my parents had a crash, I could do what I want to do." It's ashaming, but it's true.'

'The main way we get our frustration out is through music. It's a universal language, isn't it? We've formed our own band "De Facto 3" so that we can write our own stuff – "Adam Took the First Bite" (all about the apple, and we're going to end in the mushroom); "Noitulove" (which is our theory of evolution – it's "evolution" spelt backwards); and we've got a song called "RastAsians" which has got some of the culture stuff:

> *Culture, culture,*
> *You've got a new culture:*
> *You're not so black, and you're not so white:*
> *You've got no right, and you never will fight.*

('Cos we're all pacifists – that's not in the song.)

> *We are the RastAsians,*
> *We are unknown:*
> *We're here to stay,*
> *People look and say:*
> *Who are you? You are you. You are now.'*

It was mid-afternoon when I took the Fosse Way out of Leicester, past Memory Lane with Christ's Gospel Church grimy and window-grated on the corner, over a flyover designed to make the cyclist feel like a fly, and up Melton Road – in which Sid Atkins (Pork Butcher) was cheek by jowl with confectioners which were kaleidoscopes of sweetmeats from a far continent, and two delicate girls in saris were chatting outside the Melton Hot Potato Shop.

I had company all the way out of town, for I came up with a tall, thin man cycling home to his village. He had sold his car, he said, because he had been out of a job for the last three years, having been kicked out of his own business.

'People keep on saying how fit I look now,' he told me. 'Of

course, I've lost all the stresses and strains of running everything. I wouldn't have looked for it, but now it's been forced on me, there's nothing like it!'

He laughed: and so engrossed was I talking to him (for he knew of the Viking Way, which is the top end of Ermine Street as it nears Lincoln) that I missed my turning to Melton Mowbray, and went careering off miles up the Fosse, which I was not due to travel until the next day. I had to turn round and take the quiet lanes to Thrussington, with gleams of late sun on the cornfields, and the swallow flying low after the evening flies. There is nothing in particular to an unpretentious village like Thrussington – some decently aged red brick, the odd bit of half-timbering amongst it, roughish country around – but the scale is right: people are not oppressed by too many neighbours or suppressed by over-size buildings, and they are not too pressed for time which passes at an easy clip-clop, like horses in the street.

Over the muddy river, by which several small boys were plodding home from a hard day's fishing with baked beans in their imaginations and a weather-eye open on a pair of huffy swans, I came to the road I should have been on in the first place, winding along the slopes above the river Wreake. A lot of land was down to repetitive fields of grain, and in the more open and low-lying stretches it felt the sort of place which would be distinctly unwelcoming on a wet winter's day, but across the valley was a hazy, hotchpotch landscape of meadows, trees, hedgerows – a hamlet with a church tower here, a spired village there – which felt fuzzy-edged and random enough to be properly English.

I was still five miles from Melton Mowbray when my right pedal creaked, stiffened, and fell off. I cannot imagine why I should have stopped to pick up the useless remains – a conscientious instinct for litter-gathering perhaps, or a feeling that it would be somehow disloyal to leave the companion of so many miles rusting on the road – but when I set off again, my progress was not as it had been before, and I was substantially hindered from appreciating the countryside.

It is always a difficult moment when a pedal breaks off and as a rule there is practically nothing you can do, unless at least one foot – and that the appropriate one – is prehensile. If you have toe-clips, however, there is still hope – though of the same kind experienced by those shipwrecked in a rubber dinghy in the middle of a shark-infested ocean – because this is the one situation in life when it really is possible to pull yourself up by your own bootstraps – or bootstrap, since you have only one remaining (usually the left-hand one, because it is more awkward if the right-hand pedal breaks off, unless you happen to be left-legged).

The sensation of single-pedalling is fine from the top of the stroke to the bottom, but at aperihelion the change from a downward motion of thrust to an upward direction of pull causes the knee to feel as if it has become momentarily multi-jointed, like a toy train, after which the sensation is of trying to extract the leg from a quicksand with a bucket tied to the boot. Having nowhere to put the right foot, you attempt to balance it on the stump of the pedal remaining: it falls off again (since of course the pedal-stump is constantly in jerky motion, in sympathy with the other side of the crank). This makes it impossible to bend down sufficiently to tighten the left-hand toe strap so that the foot slips out and the motive power is cut off every few revolutions.

It is extremely uncomfortable resting the right foot upon nothing and upsets the general equilibrium so that you tend to wander from side to side even more than you might through being preoccupied with trying to get the left foot back under its strap. This is worst going downhill which you have to do extremely fast so as to gain maximum momentum, but you don't have to pedal then, so you can ease the cramp in the right leg by waving it a bit, until it gets caught in the back wheel (but you can be sure there is no danger of this until you are going *absolutely* at top speed). Gear-changing is difficult, so one tends to remain in whatever gear one was in at the last hill – which, since one has only half the usual number of legs, is usually the lowest.

So it was that I entered Melton Mowbray travelling extremely slowly, but pedalling with one leg at a prodigious rate. I was beheld by an audience of one – a fair-haired man sitting seriously on a wall, who turned his head in precision with my passing but allowed no vestige of greeting, comiseration, interest or even mockery to cross his features all the while.

'I pedalled one-legged for quite a lot of the way,' I remarked

to Jenny nonchalantly, while restoring myself in the bar of the
Harboro' Hotel.

'Pull the other one.'

'I did. At least five miles.'

'Well you picked a good day for it,' said Jenny, ''cos I can't
find the flagel anywhere, and your hair shirt's in the wash.'

'I mean, one of the pedals fell off, and I *had* to.'

'You *didn't*! Did you? Shit!' said Jenny, capitulating in tones
such as one might use to remark, 'All the way across the Alps:
and with elephants, too?' It was fairly gratifying.

A limb-comparison test the next morning showed no signs
of abnormal development.

In food, in people, in tradition, Melton Mowbray is as solid as
anywhere in England. When I went out to buy a new bicycle
pedal the next morning, some of the people in from the
country to shop were so substantial that it was as if sides of
meat had got off the butchers' hooks, and had gone off
walking down the street. In such a mixed country as Britain, it
is ridiculous to make too free with the way people look – and
well over half Melton's 24,000 people are quite recent immigrants anyway – but I had a feeling that a raw, red, slab-like face
with jutting bones and popping, staring eyes had been seen for
centuries among the Leicestershire woolly-backs and bean-
bellies (for these country folk were known by what they
grew). It is a face that is much more ancient than that seen
sometimes among Midland townspeople, which still has the
diet and hardships of Victorian factory life distorting it. This
one looks as if it is waiting to play the part of a bumpkin squire
in Restoration comedy, and it goes perfectly with a town
which might be a model of that in which Mr Pickwick passed
the Eatanswill by-election.

None of which is to belittle Melton Mowbray: it is only a
market town in which most houses with three storeys feel as if
they only have two, and the Corn Exchange cannot manage to
stay stone all the way up, but declines at the top into a yellow,
clap-boarded clock-tower. It has nothing great, little that you
could call beautiful, and quite a lot that is moderately ugly in
its own small way: but in it, most things have grown together

into a homely reality that does not oppress the people.

Melton is a town with a long pedigree, and strong animal connections. There has been a market there for over a thousand years and, since 1322 at least, it has been held on Tuesdays. The market-place is a little umbilical no-man's-land of neutral territory, between three of the most famous fox hunts, the Quorn, the Cottesmore and the Belvoir, and at the beginning of this century, before the Great War began to diminish the leisure of the leisured classes, there was stabling for 900 horses in Melton so that the aristocracy could ride to hounds. The expression 'painting the town red' comes from eighteenth-century Melton, suffering the artistry of a band of upper-class drunks who came by chance upon paint and paintbrush after dinner one night: their daubings have worn off, but the pink hunting coats are fresh every year, and the dominant colour is the same.

Having long been associated with the upper classes, Melton has taken on a rough polish, like the lustre of an old saddle. My hotel, the Harboro', offered me a hunt breakfast of cold meats, pork pie and pickled walnuts, if I preferred it to kippers, or kidneys and bacon; it even had pleasant pictures on its walls, eighteenth-century prints and flower-engravings; it gave good service without too much deference, which is what good service in Britain ought to be, and if the waitress at dinner had been seriously confused by the lychees, so that she had to write the name on her hand to remember it, it only added to a charm which was already so full of natural friendliness as to be quite considerable. Besides, she was extremely pretty.

'The waitress,' I had remarked in philosophical tones, 'is one of the glories of Britain.'

'Yes, I noticed you drooling round to that conclusion,' said Jenny.

Melton Mowbray is traditionally a place of good food. The area is the only proper home of Stilton cheese, although that gets its name from the Cambridgeshire village where the landlord of the Bell Inn superintended it on to the London stage-coach on behalf of his sister-in-law, a Melton farmer's wife. The original Melton Mowbray Pork Pie has lost its title too, and may now be a pie mass-produced anywhere, much to the disgust of the local pork-pie bakers. It was their own fault, I was told by the manager of the most celebrated MMPP maker, Dickinson and Morris: they were so busy scrapping amongst themselves, they never registered the name.

Dickinson's still make the MMPP according to the original recipe of Mrs Dickinson who carried the first MMPP of all over the road to be cooked in her grandson's oven a century and a half ago. Pork pies were made the country round, an inevitable by-product of the cheese industry, as Parma ham is of Parmesan, the pigs being raised on the whey. The MMPP is also raised – that is its peculiarity – the pastry being formed on a wooden block: the saying is that 'Melton pies stand up for themselves, and so do the Melton people'. The MMPP is best made from a bacon pig, ideally one from the Melton area, the pork-pie maker and his father told me: the meat should be diced (never minced, which can hide a multitude of sins) and should not be pink inside, for that is the sign of meat from an old pig, or the addition of some coloured rusk such as may be included in Lancashire pies, but which in Leicestershire is not respectable. The seasoning is simple salt and pepper, but the pepper must be white and of the best quality (which was difficult to find, I was surprised to learn): the shell is boiled paste. The jelly, which is more liquid and tastier than that in mass-produced pies, is called 'souse', and once made Melton popular with tramps, it being a cheap flavouring they could beg with their bread.

Local foods are like talents: if you have any at all, you are likely to have several, so from within a fifteen-mile radius come Stilton and pork pies, Red Leicester cheese and Melton Hunt Cake, which is rich enough in fruit to keep for years – and which, learning from the pies, has had its name registered. It is a good cake, though not very different from other rich, dark English cakes. Dickinson's send some to Paradise, Nova Scotia, every Christmas, from which they conclude, said the pork pie maker immodestly, that even Paradise is incomplete without a Melton Hunt Cake. The cake was eaten with the stirrup cup, a slice of sugary energy at the start of the Melton Hunt; the pork pie was the ideal convenience food for a gentleman to pack in his saddlebag to keep him going during the day, and at night, the Stilton tickled up his palate for the port so that the food of the area could not be more closely linked with its traditions as they developed during the nineteeth century than if it were a fricassée of dead foxes.

I met the local historian of the 'hunting metropolis' – whose name happened to be Philip Hunt – and it was his opinion that the long familiarity with the great and titled had bred independence. In the fine old English tradition that everyone loves a lord, but that if he does not tip properly, they spit in his tea, George IV was pelted with snowballs by the Melton bell-ringers after he had failed to reward them for a peal in his honour.

'A certain democratic spirit came out of the good relationship between hunt servants and employers. You'll think it a bit strange, perhaps, but it's a fact that the moneyed people cared less for the staff that looked after them than they did for the staff that looked after their animals.'

The grooms were part-timers: when the hunting season was over they went off for a summer in the building trade. They saw their betters even more on holiday than usual – drunk, deshabillé, and dumped in ditches. They were the proprietors of the expertise of locomotion (even today all men are equal in the sight of a garage mechanic when the car won't go). So it is hardly to be wondered at that they knew their own value, even as they called their employer 'master' (a form of address that has not yet quite disappeared from the countryside). To this day, Melton is independent enough to have its own subsidiary local authority. The Melton Town Estate, which plays a role assumed by the council in most other places – providing such amenities as playing-fields, and administering the market I and Jenny walked through on our way to the bicycle shop.

Having bought pedals and pork pies, we lunched next to Dickinson's cottagey bakehouse, in the narrow courtyard of the Half Moon, looking out beneath the arch to the sunlit street full of silhouettes of people with shopping bags, flitting solidly home from market. The genuine MMPP turned out to be a recognisable improvement on the supermarket versions, the jelly very liquid in the summer day; crisp, fatty crust, the diced pork a considerable advance on the usual spludgy mince, and the seasoning a little stronger, though still bland to my taste.

'I expect they hang you from the lamp-posts hereabouts for saying it,' I remarked, 'but if I was Her Majesty's Comptroller-in-Chief of Pork Pies, I'd send the lot over to France and get them redesigned with garlic, spices and delicate pastry.'

The Half Moon had a graffiti in its Gents which said: 'Godot, we're in the bar', which seemed like a very English response to Samuel Becket. Eventually a crying baby and an electronic game in one of the bars which played 'Colonel Bogey' and 'Down in the Glen' alternately and continuously drove us out into the afternoon again and down past the little clutch of ancient stone houses by the church.

There is in Melton churchyard a curious tombstone, an obelisk topped by a woman's hand – somewhat verdigrised and orange-lichened – that points a single finger to the heavens, and is inscribed 'In Memory of Mother's Love'. I was snapping this dictatorial monument when an old lady came up to me, and asked if I would photograph some flowers she had in the church in memory of her son.

We went round to the church door, but there was a service just about to start. 'Are you come for the funeral?' asked the usher. 'Oh, it's Mrs Simmonds . . .'

'Just come to look at Eric's flowers, that's all. I can have a look at them, can't I?' said the old lady with determination.

'Well, yes,' said the usher, contriving to sound guilty, doubtful, affirmatory, friendly and impassible in the same breath. A horrifying vision came into my mind: in it, I changed lenses, measured exposures, clicked, whirred and flashed across a coffin, while the vicar preached, the mourners wept buckets and steamed up the viewfinder, and Mrs Simmonds stood by to make sure I did the job properly; after which the bereaved tore me limb from limb and buried my fragments along with the corpse. Hurriedly, I arranged to come back with my camera when the ceremony was over. Jenny took Mrs Simmonds on her arm, and led her away through the churchyard.

'It's the anniversary of his death: I send a donation each year and get some roses, 'cos Eric he left school early, and went to work in rose gardens. He biked seven and a half miles each way, which for a fourteen-year-old was a big thing to do. I gave him a week to work and a week to give in his notice, but he stuck at it, and he worked his whole life among roses. He loved all flowers, but roses especially, so roses to me are a very special memory. The Flower Guild have done them lovely, and I would love a snap of them. Eric Wilfred Simmonds: it's eight years ago I lost him. I wouldn't wish him back. We have so many happy memories, but it still brings its heartaches. I shall be all right now, dear. Don't take too much notice of that eye weeping: it always weeps. I can't see out of it.'

Behind the tall windows of the church, some heavenly stage-manager directed the organ to begin.

'I live in the little row of houses belonging to the church – very old, built in 1640. I live upstairs, but my door faces that top window, with African violets and flowers in it: I still like my few flowers. Thank you dear, very much.'

We had to run to our afternoon appointment which was at the most important place in Melton Mowbray. Such as Lily Langtry, Disraeli, the Duke of Windsor and Mrs Simpson have come and gone, Prince Charles is around sometimes, but what matters in Melton nowadays is cuisine for cats and dogs. From the factory chimneys, a fragrance of cooking meats wafts over you if the wind is in the right direction: it is the gentlest possible odour, as if a tin has been opened across the room, but it is pervasive – as any aroma that provides prosperity for one family in three must have some excuse to be.

Pedigree Petfoods – usually known in the town more tersely, as 'Petfoods' – are part of a multi-national company that could have put the plant anywhere, but by happening to choose Melton Mowbray, they capped its whole history with a splendid but appropriate irony. To a place that cooked for people came cooking for animals; to hunting country came a company that cared for pets; to a playground of the aristocracy came the work-place of a new élite; to a community whose prosperity was based on the British class-system came an American-style democracy.

Petfoods is run by the principles of Forest Mars, members of whose family have been known to descend on the place at odd hours of the day and night, and sample the product with as much dedication as if it were chocolate bars. Everyone who works at Petfoods is not an employee but an associate, with the same canteen, the same washroom, the same parking spaces – and is on first-name terms with all the others. I was told that it had been known for a cleaner to interrupt the Managing Director's conversation with the request: 'Come on, Les, are you coming to this bloody meeting, or not?' In the open-plan office, I noticed that Les did actually enjoy a slight distinction: he was privileged to have his desk in the very centre of the savannahs of green carpet inside a stockade of filing cabinets which, the office manager told me, she had had to build round him to stop visiting salesmen who didn't know him by sight charging all over him in the middle of important conversations. Generally, the office reminded me of the Elysian fields, there was such angelic hush and tidiness about the place: it was all in aid of petfood, but any dog's dinner was elsewhere.

The factory was full of such surprises, the first of which was that the gate-keeper was a heretic among gate-keepers, in that he looked glad to see visitors: the second of which was the charm of Eric Scammell, my guide round the plant, who was a man of such competence and sincerity that, if he had been a crocodile, I would have given him my baby to carry across the river.

I found it disturbing at first that anyone could be very sincere on the subject of petfood: it did not seem appropriate. But, as Eric said, it could have been any product – although he thought he might object to producing nuclear bombs. The thing was to do it well. From what I saw, they did it very well. At the end of the day, I was left with the impression that the cannery for cats and dogs surpassed many a cannery for humans in output, efficiency and cleanliness: I did not dare ask whether it surpassed most of them, for fear that the answer might be 'all'.

It is horrific to think what working conditions could be like in a factory into which meat and bones and blood pour by the hundred tons and emerge in the form of four million cans a day. But the kitchen of many an expensive restaurant is dirtier than the plant I saw that hot afternoon – all stainless-steel and computerised from where the twirling fork-lift drivers loaded the hoppers to the very end where the shining cans rippled into their labels and quietened down at last after a hectic life somersaulting from the roof on helter-skelter runways like a silver river in the air. As there were house plants throughout the offices, so there were similar house plants decorating the factory. More than that – the same spiky pink flowers were at precisely the same stage of development everywhere: it was all extremely efficient. Everyone wore white, as if they were going to play cricket, except for the maintenance engineers, who wore green, as if they were in a hospital operating theatre – maintaining people, instead of machines.

There were no flowers where the food was mixing, for it would be unhygienic to get a petal in the poultry-mix which fell into the hoppers through sluice-gates, like pale pink clay. I thought that pâté de foie gras would probably look the same if it came in shovelfuls. There is a school of human cookery that grinds everything up and then packs it back together again as a different shape and a different texture: this petfood was like that, a terrine of lumps of mysterious minces.

'No one's being very precise about the details of the recipes,' said Jenny, whose admiration for Petfoods was tempered by being told by a senior executive that women were better for cuddling than holding senior positions in large organisations.

'I saw a list on a computer screen,' I said, 'but I think they're worried about industrial espionage.'

We passed a rattle of little red pellets, bouncing out of their retort along a vibrating pathway of stainless steel like blood-coloured dried peas. These, I learned, were HAEC – High Acceptance Extruded Chunks.

'Are they chewy? Are they crunchy?' I whispered to Jenny. 'Why are they accepted so highly?'

'I don't think I want to know,' replied Jenny, but as I passed, I noticed one of the white-coated line managers dipping his hand into the hopper for a titbit, just to make sure they were acceptable (not that there was any way of telling that he was a manager except by inspecting his bank-balance). Democracy of the pay-packet was not included in the Great Egalitarian Millennium: Petfoods paid everyone well, each after their kind, with 10% on top for punctuality – a payment carefully defined as a bonus so that nobody could feel they were being punished for being late.

Perhaps because it was all so wholesome, spick and span and dedicated, I found myself beginning to feel that my sense of values was being turned topsy-turvy. If, for example, I were to find myself the survivor of a shipwreck floating on a raft in a shark-infested ocean, with the choice of rescuing either Beethoven or a tin of Pedigree Chum, I would have to break the news to him gently. Personally, I do not approve of excessive devotion to organisations, because so few (if any) organisations deserve it. But I have never seen any firm try so hard to organise well, and give people the environment and dignity which will encourage them to work well with each other – and, in the process, produce good profits. It might be paternalism sometimes, but at least the father was good at being a father.

'Trust, confidence and co-operation are the sort of things that used to keep families together,' said Eric Scammell. 'I don't see any reason why a team within industry shouldn't use the same attributes. We started a new company with new philosophy and few people: you can spend a lot of time on those people, and they inculcate the principles in others. It would be very difficult, if not impossible, to inject our system into established companies where people have entrenched positions: but for us, it works.'

'But it's not the sort of system that would produce a genius, is it?' I asked.

'I don't know that I'd recognise one if I tripped over it. The world is made up of minutiae, and it's the sum of the skills and abilities of our people that produces a result that may be close to genius – though it's not the Eureka type of genius, but a constant performance level.'

It was not quite the sort of genius I had in mind, but perhaps petfoods are not the right elixir for flashing eyes and floating hair (though they are a surprisingly complex subject). There is an animal studies centre out in the countryside, where they try out the latest recipes on some seven hundred cats and dogs who live a life that is the pets' equivalent of a cross between a commune, a centre for researching the common cold and a three-star hotel: for, while anyone can make a good petfood out of fillet steak, the art of making a profit – as with cooking for humans – depends on balancing up the taste and food value of much cheaper ingredients.

There are five hundred moggies and two hundred dogs – shaggy Newfoundlands, dachsunds, beagles with eyes in eternal mourning, terriers, gobbling Labradors and old dogs like Sally the Great Dane (who is the undisputed queen, for though in Petfoods all humans are equal, some animals are more equal than others) and puppies so tiny that they lie sucking at their mothers as formless as tiny woollen bolsters. In palatability tests, dogs are less discriminating than cats, whose taste is much more idiosyncratic. If a cat is choosing between two bowls, it will almost invariably prefer food at body temperature rather than food from the refrigerator, and a small number of animals cannot be used for such testing because they have a right- or left-hand bias which always sends them in the same direction.

Talking to the man in charge of the centre, Derek Horrocks, I learned that it was no good putting catmint in cat food and aniseed in dog food, and expecting the pets to go mad over it: they are for smelling and rolling in, respectively, not for eating. Petfood recipes are different in different countries – German cats in Germany, a relatively land-locked country, are not so keen on fishy flavours, for instance; American dogs demand spicier foods, as do French.

'Not garlic, surely?' I asked. 'On that basis, you would expect British cats to like fruit cake.'

'Cats seem unable to taste the sweet at all: but, certainly, British dogs like fruit cake,' said Derek Horrocks.

The proof of the pudding is in the petfood. Certainly, the blandness of British taste was well-reflected in my mouthful of Pedigree Chum, which I found very short on salt and pepper: it was a bit like under-flavoured lucheon meat, only vaguer. Line One Whiskas, which I also tried, was more alien but more interesting, having a meaty flavour lower down on its spectrum with a highly aromatic top-note which, though I assumed from what I had been told that it was not catmint, had the same sort of thin, penetrating quality.

My appetite for Petfoods satiated, Jenny and I went back to Melton church to take the photograph of flowers for Mrs Simmonds, only to find the door locked. We dragged several citizens from their tea to tell us where we could find the verger to open up; then we dragged him from his tea. He was very understanding about it, which made it worse.

It was almost seven o'clock by the time I got back to the Fosse Way, and headed for Newark. It was a sultry evening – no wind, but the still air was a jumble of infinitesimal movement, for the storm-flies were out. My shirt was quickly bespattered with a twitching pattern of living black polka-dots. The distance was hazy and drained of colour as if seen in ground glass. The hot air aromatised smells of woodsmoke, smells of hay.

The Fosse is unrelievedly straight here, and there is something about cycling along lengthy stretches of dual-carriageway that infuses its own boredom into the countryside around, diminishing the landscape. At first, there were trees to either side of the road, stretching uniformly into the distance towards a narrow strip of clear sky between them – and as I rode, even that narrow strip of sky remained the same. Then the trees were gone, and I no longer rode over the wold so much as amongst its fields. To one side, a pasture of lambs conscientiously and obliviously fattening themselves up on tussocky grass; to the other, the eternal arable of grain.

But there was still a crude humanity to the farmland – wood-pigeon in the thorn hedges where there were crab apples, yellowing hips of the dog-rose and hard green sloes – and it lasted until I came to the edge of Cotgrave Wolds, where the road breaks its back. For there is only one major change of direction in the whole of the line of the Fosse Way, and this is it: the Fosse is heading straight for the Humber (and has even wandered slightly west since Leicester, as if in hopes of hitting an easy crossing-place upstream or going direct to York) when it changes its mind. Some Roman surveyor stood on Wolds Hill, or Owthorpe Hill or Windmill Hill, and decided he must bend his road by almost forty degrees towards Lincoln and the coast instead. No one will ever know, but I am sure he heaved a sigh when he had to do the sensible thing – for it was the ruination of a grand and exceedingly straight design, and at Lincoln the traveller would have to go north on Ermine Street, which was another surveyor's road.

I whooped down Cotgrave Hill at breakneck speed (narrowly escaping being driven into deep potholes at the bottom by a passing car), and near Cropwell Butler there was some attempt to add dignity to the land with a small crop of park trees and an infant avenue curving up to a white house, tiny in the distance (it seemed odd: perhaps an avenue only really becomes an avenue when it reaches a certain height but if so, what height?). Then life began to get dull: the countryside ever flatter, and ever more brutally practical. The sloe hedges, having first been savagely slashed back by the steel of some monstrous hedge-cutter, soon went altogether. In the few farms that there were, there was a tendency for the outbuildings to be more important than the house, and neither attractive. For a mile at a time, there would be not a single flower to be seen in the verge, but there were little weedy cabbage-plants as if Nature herself had given up the struggle against agriculture, had decided to become productive to satisfy her accountants, and had failed.

You could look across the land for miles, and when you did, there was nothing to see for your trouble. Only the sun put any drama into the flat, growing as it lowered itself down on the horizon like the opening of a furnace door. They were burning stubble in the fields, the fire crackling in the straw as it ran a thousand ways at once, like mice at harvest time trying to escape the last square of corn. The smoke drifted over the road with a hot straw smell and hung far over the fields until it merged with the misty horizon. With the smoke, the fire and the low sun reddening through the haze, the air was tinged with pink, as if the colour of the rose bay willow herb along the roadside was reflected in the sky. With the air full of flying creepy-crawlies, the general effect was like being in Mrs Satan's boudoir. A giant freezer lorry rushed in a devil's progress down the road towards me, with the sun semaphoring on and off in the juddering windows, like the flashing of a pair of red eyes.

There was a patch of parkland at Flintham, and a wood with a smell of undergrowth and a welcome coolness among the trees, but the only interesting object all the rest of the way was Elston Towers, an extraordinary dull-bricked would-be Gothic mansion across a field of long grass. There were mysterious outbuildings at the back surmounted by a modern steel chimney mounted on the top of a Victorian tower rather in the style of a *campanile*. But the front – although it had both a very tall slate roof surmounted by an architectural tiara of very ornamental ironwork and an extensive baronial terrace – could only manage a single storey in between which, I reflected, probably made it the only Stately Bungalow in the British Isles.

I came in sight of the Trent, its banks pretty well as flat as the rest of the landscape, fringed with weed, very calm, and gleaming lightly with the sunset sky: then there were market-gardens, with stripes of marguerites and bright yellow weeds where sections had been left to go wild (for horticulture is the last refuge of medieval strip farming); and then at last a tall spire ahead, at first no more than a shadow in the haze, and that was Newark.

VI

THE TRUMPETER AT THE GATES OF SCUNTHORPE

TO SCUNTHORPE via LINCOLN

I woke up in my hotel at Newark to discover a spider of exceptionally active and perverse tendency in the basin. It continually rejected the blandishment of the escape ladder of pink lavatory paper that I offered it as a proof of loving-kindness, and scrabbled on the spot instead, going nowhere in a slippery white universe. Impatient, I eventually succeeded in cornering it with the aid of a polythene bag, whereupon it ran rapidly up it towards its benefactor who, appalled by such aggressive behaviour, dropped the bag in a symbolic affirmation of principles of non-violence. The spider scuttled off across the floor, and was last seen trying to get into the bath.

'You'd never get a job at Petfoods,' I told the spider, 'you anti-social beast.'

Newark is a town of pleasantly unassuming antiquity, with a cobbled market square beneath a church which is higher than it is long, all upwardness to the very tip of its pointy spire, and castle ruins with the remains of a very fine drawing-room window looking out over the river. The drawing-room itself unfortunately vanished in the Civil War along with most of the rest of the castle, and the area is now carpeted with grass, but if one had to choose to have part of a drawing-room, the window would probably be the best bit to have since one could see out of it. One could not have a ceiling without the walls, the wallpaper would quickly be ruined without a ceiling, so the only possible competitor to the window would be the fireplace, which would be unlikely to draw properly in the open air.

Sweetness surrounds Newark. A great event of the local year is the Campaign, when hundreds of people work seven days a week for three months to harvest sugar-beet for the sugar factories. Before that, the town was called 'The Metropolis of Malt' – although the closest thing to the production of alcohol that I came upon in the town was a home-brew shop where they make and sell such wines as may be based upon grape concentrate and country ingredients – elderflower, orange, peach, strawberry and the like – which they draw from plastic vats and sweeten to your taste while you wait.

The maltings, boxes of old red brick topped with the high slate hats of kilns, sit beside the Fosse Way with all the solid confidence of a Britain in which a sovereign was a golden sovereign and always would be: one had furniture in it, and another next door was a barley store, though it had been working up to two years before I saw it. It was far from derelict: there were men on the roof busy making it watertight with buckets of pitch. Inside, everything was still there: the water-tanks, the old iron pulley-wheels and chains hanging dustily in the roof; the spreading galleries of the malting floors were supported on a regular forest of cast-iron pillars, and were so low that they felt like the gun-deck of the *Victory*. Trevor Havard, the maltster who took me round, told me how modern pneumatic methods of malting had largely taken over the industry, but how floor malting produced high-quality malt, and was more fun.

He took me climbing up wooden companionways to the top of the maltings where the beams had grown so dusky over the years that the wood was almost red, past cooling ducts in black-and-white match-boarding, grain shafts with control shutters that pulled out like the darkslide on a plate camera. The floors had been well-swept by the last workmen to leave: there were wooden slats over the windows to keep out the sparrows, and only a single orange butterfly had squeezed in to get lost among the pillars of dusty sunlight.

'With all this grain about, don't you get problems with mice?' I asked.

'Never,' said Trevor. 'Never any mice.'

There was a voice from heaven, the man mending the roof just above us: 'We've got a foot-long dead rat up here,' said the voice from heaven, triumphantly. Trevor and I descended to ground level once more.

Floor malting is malting as it has always been: moistening the grain, spreading it out a few inches deep over a large floor until it germinates just enough for the insoluble starches to turn to the soluble sugars the brewer wants, and then drying it in the kiln. The art of the maltster is to control the growth throughout the 'piece', as each stretch of barley is called, turning it over and ploughing it to keep the process even: which in the past meant back-breaking shovelling from morning until night. A working malting-floor smells like a vegetable dairy – fresh, like cucumber; looks like the most golden of sands, and feels like eating bean-sprouts with your feet when you walk on it (for a maltster will follow the growth of the grain by treading it, as well as chewing it and rubbing it between finger and thumb – hard to begin with, then rubbing to a silky powder when it is ready for kiln).

The first samples of the season's barley were just coming in. They were chemically analysed, but Trevor carried his laboratory in his head, recognising the variety and the quality from a quick glance into a handful.

The corn merchant, who looked rather as if he had been barley-fed himself, told me he could go to five farms within three miles, pick up five samples and every one would be different. It was like grapes varying from different slopes of the hill.

'That looks a bit hard,' said the corn-merchant, peering into a handful of grains seemingly identical to every previous handful. 'Steely, isn't it?'

'I've got a much worse one than that,' said Trevor, 'from Snitterby.'

'It's very heavy land is Snitterby land,' said the corn-merchant.

I left them to it, and went back to the Market Square for lunch at the White Hart. It was humid, and the barmaid found me some ice for my drink as a special favour.

'Don't let anyone else see those ice-cubes,' said the barmaid of the White Hart conspiratorially, ' 'cos I found them, and I've had them hidden ages.'

The news was of floods and storms everywhere in the country except where we were. 'It's like being in a time bubble,' Jenny said.

In the pub yard, people had gone all asprawl in the heat, their ploughman's lunches melting on the tables before them. Stomachs bulged through shirts like Iron-Age hillforts: sweat flowed over the ridges of corsets. Children were bored and surly behind their dummies, which were common even when the children were quite grown beyond tot-hood.

'That's a sight you don't see very often,' said a small person in an even smaller pushchair, eying my legs.

'There was a time when one could have taken young lads such as yourself and torn their flesh with heated grappling-hooks,' I said to the small person.

'Get stuffed, mister,' retorted the small person, recognising an implied criticism.

'Don't you make faces at me,' I said.

'Wasn't,' replied the small person, putting out his tongue, thereby drawing himself to the attention of his mother who paused in her conversation to slap his ear, and incapacitated him from further discourse by slapping a dummy in his mouth.

'I know you weren't,' I said.

In a grey late afternoon, I left Newark for Lincoln. A few
angry spots of rain had fallen as I was putting the bags on the
bike: 'Well, that's the end of that summer,' Jenny had said as
she felt them, but it kept dry. The heavy skies oppressed the
dull landscape: it was grain and stubble, grain and stubble – so
that I was glad of even a march of pylons off to the power
station across the river to break the monotony. They stood
like people with broken elbows, stretching out dangling
forearms either side.

The scarlet runners in the allotments before the maltings
were the only colour for a long while – they are flowers that
always seem the brighter for drab weather or dreary surroundings, which may be why they are traditionally often grown in
city plots and basement areas – the poor might just as well have
cultivated french beans, which taste better, but runners are
more cheerful. Out in the country, there was the same utili-
tarian air to the verges and dearth of hedgerow flowers that I
had noticed the day before.

Not only the skies threatened as I began my journey, for my
entire twenty stone plus bicycle was almost blown off the road
by a thundering meat lorry labelled 'The Abbatoir' in blood-
red letters: thereafter, hunting parties of juggernauts and
monster trailers pursued me all the way to Lincoln – and might
well have bagged me, but for my extreme humility in keeping
to the gutter. Then, when I stopped to take a photograph of an
interesting Gothic cottage with a large pink dahlia before it, a
fearsome lady of the house emerged like something nasty out
of Anglo-Saxon literature, and stood, a plebeian Grendel, at
bay in the doorway, with her eyes shining like silver pennies
behind her spectacles, until I had gone off again.

It must have been fancy that the county boundary of
Lincolnshire brought touches of nature back to country which
was generally unchanged, unless it was simply the difference
between one brand of selective weed-killer and another; but
there were poppies in the verge, the occasional twine of
honeysuckle in the hedge, and even a red rose which I stole
from a scraggy bush before realising that what I had thought to
be roadside belonged to an over-extensioned pub called the
Halfway House, and was an attempt at a garden. It seemed that
the North Kesteven had been allowed to exist just a little more,
with trees from time to time and some pasture varying the

texture of continuous grain. There were now little brick enclosures for rubbish in the laybys, instead of rubbish and warning notices, and although Lincoln began like many another town, with a ribbon of villas, there was neatness and a cared-for air about them even before I came to the bigger, older houses closer in, where a stream runs by the roadside. But the astonishment was Lincoln Hill, with the cathedral towers ghostly in the fading light: even if Christianity had never been invented, it would have been necessary to build something exalting on top, out of simple gratitude for that vertiginous relief from the boredom of the plain.

A friendly policeman on a bicycle (bicycles are even better for policemen than they are for the rest of us, since they take away that sourpuss pomposity which they often seem to mistake for dignity of office) directed me past a strong smell of frying crisps from Smith's factory up the only other hill in the place, which is also good and steep.

I stopped outside a house called 'Hill Rest' (which seemed to show optimum geographical positioning on the part either of myself, or of the house) and looked back over the dusky country through which ran the shadow of the Fosse Way. It was strange to think that the road which had run straight for so long had served its purpose, that I had seen the last of it (I thought), and that another Roman road would shortly take its place. My hill turned out to be not a hill at all, but the edge of a plateau, and over it I made my way to Branston, pausing only briefly in a patient traffic queue waiting while the leading driver, an iron-grey lady from a Morris Minor, did traffic duty for a duck and a file of ducklings crossing the road.

'We thought you'd arrive exhausted,' said the hotel manager, helpfully, 'so we put you on the ground floor – in the Disabled Room.'

I had hardly put down my panniers before there was a pattering from the lane outside the window, and great spots of warm rain began to fall. The skies were violet, lurid at the edges; soon, they split open with thunder and lightning. I went out to put the bike under cover, and found a ginger-haired old lady hovering in the corridor.

'I'd rather have it now than tonight,' the old lady announced.

'I expect many people would say the same,' I said, cautiously.

'I can't be in my room alone.'

'What, never?'

'When there are thunderstorms: I'm terrified.'

It was clear that the demands of humanity were not going to let me get to the bike. I asked, 'Is it the thunder or lightning that frightens you?'

'Both.' There was a flash that sent the old lady scurrying away from the glass door: then a boom that sent her back again. Her face went brick-red, which made a very bad colour-match with her hair. 'Sheet!' said the old lady, violently.

'I beg your pardon?'

'Do you think that's forked lightning or sheet? Forked lightning's the most dangerous, isn't it?'

'Sheet. Definitely sheet.'

The lights flickered in imitation of the sky. 'Don't you dare!' exclaimed the old lady, shivering, before going on to comfort herself with thoughts of disaster, 'A surprising number of people have been killed recently: that poor man on his bicycle . . .'

'Really?' Outside, the downpour was tearing at the leaves of the cherry-trees; at my feet, the doormat was turning black with wet.

'Oh no, he was jogging. Still, we can do with the rain,' said the old lady unconvincingly, 'the garden's getting very dry.' There was a terrific bang, that made the old lady hop. 'Was that a thunderbolt, d'you think?'

'No. It's right overhead now: it'll go away soon.'

'*Right* overhead?' The proximity made her jump a yard at every thundercrack, though she was uncertain about which way to do it – towards the strange man, which might be improper, or away from him, which was not what she wanted at all. So she dithered between the two.

'They say it's safe in a car, but I'd rather be indoors. You mustn't telephone though: it gets into the wires. Gosh! I'm standing in it!' Water pouring under the door like the march of a column of liquid ants was meeting another stream coming from the bar, and joining forces in a lake. The storm was very loud.

'And yet I was in Africa for two years, and this was mild to what they get over there,' continued the old lady, flinching. 'I was glad to get home. Oooh, look at that pouring in! They say it's not so dangerous when it's raining: it makes a good conductor.'

'Yes, it does,' I replied, looking at her standing with her feet in the water. Above us, the storm was passing away. I opened the door to watch it go, unaware of the reservoir that had been building up in the garden on the other side, and which now gushed in, wafting the doormat into the interior of the hotel. I shut the door quickly and guiltily.

'As long as we get it over before tonight: I can't go to bed otherwise,' said the old lady, retreating with the thunder. 'If you hear a yell, you'd better rush in and rescue me.'

'Of course.' I padded back to my room to find it dry, but the corridor carpet had an interestingly springy feel to it because it was floating on water.

That evening, Jenny and I thought it prudent to go into Lincoln for supper: we drove past well-washed cornfields on roads lined with long, shining puddles, and fetched up eating jumbo prawns with garlic in the bar of the Wig and Mitre, beneath a blackboard on which was chalked the menu and a quotation from Walter Lippman: 'Let a human being throw the energies of his soul into the making of something, and the instinct of workmanship will take care of his honesty.'

'What an obscure quotation,' I remarked.

'Sometimes is, sometimes not,' replied the frizzy mid-blonde behind the bar: 'all depends how the manageress is feeling when she chalks them up.'

Obscure or not, the quotation had to be true of the cathedral bell-ringers, who started up at that moment. For anyone who believes that 'Satan finds some mischief for idle hands to do', campanology is the answer – in that both hands and the mind are occupied. I stood beneath the arch of the cathedral gateway, listening to the bells and watching the rain flash past the ranks of statues on the front to hiss against the floodlights in little puffs of steam as though inside each one was the Lincoln Imp with a little piece of hell. When the ringers came down from the tower, their captain told me that the company claimed to be the most ancient of all, having been founded in 1612; the bells were from the present century, however, the first of them being hung in 1913. The senior member of the company started ringing eight years before that, and was still ringing at over ninety.

'It's not the ringing that bothers me: it's the steps,' said the senior member.

'He's up 'em three times a week,' the captain told me. 'There's two hundred and thirty of them.'

Set at the top of Steep Hill – which deserves its name, being one-in-seven – Lincoln Cathedral makes people look up to it. Tom Baker, Chairman of the Lincoln Civic Trust, told me that traditionally the top of the town had been at odds with the bottom, for the clergy and professionals lived round the cathedral, while the workers and more commercial folk lived below. There had been great rivalry between uphill and downhill schools in his day, and major battles in the past.

'Lincolnshire people are insular – you defend your patch, don't you? It's an area that's cut off – by the Humber in the north, the North Sea in the east, the Wash and the fens to the south; it give them a certain independence that colours their character.'

'Lincoln green, presumably?'

He told me that the Lincoln green that Robin Hood wore might not have been green at all, but Lincoln graine, which was red. If it was green, he said, it was probably made by mixing the yellow dye from the wild mignonette with woad. (Woad is the same blue as police uniforms, which were dyed with it until well into the twentieth century, so producing an interesting link between the constable on the beat, and Boudicca.) As for the people, they were 'Lincolnshire yellow-bellies'.

'Of course, the frog has a yellow underbelly although there are not so many frogs in the county now. Lincolnshire coaches had yellow paintings on the underside of the body, the Lincolnshire Regiment had yellow waistcoats. But I think the story goes back much further than that – to the middle ages, when the fen people were subject to ague which is a disease very similar to malaria, with fever, shivering and, in the advanced stages, a yellowing of the abdomen.'

On Friday morning they were still trying to dry out the hotel carpets by blowing at them with an industrial heater like a junior dragon that had not yet received its diploma for breathing actual flames, but was making excellent progress with temperature. It was a delightful feeling that since I was a paying customer I was prevented from offering to help, and it looked as if the hotel staff had succeeded in discovering one of the more unpleasant ways of passing the time between the cradle and the grave.

Before leaving Lincoln, we made a modest pilgrimage to the nearby village of Holton-cum-Beckering where there was a little dairy – a couple of rooms made in an old brick barn. It was run as a sideline by a food technologist, Helen Hinch, and staffed principally by two girls who were shrink-wrapping cheeses in the outer room, surrounded by that distinctively dairy smell, fresh and would-be sour both at the same time.

'Grace has a degree in maths, Jenny an HND in agriculture, and last year our van-driver was a lecturer in philosophy,' said Helen Hinch.

Though small, the dairy was remarkable in that it was devoted to producing English soft cheeses. It has always puzzled me that France has so many local varieties, while this side of the Channel there appears to be none. Since cows are cows, bacteria bacteria, and tastebuds tastebuds in either country, it did not make sense to me, and I hoped to discover what had gone wrong.

Helen Hinch gave me a white coat which could just about be persuaded to cover my shoulders, and a little white cap for my hair. I asked for something for my beard, but it appeared that that particular piece of hygiene technology was as yet unevolved.

'If you're not clean and orderly, you're not running a good dairy,' said Dr Hinch, leading the way with a thump of gumboots.

She knew of English soft cheeses, she said, both as the daughter of a dairy farmer and because she had made them as a student at the University of Nottingham Agricultural School. A village near there was the origin of her main product – Colwick cheese, a white skimmed-milk cheese shaped like a tart and designed to be filled with soft fruit such as strawberries, although a popular Nottinghamshire Sunday tea was Colwick cheese, salt, vinegar and cucumber.

'Colic all right, with that lot,' I said.

'It is rather an unfortunate name,' Dr Hinch agreed.

There had been many such cheeses throughout the country, she thought, though not of the same shape: they had died out with hand-skimming, for machines were so efficient that they left skimmed milk with virtually no fat content which made a drier, harsher cheese, which was less palatable.

Being a fragile shape, Colwick cheeses were very difficult to pack and transport: nor did the cabbage leaves, on which the farmers' wives traditionally sold them, travel very well. Local markets fell away: it became more profitable for farmers to sell milk in bulk rather than processing it themselves. Colwick cheese vanished into acadaemia: many another soft cheese just vanished.

'There's no mystery about cheese-making, but there's a great deal of skill: it's like baking – two people can make the same cake to the same recipe, but it won't turn out the same.'

It seemed, however, that there was no such thing as a lost English Camembert. All Dr Hinch's products were very fresh-tasting, lightly salted, slightly sharp: the Colwick (best eaten straight from the dairy); a farmhouse curd cheese like Yorkshire Curd; and a future addition to the range, Cambridge – a striped cheese, white on the top and bottom layers (which traditionally were skimmed milk), the centre layer yellow (traditionally of cream cheese).

'Cheeses will never again be as local as they were. I remember my mother saying to me as a child that they used to get very tired of Stilton because that was the only cheese my grandmother made: those days have gone. In those days, milk wasn't bulked, but came from an individual herd: it wasn't pasteurised, so each little dairy had its own particular bacterial flora to give differences in flavour between cheeses – even today, a cheese grader can tell where a cheese is made because of the slightly different flavour from each factory.'

We left the dairy and went to the house to drink tea in the company of the next-door farmer, Howard Crapp. Grace had brought me a photograph: taken around 1968, it showed a sign outside the village announcing that Holton-cum-Beckering was the end of the Fosse Way.

'I thought I'd finished with the Fosse,' I said. 'What is the truth?'

Mr Crapp told me that the local council had put up the sign only to have it taken down again after a couple of years. 'So we don't know what the answer is now. Looking at it on the map, it's straight in line: we think the road went right through to the coast, where they had salt pans.

'But how was it made so straight?' he went on. 'It's always intrigued me. They couldn't see from one end to the other. When they were standing in Lincoln, they didn't know where Exeter was – they had no theodolites, no maps, not even the stars would have told them. The only way I think they could have done it was to have men from Exeter to Lincoln, about two hundred miles – all in a long line so that they could see each other – and they kept lining themselves up till they got straight.'

'It would be a lot of men – and they'd have wanted shifts as well,' I said. 'One man to have his lunch and another to stand there for him.'

'Like the army at drill,' Mr Crapp continued. 'Each one would have lined up with one either side of him, and then when he'd moved, they would have lined up with the one each side of them.'

'That sort of thing, I suppose,' I said, downing my tea, since I was eager to get to Ermine Street, and on to my next destination.

'To Scunthorpe, then,' I remarked to Jenny, when we were back in Lincoln, and I was fixing my bags on the bicycle. 'It's funny how that name rings in the ears.'

'Like most names when you've never been there.'

'No, some are special: the Taj Mahal, Mordor, Timbuctu, Narnia, Eldorado, Poictesme, the Yangtse-Kiang; Christopher Robin's Secret Place at the Top of the Forest, Skegness, Cheam and possibly Neasden. "We take the golden road to . . .".'

'Yes you do: and you take it now.'

'I must enquire of the burghers why it is that the name rings like that. Look!' I exclaimed in horror, 'my sprockets have gone all rusty.'

The Golden Road to Scunthorpe led up Steep Hill past the cathedral front to the pottering shopping street at the top where they have let circles of granite setts into the roadway at intervals to mark the places where Roman pillars once stood. There I asked for Ermine Street, and held an interminable discussion with two mathematically-inclined housewives interested in exploring all the possible permutations of Ermine/Ermyne/Street/Road/Estate, and the best way of getting to the seaside (which got into the conversation at an early stage, and insisted on barging back in at intervals thereafter).

Eventually I came to the conclusion that, whatever it was, I was probably on it and made a triumphal exit from the city through the Newport Arch, which is Roman, and feels so – although it is rather on the small side to one accustomed to the films of W. D. Griffith, since the first eight feet of it are below the level of the present road. A cynical gentleman in a stripey shirt who passed me taking a photograph said that I mustn't mind it having been rebuilt in the 1970s after a lorry with a high load got stuck under it. I said he was not to shatter my illusions: he said no, he hadn't shattered it, it was the lorry. I told him he was too late, anyway, since I had already made my triumphal exit, and saw no means of downgrading it retrospectively – and left.

It was an ideal cycling morning, with the air just warm enough to still feel fresh as you moved through it, the road dry but the rain still on the grass in the fields: the moisture in the air made the distance misty and muted its colours. There was a slightly disquieting feeling about having gone up Steep Hill and stayed up (rather like being an apprentice to the Indian rope trick on your first big day) for Ermine Street ran straight off across a plateau even flatter than the low country I had travelled from Newark.

Just beyond a cottage which was trying hard for the Best-Kept-Kitchen-Garden-in-the-World Award, I passed the Lincolnshire Show Ground which was doing an imitation of the Field of the Cloth of Gold, except that this was a field of cloth of green, cloth of red, cloth of orange, cloth of blue – all the bright colours of tent fabrics in a cross between a shanty town and a medieval tournament – an international camp for scouts and guides. Its name was on a big sign at the gate, next to a smaller one that said 'Guard Dogs Patrolling'.

There was something ironic about the novitiates of the Great Outdoors having to be protected by surrogate wolves, and when I chatted to a small lunch-party of guides, it seemed that a certain refinement was making its way into camp-fire catering: they had had barbecued ribs the night before, they told me, and Boeuf Bourguignon and Poire Belle-Hélène were on the menu for that evening. However, as far as I could see, the humour was traditional: a wellington boot hung over the entrance as a symbol of some inscrutably complex inter-group rivalry.

When I told the guide-leader how difficult I found it to understand the relish with which some adults enjoy children's practical jokes, she shrugged her shoulders: 'You just have to join in.'

'What do you get up to, then?' I asked her.

She said that it had been known for plastic lizards to appear in people's beds. I looked around the bevy of young faces with some alarm, wondering what this sort of childhood might do to their future sex life. In ten years' time, would there be homes throughout the country echoing to the cry of, 'Come to bed, dear: I've put the plastic lizard in to warm'?

I left the field of many-coloured tents to the barking of the loudspeaker system calling for an assembly of all members of the concert party: shortly after, there was a large sign by the road bidding me to 'Beware Camp Entrances' – excellent advice, but relating to RAF Scampton which keeps a Second World War bomber at its gates, and has actually gone to the trouble of planting trees among its buildings so that, within the limited standards of RAF camps, Scampton is reasonably aesthetic. Of course, nothing can erase its responsibility for having created round its runway the only bend in Ermine Street between Lincoln and the Humber which is known by the suggestive title of 'The Scampton Kink'.

The sun came out: wisps of steam rose from a field of sugar-beet, and with it a cloud of cabbage white butterflies. Many of the fields had been cropped and reploughed – with the hedges grubbed up and so much brown earth stretching to the horizon, I felt like a flea on the back of a Guernsey cow. But this was a geometric cow bred by God the Farmer out of Man the Accountant, and there was no delight in it more than an infinitesimal, clinical graduation of shade and texture. Even if contours are unalterable, crops unchanging and trees anathema, why does every field have to have ninety degree corners? Why should they not be grown in circles, ellipses, in the shape of a rose, or the hat of Napoleon Buonaparte? But the fields of the new age are shaped without imagination: not by people who quite like a pretty pattern or mathematicians but by a dreadful hidebound creature – the Mathematicon, the Automath, who thinks in rectangles; to whom a curvy line is an offence and a triangle dangerously unpredictable.

In traditional fields, straight lines are a useful aesthetic formality to contrast with the random bulges of Nature: but when there is little Nature left, why should farmers not have the imagination to design the landscape with a little variety, put their own patterns on the land, or hire artists to do it for them (since they have money, and artists have none)? Then we should see that Farmer Jones fantasises about breasts because he always ploughs in semi-circles; or Farmer Giles really wanted to be a sailor and go to sea because his sugar-beet is serpentine; or that Farmer Joddrell will go to heaven when he dies because all his fields come to a point, like a spire, and if he could he would plough them up into the sky. And people passing in aeroplanes would wonder that people could care so much about art, variety, pretty patterns, and about being their odd but precious selves.

It was no country for a man reared on Wordsworth: indeed, it was no country for any man, for in its own way it was as inhuman as a robot mill, where no one goes in the space between the machines because, while they run, it is not a place where people belong. Here the space itself was the robot: only the occasional clump of trees hinted that Nature lurked beneath the land and – while temporarily responsible for growing money – might still be capable of extemporising a clump or two of undergrowth, if people would only stop planting potatoes. The fields of potato foliage had a humpy, whooshy look to them, like a green sea being agitated from beneath by huge jets of gas. They were malodorous: and in the distance a gigantic spray spurted black sludge in a crude parody of a fountain. A sign pointed to 'Danby Pig Unit', pointed in the direction of vast hangars away from the road: but no sign was necessary. The old rhyme appeared to have at least one true line in it:

> *Cheshire for Men,*
> *Berkshire for Dogs,*
> *Bedfordshire for Naked Flesh*
> *And Lincolnshire for Hogs:*
> *Derbyshire for Lead,*
> *Devonshire for Tin,*
> *Wiltshire for Hunting Plains,*
> *And Middlesex for Sin.*

Remembering what I had learned from the perfumer, I waited for my nose to get fatigued, but it was still wide awake to the waft as I entered the Moncks Arms at Caenby Corner. It was so sad, however, with its big, dowdy rooms and never an airman to fill them, that I took my pint out to the odorous roadside and waited in vain for Jenny to come by, with my thoughts running on the days when the pub was crowded with bomber crew giving themselves a hangover to carry over Germany. During the war, people died just as thoroughly in the army and navy, but the bravery of the war in the air had a special romantic quality to it – although it wreaked more havoc on the innocent. I thought this must be because of the vulnerability of the crew and their small numbers which is easier to focus on than the amorphousness of an army. England is a country of old airfields: centuries from now, archaeologists will dig them up and find them all the same, and go on to dig up another one; more ordinary people will never have heard of the Battle of Britain, but they will see the shadow of a runway in the grass, and it will be as boring, as incomprehensible, and yet somehow resonant as the Roman marching camps are to us.

Just over Caenby Corner (which is so called because it is a cross-roads, for this part of Ermine Street tolerates no such thing) there was a tiny oasis in the desert of agricultural productivity – park trees, what looked like a walled garden in red brick, a few green fields in which a herd of Friesians were galloping behind a tractor with un-bovine levity in expectation of food. The abrupt change made it very obvious how artificial the English landscape is, with Nature created in our own image according to the values of the time: but soon the green was gone, and I was back in the Land of Nothing again, created according to ours.

I was a country child, and had always thought that in some tiny way, rural England belonged to me – I did not expect to walk over other people's farmland as if it were woods and wilderness, but a fraction of their pleasure in good land and growing things was mine too.

Riding the length of England changed my view. It made me feel that I was excluded from the land as firmly as the medieval peasant whose hand was cut off for poaching, or the eighteenth-century labourer who lost his patch of pasture to the enclosures: for the land is wealth, and wealth has never belonged to the people – and probably never will, while there are too many people for the share-out. But among all the keener injustices of past ages, the land was loved more for itself, and not only for the money it could make, or the subsidies it could attract. Today, we have lost the refinements of élitist society, while the labourer is as dispossessed as ever and even the farmer may have no hope of passing on the farm to his son, so great is the value of the ground. Land ought to be controlled by people who care about it, and work with it.

I found myself feeling rather lonely on the great, straight road – a thin river of movement over a blank landscape of things that simply sat there and grew. It was a relief to pass a few men stripped to the waist felling the stump of an ash tree with a petrol saw – although of course they were making the landscape even blanker: nowadays it takes so few men, such little machines, to change so much. The afternoon sounded like dying artillery: though it was still sunny, there was distant thunder. Further along, they were grubbing up more trees: each one seemed as if it was the last one on earth. A single pylon – some old radar tower perhaps in this country of airfields – watched over it all like Wells's Martian fighting machines rusting in Hyde Park while children ran in and out of their legs; but in the war of this world, the Martians had won.

Then the change came: off went the main road to Brigg and the Humber, and I and Ermine Street adopted the sort of existence in which, instead of us crossing other roads, other roads crossed us, which seemed less pretentious and more pleasant. There were verges again, one or two flowers in them, and someone had been so frivolously unproductive as to plant two cherries and a couple of young ash trees, and to suffer a hedge. Outside a little red smallholding, a bad-tempered old cock, all comb and glaring, chivvied his wives and their brood through the grass. With each crossroads, Ermine Street got smaller and wilder, till it was lined with poppies and grass grew through the tarmac in the middle. Ahead, there was a cottage in Victorian red-brick, and a gate across the road.

As I came up to the level-crossing, I saw that the cottage was empty and the garden overgrown, but opposite stood a wooden hut about four times the size of a sentry-box, and an even smaller plastic hut next to it, with a notice on it saying 'Portaloo'. From the larger of the huts came the sound of a trumpet which stopped short as I approached: when I peered in at the door, all that was to be seen was a rather short man with smoothed-back silver hair sitting innocently at a wooden table in his shirt sleeves. On the bench beside him, the corner of a black instrument case protruded from beneath a cushion.

'There's nothing about – you're all right: we've been a bit shy this afternoon,' said the crossing-keeper, full of good-humour. He had a great big smile, and a discreetly expansive stomach to go with it: his name, I afterwards learned, was Percy. 'Would you like a drink of water? It's all I can offer you, but it's nice and cold in the tap.'

'That's very welcome,' I said, and meant it: it was better hospitality, after all, than a bottle of champagne from a public relations man. 'You're a musician?'

'I keep me eye on this crossing here in general, and all aspects appertaining to British Rail,' said Percy instantly and officially. 'I'm here today for twelve hours – six in the morning till six at night.'

'But if you did happen to have any leisure time?' I said.

'Since I've been interested in the musical side of the business, I sometimes sit down and jot a bit of manuscript out. I started at nine years of age learning to play the cornet in the brass band, graduated to dance band work, then I had a yearning for another instrument which I took up about nine year ago this coming January – alto sax, doubling on that like: and just to go on better still, I've took up taking lessons on the electronic organ.'

'British Rail wouldn't approve, I imagine, but it would be a good place to practise.'

'I like solitude and quiet,' said Percy. He reached under the cushions and drew out a shining brass trumpet.

'But after hours – say you were stuck here for an hour when you'd finished work, then you might . . . perhaps?'

'It would be permissible with British Rail then. After time. But then again, the question would come that if and when you'd been relieved, then you'd been relieved and your job is get into your vehicle and away home to your own fireside: in other words, you'd be trespassing if you stopped here after six o'clock.'

'Hard masters, British Rail – you didn't say it, I said it.'

Percy laughed. 'I'll tell you a bit of a yarn: at Christmas time when it's pitch dark and the stars are out, I can stand out here, and they can hear me at Kirton Lindsey if the night's still. I love it.'

A regular customer came up the level crossing and joined the conversation – a man in dusty blue overalls on an ancient bike. His face was weathered and he gripped his jaw as tight as if he feared the bottom half might drop off. He worked at the local cement factory, he said, except that it was a factory no longer.

'Used to make our own cement, but not now. They shut it, it's a depot now. We don't want this line closing, or else we'll be out of work,' said the man in overalls. 'Once, you could get work on a farm any time, but now you can't: it's all getting modernised.'

'Enormous fields they are,' I said.

'There could be twenty acres of beet on the way to work in the morning at a quarter to seven, and at five at night on the way home the beet could be gone: machinery and three men could have done it. Before it took us all winter to get a row of beet up.'

Percy swatted at himself. 'How long do you think it'll take them to clear this field of wheat, then? And all these damn black flies with it.'

'If there's two combines, less than a day. One will nearly do it – a combine will do thirty acre a day.'

'I'll be very pleased to see it when it does then.'

'That black smut on it, that's flies, isn't it?'

'Only half of them,' said Percy. 'I've got the rest in this cabin here. But give me this part of the country: give me Lincolnshire.'

'It's level, and you don't get the winters you do anywhere else,' said the man in overalls. 'Lincoln's fairly homely to everybody. The land's all gone down the families: they've nearly all married sisters and brothers, like.'

'Other people's, I hope,' I said.

'But near Caenby Corner, the hedges are being torn up and great big fields made,' he went on. 'That used to be two or three farms, three thousand sheep and all big partridge shoots, the old-fashioned partridge rearing. You didn't rear them at home and let 'em go like they do now; it was hedge bottoms then. My father was a game-keeper and in the summer time he had to go all round that estate with a horse and cart and a barrel: there were rubber tyres cut in two, and he'd fill 'em with water for the partridges. You don't see it done now. They used to lay the stubbles until Christmas for the pheasants and partridges, but now they burn them – burn all the seeds and everything, so there's no living for owt.'

There was a toot from a little white mini van: with a quick glance at his indicator, Percy ran across the track to open the gate as if he were resolved to do the job as efficiently as possible so that he would not have to give any more of his life up to it than was strictly necessary. I quizzed the man in overalls about the road ahead, and particularly the river crossing, in case there was a more romantic alternative to going over the Humber than a modern suspension bridge.

'You'll be all right when you get to Whitton,' volunteered the man in overalls. 'That's where they used to go across with the horse and cart. They used to reckon you could walk it. We said that's where the bridge ought to be.'

'Aye,' said the returned Percy, 'instead of where it is now.'

'That's what the Romans used to do – used to go up to Edinburgh, didn't they?'

'I hope so,' I said, 'because I am.'

'About three years ago, they were digging for skeletons where the Romans had been, in that field there.'

'It'll be longer'n that when they found that skeleton near the war memorial in Winterton,' said the man in overalls, not to be outdone in archaeology. 'Me brother-in-law was working on the council then. But they changed the old Roman road to Lincoln, didn't they? Bypassed Scampton aerodrome. That was where Wing-Commander Gibson won the VC. There were three VCs at Scampton: Sergeant Hannah was the first, Leroyd the second, and Gibson the third: he was in the Dam Busters, was Gibson.'

'Yes, I saw their names on the barrack blocks as I came past.'

'I've seen two hundred airmen down at Caenby Corner at night: they mixed with you, and they didn't care whether they were going to live tomorrow – well, they didn't know, did they? I've seen the barman – he was an ex-navy bloke from Barnsley – get a bucket and fill it up with beer and give it the airmen; he didn't care how he got paid, but that's what he did. It was a good pub then.'

The man in the dusty overalls crossed the line, climbed on to his bike, and cycled off. On the horizon, the skies grew blacker and blacker, and began to fulminate a livid fringe that promised storms. But I couldn't leave, and snub such a friendly conversation.

'Apart from the trains, I don't suppose there's much here to distract you from your music,' I observed.

'Wild birds what I've never bothered about before; but at this later stage in a lifetime, you're aware of a lot of things you didn't bother about when you were young. Yellow-hammers, robins, dozen and dozen of sparrows, blackbirds, thrushes. About three week ago, I heard a hell of a row in this wheatfield here, and there was a stoat or a weasel got fast hold of the back of the neck of a young rabbit – and if it hadn't been for myself and another railman, that poor little rabbit would have been no more. But we played up hell with this here stoat and liberated the rabbit, and I hope it's still alive. There's times when things get quiet about half past ten at night, you can hear a mouse run across: and sometimes you can hear the bleating of the sheep.'

'It sounds like a job that has its compensations,' I said.

'This crossing, it's home to me. It has that feel about it: home. I spend quite a while here, days – and nights as well. The previous crossing-keeper was a lady, Mrs Twells: at least twenty-seven, twenty-eight years she lived in that house that's now standing empty, and since the good lady retired, us relief men have had to keep the job manned.

'But giving just over a year, I shan't be on British Rail any

more. Sixty-four . . .' A train went past and drowned the rest
of the sentence. '. . . and I don't mind if British Rail does
know it: but the last day I finish, I shall come in civilian clothes
in me car there, and I shall shed these that I stand up in and burn
them at the stake, whatever crossing I'm at. That's how I feel. I
have to go along with things as they are today, but I'm far
from happy. I stepped down from being a driver seven years
ago, and I belonged to the railways when it was railways
proper, when there were good bosses you could respect and
think a lot of, and good men to work among. It's the truth, and
any of the older fraternity would bear it out. What we see
about us today, I'm sorry to say, is but a load of rubbish.'

'So what will you do then? Take up music?'

'There's an award for senior citizens – you've got to be over
sixty-five: lovely trophy, fifty quid in money, I believe, with
other perks what goes with it, and I've set my sights on that.
When I'm eligible to enter the first round, I'll be in like a rat up
a pump. I shall walk on to that stage as a multi-instrumentalist,
just a nod, and away we'll go. I'll pick the trumpet up like this;
have a look round the audience to see whether they're elderly,
fifty-fifty, whatever it is, and choose what I think will go
home. Then I'll put the trumpet down there on the stand, pick
up the alto sax, give 'em a nod, and away we'll go with
something like "Trees" – 'cos I like to work in the higher
octaves on that. Winding up then, just go across to the organist
and request him to get up, like, which he will do: slide into his
seat and end up on the organ. It'll all be pre-arranged. I've had
three courses on the organ at Scunthorpe, and now I'm getting
to the stage where I think I'd like to have an hour's intensive –
someone to really turn the screw on and say, "Whoa! That's no
good" and really make me do it right.

'I'll have the alto sax in the car tomorrow, and as long as I'm
sat there watching those indicators, as soon as a train comes in
section I can drop the instrument and watch how things are
going. That's the reason I like being here, because the nearest
place I have to me is a little farmstead right in that hollow
there, so I'm not disturbing anybody with scales and so forth,
which are a bit monotonous for anybody to listen to.'

We were interrupted again by a van of fruit and veg, whose
driver gave a musical toot as he crossed.

'I've got a nice sentimental ballad I composed myself appertaining to the number one I have at home, and think the world about. The words came easy, being blessed with such an exceptionally good partner as I've had for forty odd years (we had our ruby wedding last December) – I couldn't have had better if I'd scoured the country from top to bottom. I've got a twenty-two carat plus, and am very, very proud to say so. I've not regretted any moment of it: if I had exactly the same chance with the same girl, I'd do exactly the same again. The Bank of England may be a lot richer with its gold bullion, but I think to meself that I've got far greater than what the Bank of England's got, with my partner. D'you see?' asked Percy, as if he really wanted me to.

'I thought to myself: Supposing (which is not remotely impossible) that she suddenly took you for a ride, as it were, and said, "Goodbye, I'm off": what a shock it would be. I more or less frightened myself with it. That's how I got the idea of writing this song: "Don't Make a Fool of Me, Sweetheart". The title came as easy as that, and the words just flowed along, in a nice slow foxtrot tempo. The fellow who has the tickling stick, Ken Dodd, I'd like to send it to him, and I'd be tickled pink if he could do something with it.

'I wanted to go to the Kneller Hall school of music, but I missed the boat through no fault of my own. My parents wouldn't let me go as a bandsman but that's what I've always been dead keen on; I wouldn't have been pestered with this damn job then.'

'You must feel quite sore about that,' I said.

'I often do. But there's no turning the clock back: that time's gone. But I still want to make a success in the musical field as far as I can in my own amateur sort of way, and it'll not stop me from trying, until Somebody Else says "Time's up," like.'

He sang his song to me, and trumpeted between the verses. It was getting late, the skies were darkening, and the thunder was getting more insistent.

I wheeled The Roman Philosopher across the track. 'I like it,' I said.

'Do you?'

'Yes, I do. Good luck.'

'Bye bye,' said Percy. 'That's what I'm going to do.'

Briefly, the little road was like a garden running through the fields – the wide verges covered with ferns, blue vetches, clovers and dead stalks of cow parsley. A grouse popped out and zigzagged ahead of the bicycle in a great state of anxiety, shooting its legs out sideways in a frantic Charleston. After a crossroads with a sign for a cul-de-sac, the road came to an abrupt halt on the embankment below a motorway round-about. But some historically-sensitive civil engineer had not only made a path up and over, but in the grassy centre of the roundabout had left a token stretch of tarmac to signify that Ermine Street went on. It would have been just as quick to cycle round, but I waited for a break in the traffic and trod that tiny segment of roadway on principle. Then I went straight on for, although there was a shorter way to Scunthorpe, it was dual-carriageway while Ermine Street ran peaceably among trees.

On a woodland track by Broughton, three girls dressed up to look very daring posed on the cemetery wall until I approached; then they vainly tugged at their mini-skirts in an excess of modesty and said hello like the children they still almost were.

The woods were tall beech and pine, smelling sweet and spicy: I hadn't expected the country to be wilder the nearer I got to an industrial town, but there seemed to be a logical connection, for strange humps and holes appeared among the trees like the burrows of dwarfs, and in the open country there were heaps of golden sand dug out of the ground. As I turned off towards Broughton Slag Works (wondering what it did, for I had always thought that slag was something that had been worked already), the signs of industry began to jostle the farmland for supremacy: more sand, a railway, the Santon Mine, derelict, with its windows boarded up, a row of grubby houses.

There was a distant rumbling in the air and a pronounced chemical smell. There were vast chimneys and cooling towers covered in a haze that I suspected was not the same haze that covered the edges of the countryside before; massive metal towers which had all their intestines on the outside, and steamed and smoked like rockets about to take off; while conveyor belts marched high over grey heaps of slag. It was immensely impressive and immensely awful, and in it all, there was not a single creature of flesh and blood to be seen.

Beneath a strong, unpleasant smell from the coke ovens and a spray of what I hoped was water from the cooling towers, I came to Redbourne General Tip. There were heaps of rubble, dunes of old bricks as if they had rained there from the sky, rusty, contorted iron, lonely embattlements of concrete. The desolation was cosmic: it was as though Cecil B. de Mille had set himself up in the demolition business. A fading notice on a low brick building – derelict, but not actually demolished – said 'Counselling Centre': I stopped to take a photograph of it with the rubble in the background. There was a voice behind me: I turned to find a security guard in a helmet looking officious.

'And why are "photographs not permitted"?' I asked.

'You're on British Steel Property,' replied the guard with capital letters, as one might say, "Know, stranger infidel, that you have trespassed upon the Holy Mountain with unclean socks; and lo! the High Priest is now going to cut your feet off." I was unimpressed.

'If anything happened when you're on British Steel Property,' persisted the guard, religiously, 'you're part of British Steel's responsibility.' It seemed unlikely, but he was as pleasant as is possible for a member of a private army to be, with a much-cherished curly moustache and flowing hair under his helmet, and he now had me tagged – not as a criminal likely to make off with half a hundredweight of old bricks in his saddle bags – but as a well-spoken member of the middle classes who might possibly make trouble. 'Sir,' said the guard.

'What are they going to do with all this?' I asked, quickly changing the subject, 'apart from stopping people from walking over it.'

'It's the old Redbourne Coke Ovens: was the counselling centre for all the redundant men just before it was demolished last year. Now they're filling it in with all the rubbish.'

'And then?'

'I don't know: it's possible they may redevelop . . . in some sort . . .' He seemed unable to imagine that anything might ever be redeveloped again and, looking around, I felt inclined to agree with him. I left British Steel Property before my presence caused an earthquake, and I bicycled off wishing that

I had had the presence of mind to call him 'my man'.

'With all the ramblers you must get round here, my man,' I said to myself, 'don't you think you really ought to get out a few brochures, establish a luxury hotel?'

The road was hemmed in by black-encrusted chainlink fences, protecting people from going where no one could possibly want to; when I leant my forearm against the wire, it came away patterned in diamonds as if it had been seared on a barbecue. The same grime lay in drifts at the sides of the road: a few blades of grass made their way through it with difficulty, and got covered in grit for their pains. You could see the hardness and sharpness of the particles of dirt, like the sands of a black seashore. The railway next to the road was rusty – the track, the waggons – and weeds grew between the sleepers. There were bus shelters where no bus had stopped in a long, long while, filthy, with spikes of glass along the edges of the empty frames; and a crazy, dirty signal-box with broken windows.

There was one building where some form of manufacture seemed to be conducting itself – for there was nobody visible to do it – in a graveyard of old pallets, dusty corrugated iron, abandoned oil-drums, forgotten castings rusting away where their faces were turned towards the weather. Over it all sagged the limpest Union Jack that ever depressed the spirits, as melancholy as the sun hanging on the horizon now that the storm had gone elsewhere, for it could hardly get through the haze: it was only half a sun, weakly red as if it were coming out in sympathy with the Redbourne Coke Ovens, as ironic as the fiery sign on the Furnace Arms.

Through the chemical effluvia came a smell of spice from fennel growing by the road – it was not the sort of fennel I would have liked to have put on any fish, but it was growing; rose bay willow herb, soap-plant (ironically) and little marguerites had sprung up on waste ground where they could, but their brightness had to fight the grime so that even the daisies were grey. Nothing moved on the railway sidings, little moved on the road – a dumper truck like a wheeled frog, a motor cyclist wiping grit out of his eye.

Then a church tower ahead at the end of the long straight suggested the possibility of something cleaner, and beyond a signal gantry for the railway and a scrap-yard was a windmill (sail-less, but a windmill all the same) while an ornate school-house in the Dutch style tried bravely to keep up aesthetic appearances. I came to a much-designed, brand-new shopping precinct, but the deserted streets were littered as if the habit of demolition had extended to the people themselves. One cheer-ful-featured man strode briskly down the pavements, and I asked him the way to the Royal Hotel.

'As sure as blazes, you go into a strange town and the first person you ask is a complete stranger – thousands of times,' said the cheerful man with Irish courtesy. 'It's a week I've been here, and not a day more. Now, the Royal Hotel, is it? There's a big one up there, a good one – oh, yes – but it's not the Royal. It's the Royal you want? Then why not go up there – follow that car – you can turn any way at the top, and most likely you'll find the Royal close by – and a fine hotel it'll be, that I'm sure.'

I followed the car. It took me past the offices of the Scunthorpe Star, which twinkled not very brightly, the Las Vegas amusement arcade, the Showboat amusement arcade, Funland (with three teenagers sitting on the step looking anything but funny), Tiffany's Dancing, and Scunthorpe Rollers – from which as I passed came the faint but distinct shout of, 'Get pedalling, you fat bastard.'

However, the Royal Hotel turned out to be hospitable, with a fat barmaid with a smile like a cream tea. She had been a graphics designer in British Steel, she said, before she was made redundant.

'I've been one of the lucky ones: I love this job, I really do,' she said. She had bright eyes, a silver laugh, and warmth inside and out for the evening was hot, and it made her blue-and-white print dress cling round her like an over-officious wrapping.

'And I love this town – wherever you go, there's always a welcome,' said the barmaid of the Royal Hotel, her face gleaming.

I said that I had already been welcomed at Scunthorpe Rollers.

'They've sprouted up in the last year, penny arcades and places like that. The bingo across the road is brimming: people have got to have something to do, they can't just sit at home and mope.' She went on to tell me that Scunthorpe had had a great reputation for entertainment during the war, when all the airmen from the Lincolnshire bases came in for the dances, and the local music-hall which was celebrated – the top comedians who played there were the reason the name of Scunthorpe became something of a joke.

'If you can't laugh at yourself, you can't laugh at anyone,' said a sandy-haired man next to me. The barmaid introduced him to me as a local businessman: the business turned out to be fish and chips.

'I'll fry black pudding, pineapple rings, saveloy, beanos – anything the public wants,' said the fish and chip man, non-chalantly. 'Cod roe – I tell the public that's just a cheap version of caviare, they're getting a bargain.'

'It's a very happy place still – despite the depression,' the barmaid told me. 'Cosmopolitan – we've got a lot of Indians, Pakistanis, Italians, Polish. They mix well 'cos they all used to work in steel. It's a town that was built on steel – people came from all over England, all over the world.'

'But if you'd come in from Doncaster way, you'd never assume it'd be a steel town,' said the fish and chip man. 'It's like a garden.'

'You'd hardly assume it anyway,' said the barmaid of the Royal Hotel, between pints of lager. 'Not with so many out of work. There's foreign steel coming in down at the wharf – from Sweden and Japan and all over – and yet they've closed two steel-works down, and part of another. There's only one steel plant left, and it doesn't employ many – so there's fathers out of work, sons out of work, whole families on the dole. Go down town, you'll see men doing the shopping, men just wandering around, nothing to do, depressed. You can see it in the faces of the little gangs on the corners. Crime is going up – it used to be a very good town.'

'It was the five-pound-note town once,' said the fish and chip man. 'Now men will have one or two pints where it would have been four or five: instead of going out at eight o'clock, they'll got out at half-past nine. There's many businesses closed. We've noticed that people who used to have fish and chips two or three times a week, now they'll have fish once, fishcake once. It's sad.'

'If you go towards Grimsby, it's the same sort of thing now that the fishing fleet's been disbanded,' said the barmaid. 'You

can smell depression as you walk down the street – fishing-
boats just lying there rotting, great big beautiful ones, it's like
a graveyard of boats.'

'In Grimsby, they won't touch cod like they will here. They
want haddock,' said the fish and chip man.

'But they haven't got a smile on their faces like they have
here,' said the barmaid of the Royal Hotel, defiantly.

Having gone to bed early to prepare for the long ride to York
the next day, I was woken up about chucking-out time by a
sound like flapping chickens from below my window.

'Leave it out!' said a protesting voice. The chickens flapped
vigorously again. Peering down, I saw that the noise was not
wings, but fists. There were three dark shapes together, one of
which suddenly parted company with the other two, flew into
the nearby hedge and disappeared, like a snooker-ball into a
pocket.

'There's two on to one here,' cried an aggrieved voice from
the hedge.

'Too bloody right there is,' said one of the two, less critical
of the status quo. Twigs crackled, and something began to
come out of them, but the two sprang at it, and everyone
vanished back into the hedge.

'Ah,' said the hedge. (Slap.) 'Leave off.' (Grunt.) 'You
bastard.'

There was a thump of the bar door being flung open: four
figures flitted forth, light as ballet-dancers, and the three in the
hedge were pulled out of it.

'What is it?'

'All these bastards . . .'

'Leave him alone, eh?'

The *corps de ballet* joined the principals in a blur: the blur
executed a stop-go sideways foxtrot down the road. A police-
car drew up: the blur separated out.

'All right, all right,' said the policeman for no obvious
reason since everything was all wrong.

' 'E started it,' said the voice number two of voice number
one.

'Sorry, Mick. Sorry,' said voice number one with a rather

poor effort at sincerity. 'You fucking bastard.' (Scuffle.)
   'All right, all right.'
   'I'm sorry, sorry.'
   'All right, all right,' said the policeman again – adding, in a
flight of eloquence, 'Get on, please.' Whereupon, everybody
went off.

VII

A CITY OF GHOSTS AND DRAGONS

TO YORK via THE HUMBER BRIDGE

The next morning, Jenny went back to London early to get more recording tape. I heard the car start up and the character-istic Alfa exhaust note die away through four long gear-changes into the distance. A particularly squeaky seagull set up piercing the morning's dull ear somewhere about the next window-ledge but one; a motorbike went past like a mech-anised version of at least three of the four horsemen of the apocalypse; the man in the room next door took a shower that went on for such an extraordinary time that I suspected him of trying out a new method of suicide by washing away the epidermis.

It was time to get up and enjoy the world, which provided

a) what felt like an abscess developing all along one side of my jaw (grown in sympathy, no doubt, with the other jaws I had heard being thumped the night before); b) a sinister little pile of black grit left in the centre of the bath from my ablutions of the night before; and c) crystal-grey drops all along the telegraph wires. It was grey, and raining hard – a wet Saturday in Scunthorpe. Looking out, I saw a hole in the hedge, and a number of more established holes of similar size.

Having hung around the hotel until mid-morning, however, the weather lifted and my spirits with it. Even the yellow smoke from the coke ovens made a fine effect against the blue and fleecy sky as I made my way out of town, but I was not sorry to reach the outpost of industry – an electric sub-station of scrawny pylons and gawky transformers humming a duet with a treeful of cawing rooks. A couple of miles further on, I joined Ermine Street again – but even amongst the fields, it was some time before the breeze blew the fumes out of my nose.

Appleby was a pretty little country village that showed an estate influence in its patches of woodland and its distinctively folksy cottage architecture in stone edged with red brick. After it, the country opened out into wide fields again: there was a fresh, rainy feeling after the wet night, with big brown puddles shining along the roadside: one field would roll out in green waves of potato leaves with flecks of white flower on the crests; in another, a regiment of stout cabbages rocked gently in the wind with a solitary white butterfly flitting erratically above them, totally confused by the *embarras de choux*.

Ermine Street grew smaller as I neared the Humber and could make out the skeletal suspension bridge in the eastern distance, seeming as fragile as grey cotton. I stopped under a bent oak tree across a barley field from the pinnacled Winterton church, listened to the wind crisply battering the leaves, and looked ahead to the ridge of higher ground that had crept infinitesimally up the horizon – the first hills of the north – and thought I could see the sun on them. I topped the next rise, and it was all downhill to the river itself, at first hardly more than a thread of silver-grey smoke. But a few fields from the water, the road bent round towards the bridge: although that was my intended route, the morning almost gone, and York still almost fifty miles away, I had a sudden fancy to see Ermine

Street end at the water's edge. I had no idea where it did so, but it seemed logical to project the line of the road straight to the little creek at Winteringham Haven, the only inlet on that stretch of the bank.

With the innocent enthusiasm of the uninformed explorer – for I had no idea what I was looking for – and careless of the fact that it would be uphill coming back, I freewheeled past a farm which had everything a farm should have – cows cooling beneath chestnut trees, a patchwork-tiled barn, farm machinery neatly done up in tarpaulins with bright colours sticking out, chickens strutting in an orchard – and through Winteringham, which is as unpretentiously pretty a village as you will find anywhere. The road became a cinder track to the Humber Yawl Club, with the members' boats scattered at ridiculous angles along the muddy banks of the creek, it being low tide. At the mouth of the channel I stopped and sat down on the wooden piling to give proper meditative weight to the occasion.

The sun was hidden, and the light was pearl: it skated down the mudbanks and splashed about in the water among the gulls. There is a magic about frontiers of any kind – it is as if the resonances of the country you have travelled through pile up against an invisible fence so thick that you have to struggle through them to gloriously empty air on the other side. Here was old magic in a quiet place, with children's voices and the rattle of a distant pram-wheel cart on the cinder track and an occasional, unhurried hammering from one of the boats. I thought that it must have been a nasty shock for the Romans to have come unawares upon the Humber and have to get over to Brough before they could get a drink at the Ferry Inn, which has a picture of Roman soldiers lecturing naked Ancient Brits on its sign, and must therefore be assumed to have existed since time immemorial. I went over to the hammering.

'Was this the end of Ermine Street where the Romans had their crossing?' I said to the boat. It made no answer, not even a subdued tap, but I had attracted the attention of the man next door, who was enjoying the nautical life with a couple of friends, sitting on his boat in the mud.

'You're obviously a rambler,' said that mariner, fairly accurately, but with a certain disfavour. 'I couldn't tell you.'

'I thought it might have been common knowledge in the

Humber Yawl Club.' The pearly light skittered up off water
and bounced off the mariner's forehead, which was domed
and shiny.

'Having said that – ' the mariner reflected, ' – no, it's at
Whitton, a village up the road. From the water, we can see
piles of stones they tell us was the site of the old bridge. It's up
the river bank a couple of miles.' I thanked him and he
returned to whatever wheel, mainbrace or marlinspike he was
busy with. It was a setback, but not a great one: the meditation
on the Mysteries of the Past had been quite satisfactory,
although in the wrong spot, and now I had directions to a pile
of historic stones. I set off along the dyke.

The way to the dyke was marked on the Ordnance Survey
as a public footpath, and I passed two notices which confirmed
this, both of which had been thrown down by a vandal, person
in authority, or public-spirited local. The surface was rough
flints: I was afraid they might slash the tyres, and said as much
to an old person I passed.

'The tide?' said the old person. 'No need to worry – you're
on a bike.'

'No, the tyres.'

'Half-past twelve, isn't it?'

'Yes, that's right, half-past twelve.'

It was very peaceful travelling along the dyke, and even
more so when the path stopped and I had to scramble the bike
up to the grassy top, and walk. There was the measured
belling of a foghorn close at hand from a tiny red lightship
called the 'Upper Whitton', and the wind went *whissh* in the
reeds. A brace of partridge rose from almost under my feet and
whirred off over the fields; then I passed a mysterious nautical
object on the top of a pole, shaped like a flowerpot with holes
in, and looking as if it might be intended for the capture of
absent-minded seagulls.

The sun came out and made jiggling lights in the brown
water, but it was all taking rather longer than I had expected
for the grass was long, and the general effect was like pushing a
double pram full of large twins through an ill-tended hayfield
in a relay race. Apart from a certain amount of barbed wire,
there were fences every few hundred yards with stiles for
walkers, but little provision for cyclists, especially those
weighed down with luggage. Bicycle bags are like bras and

suspenders – not easy for a man to get his hands on and, when he can, trickier than you would think to undo. So to avoid dismantling the bag systems to make the bike light enough to lift over, I was forced to evolve a technique of passing underneath. I laid the bicycle on its side; I laid myself on my side; I rolled under; I pulled the bicycle through; we both went on to the next fence.

It all took time, and I was still going away from York: however, it delighted two small boys fishing in a reedy pool as being something new in the way of adult behaviour.

'Wor Rex does that,' said the smaller and cheekier of the fishermen.

'Goes through fences?'

'Rolls about.'

'Rex is your brother, cousin, father, second cousin, grandfather, brother-in-law?' I was feeling sensitive, just having rammed a large fence-splinter into my hand.

'He's wor dog, Rex. He finds summat dirty, and then he rolls in it.'

'I'm looking for an old way across the Humber,' I said carefully and politely.

'Swim. That's an old way,' said the larger boy. 'Heh-heh.' It was like something out of *Beano*.

'You haven't seen any old Roman stones in the river?'

'Don't like the Rolling Stones. D'you like 'em, mister?'

I rolled under the next fence. It seemed to be taking a long time to get to Whitton, though I could see it clearly along the dyke – all barns and the backs of cottages dominated by one tall house, three poplars and an unusual church tower in Tuscan style. The dyke and the path of some tiny railway, dead long before Beeching, converged on the village: there were everwider meadows between me and the river, and no hope of seeing anything in the water, but from the long grass below the dyke, not twenty feet away, a brown and white buzzard rose on freckled wings and sailed in an ambling flight far out over the Humber.

Many fences, and a few liftings and buckle-fumblings later, I came to Whitton, and explained my quest to a man filling a bucket at a garden tap.

'Apparently you can see the stones,' I said.

'I wouldn't imagine that's so, because of the tide, like,'

replied the gardener. 'Although we're quite high up, it's fairly wicked like on a high tide – covers everything up – within a week it's changed.'

Inwardly I cursed the Winteringham mariner. I said, 'I heard you could wade across.'

'They say it's possible sometimes, but you'd get wet, however you did it. If you get a real low tide, there's very little water to be seen, but in winter, the high tides are up within two or three inches of the banks, then they go down at full belt, and it's a bit fierce.'

'Oh well, if there aren't any stones, I'll settle for a pub. Where is it?'

'Sorry, we're dry,' said the gardener, turning off his tap.

I had not completely lost hope: I rode through Whitton towards what was marked on the map as the Devil's Causeway – because it quite often happened that later and more primitive generations gave supernatural names to Roman work. There is a Fairy Lane towards the start of the Fosse Way for instance, and another Devil's Causeway is the Roman road to Berwick. But this one turned out to be irrelevant to Roman crossings, and my way to the most likely bit of river bank was behind the gardens of two bungalows. I photographed them, just in case a Roman foot might have trodden their neat lawns and the camera reveal the impressions of the bodies of lounging legionaries among the begonias. But next to the gardens was some extraordinary ground: a field suspiciously flat and a glade suspiciously humpy with stone under the surface. It felt not so much Roman as Druidic, for there was deep-pile moss richly green among ash and elder, bramble and hawthorn, and the humps grew magical teazels: but thick rushes stretched between the humps and the water (doubtless with even thicker mud beneath them), so I could not approach the river to look for any stones that might remain uncovered.

I abandoned Roman crossing points and cycled away, stopping only to ask the whereabouts of the nearest pub from a man in an oil-stained peaked cap who was walking through the village with a little boy by the hand.

'Butcher's Arms, West Halton, a couple of mile up the road,' said the man in the peaked cap with a smile so wide that it was impossible to believe in his teeth. 'You should just find them open.'

'I'm glad of that, 'cos I've been tramping all along the river from Winteringham looking for old stones.'

'Used to be a jetty here.'

'Yes, I thought I found something pretty ancient on a bit of waste ground by the couple of new bungalows at the end: the ground was all humpy.'

'Owd railway station.'

'Oh.'

'It was the Roman crossing I was looking for.'

'That's at Whitton Ness.'

'Whitton Ness?'

'You'd have come straight past it: there's a shipping basket.'

'Shopping basket?'

'Shipping basket: looks like a sort of flowerpot on a post.'

'I saw something that looked like a birdcage for seagulls.'

'That'll be it, give or take a yard or two.'

It was nice to have positive information, but I was galled that I had walked, lugged, the bicycle straight past it without noticing. 'I must remember that next time,' I said. 'When I see a flowerpot on a pole, it's likely to be a Roman crossing-point.'

'Nay, I can't vouch for that. It's a shipping basket.'

It was after two when I arrived at the Butcher's Arms, thereby tipping the ratio of those behind the bar to those in front in favour of the customers – four of us, three of them, although the balance of power remained with the stout lady who drew my beer, and who combined the dignity of Queen Victoria with the self-assertive humour of a small volcano. This seemed to be contagious: the whole bar was seismically disturbed with chuckles and guffaws, with the exception of a nervous-looking customer who spent his time hovering in the middle of the floor, hurrying outside, peering round as if he was expecting Custer and the cavalry any moment, and trailing back in again.

'Good morning, a pint of bitter, please,' I said. 'No, on second thoughts, lager. And a ham sandwich.'

'Afternoon. D'you want bitter or lager?' said the stout lady.

'Lager.'

'I've got bitter if you want bitter. And cheese and onion.'

'No, lager.'

The bar in general sighed the contented sigh of a social group who had feared that their hierarchy might be about to be disturbed, and discovered that it wasn't: and the stout lady drew the lager with an air of modest triumph. 'What about the sandwich?'

'Cheese and onion.'

'Sure you don't want ham?'

'One of each.'

'I've got ham . . .' A slim, pretty girl trundled in a beer keg. 'Lift it up, lift it up!' cried the stout lady.

'That'll be your daughter, I suppose?' I said, ingenuously scoring a point.

'Me daughter, me daughter!' bellowed the stout lady, breaking up entirely and shaking her head with such violence that her tight white curls almost moved. 'It's me grand-daughter!' She added a long, extremely rapid Lincolnshire sentence, which was totally incomprehensible but which I took to mean that I was a delightful personality at liberty to return to the Butcher's Arms on a future occasion; and went to make the sandwiches. The nervous man hurried outside.

I explained my quest for the crossing to those assembled, who guffawed once for the fences, once for the splinter, once for the shoulder wrenched with lifting the bicycle, once for the railway station, and twice for the shipping basket. The nervous man passed by the window.

'They're not sandwiches, you know,' said a voice from the kitchen: 'they're in a bun.'

'That's all right.'

'It's a big bun.'

'Oh. Well, p'raps you'd put them together then.'

'Ham and cheese and onion, all in one bun?' It sounded like the last memsahib about to shoot herself at the siege of Lucknow. I told her to go ahead.

The landlord leaned forward: 'The last man who asked her for something different, he was clean-shaven when he came in, and had a beard like yours when he got it.'

'Do - you - want - ham - and - cheese - and - onion - all - in - one - bun?' came from the kitchen. I did not, but it was too late to back down.

'Yes.' There was a snort off-stage. The nervous man came back in and went out again.

The stout lady returned looking like Lady Macbeth about to address a conference of arboriculturalists.

'Here's your bun. Ham. And cheese. And onion.' She was quite right: it was a horrifying combination. There was a great deal of extremely fierce onion, and I felt the stout lady watching to make sure I ate every scrap. It was, I learned, anything from thirty-five to fifty-five miles to York.

'You're never on a bike!' said the stout lady with her eye on my stomach.

'Yes he is,' said the landlord. 'I saw him come cycling past the window.'

'I wouldn't wear shorts if I wasn't on a bike, would I?'

'Can't see your legs,' said the stout lady from the other side of the bar, in tones that implied that therefore there ought to be serious philosophical doubt as to whether I actually had any. Indeed, from her side of the bar, the only proof of legs in connection with customers as a whole was the nervous man, who now came back in again, hovered, and went out.

'What's the matter with him?' I asked.

'He's having a baby,' said the stout lady. The other male customer hooted like an ambulance, and everybody fell about.

I was four hours late by the time I began to cycle new ground again, travelling towards the bridge along the south side of the Humber past an interesting red-brick farm which bore the inscription: 'Pray, play and sing God Save the King 1796'. The tide was at its lowest, and the sun welded water and the shining mud together in brightness, so that it looked as if there was no river there at all: and only from the top of the steep hill at South Ferriby was I able to see the shifting patterns of water over Redcliff Middle Sand and the banks around Read's Island. As I rode across the bridge, with the pillars of the balustrade flicking hazily like a stroboscope to show how fast I was going, the water seethed and chopped below but the colours were peaceful and harmonious – mauves, browns and blues for the river, grey for the bridge, light blues for the sky and whites for the distance.

An elderly couple I met on the bridge turned out to be tandem enthusiasts who had ridden many a run with clubs in the thirties. 'We had the best of the cycling,' they said: 'it's all spoiled now – they practically blow you off, those big lorries.' They pointed out the old ferry pier, and the boat itself which almost went to the scrapyard despite being the last in the line of Humber ferries stretching back two thousand years. *The*

Lincoln Castle is now a tourist attraction on the north bank of the river she used to cross in twenty minutes for the price of a few shovelfuls of coal. The trip over the bridge is many times faster for those who need to make it, but the price was something like a hundred million pounds for over a mile and a quarter of four-lane road, whose central span of 4626 feet makes it the longest single-span suspension bridge in the world. It is not the sort of achievement to be measured in twenty-seven-inch-thick hawsers, however: it is from a distance that it appears most impressive, because then you perceive the space those ropes are conquering, while they themselves are gossamer.

When I crosssd the Humber, I gladly left behind many miles of dullness. The country was quite different, and the prospect of a range of hills invigorating, even if I might have to bicycle over them: I could not tell, as I rode back along the side of the river towards Brough to pick up the Roman road again. There were the varying shades and planes of woods and meadows above me as I rode below the brow; and as I approached North Ferriby, it was as if I had been instantly transported back to the Home Counties, with smart old houses, smart new houses, and smart in-betweens: at one gate, a tidy man was tidying his very tidy garden in a collar and tie complete with tie-clip. Even the wildlife was brisk, neat and industrious: a bucket brigade of sparrows fluttered from a copse to the corn below; hovered, dropped down, popped up with grain, back to the trees dodging the rest of the sparrow-traffic; they flittered their wings so fast that the sun appeared almost to shine through them, so quickly was it reflected. A red field-mouse bustled across the road – but it was so excited by its own daring that it ran headfirst into the kerb; rebounded, momentarily stunned; and trotted off again with a headache.

When I turned off on to my road, it rose easily on to the wolds through South Cave, which had wide coaching streets and a Toytown town hall with a clock in a self-important dome on top in its centre, and a little further on, the Drewton Country Hotel for Dogs in which the clientele were ululating for service. I could not follow Ermine Street direct to York: this section is only a dotted line on the map now, forking off before North Newbald, which sat compact in a fold of the fields warming itself in the weak evening sun; and the branch I was following (which originally went north to the Roman fort at Malton) petered out in a field of wheat after Sancton. On the surface, the village is noticeable mainly for the octagonal tower to its church, but the crest of the wold here attracts thunderstorms, and – long ago – it may have been some association of the area with the thundergod that brought Anglo-Saxons from miles around to bury their dead in the cemetery there, which is one of the largest ever found in the British Isles.

I came down into the Vale of York through an odorous Market Weighton: there were pigs before, and pigs afterwards – and the pigs afterwards produced a bouquet which had at least one of the qualities of a good Sancerre, being extremely long in the nose, and lasting until it was submerged in an aroma of frying chips from a wayside café. But even so, the Yorkshire pigs had nothing on the Lincolnshire (there is no such thing as a Humberside pig), and – though the country was flat – it was also human and pleasantly casual. Someone had tolerated a field of thistles which were doubtless very inefficient, but smelled sweeter than the pigs. In a nursery beyond, the sun was in the dahlias and chrysanthemums like holiday candyfloss, and the bright colours travelled along with me: they got into a garden and waved orange arms, mauve and red on the washing-line before coming to rest in a bank of sweet peas by a cottage at Hayton, where the black fuzz of the pea-sticks set them off to their best luminosity in the evening light.

Being Saturday, the main road was quiet, and I met few people. There was a cheery jeer from a family of very brown children perched on an old tractor in one of the world's few neatly-kept scrapyards, with the junk laid out like a flower garden. I missed the point where Ermine Street came back and the road was Roman again because my attention was distracted by another cyclist who was riding along with a baby in his handlebar bag. He looked guilty as he passed, and I made a mental note to report him to the Royal Society for the Prevention of Cruelty to Handlebar Bags. There was a marathon runner, looking ecstatically uncomfortable; a party of anglers by the Derwent setting up for the evening's fishing, tipping maggots into the palms of their hands like diamond merchants declaring a dividend – and that was all I met until I came to the twilit walls of York, just about the time they were locking up the off-licences. Very weary, I pedalled round the city for fear of getting lost inside it, to Bootham and my lodging.

'I suppose I'm too late for anything to eat?' I said.

'Yes you are,' replied the proprietress, with great confidence.

I walked out into the city again, and found a trendy junk-food restaurant with a great deal of ambiance on its menu.

'There's an hour's waiting,' said a young thing with case-hardened sweetness. 'In the cocktail bar. It's policy.'

'I bet it is,' I said.

The young lady in the next, more traditional, restaurant was hiding any true self she might have been conjectured to possess behind a face encrusted with make-up: or possibly a façade encrusted with make-up.

'Are you still serving?' I asked.

'No, I'm sorry, we're not,' said the young lady's façade in the manner of one who has found a dead rat in the soup tureen, and is going to have to be extremely firm with the staff about it.

Eventually I found an Italian restaurant which, not being English, welcomed me in. The food was awful.

Next morning, I found York to be a gracious embodiment of English civilisation almost entirely surrounded by tourists. The walls no longer keep out invaders, but bring them in. There is no such thing as the place that can survive mass tourism unscathed – since the essential principle of that particularly inessential activity is the exploitation of the one-off customer: but York copes as well as can be expected. The astonishingly medieval Shambles has not totally bowed before the law of commercial nature that any shop in a tourist centre will be useful in inverse proportion to its picturesqueness, and when I chatted to an earnestly be-spectacled American girl over Sunday breakfast, and learned that she had given up her job and was blueing all her savings to see Europe, I was glad to be able to feel that York at least was worth the sacrifice.

'Probiding you're tall enough to see the Minster ober the heads of the odders,' I told her, indistinctly – since the jaw which had begun to swell at Scunthorpe was bulging like the yolk of the fried egg on my plate.

'Doesn't he have a pulpit?'

'No, *Minster* – the cathedral.'

'Oh yes, I read that name. And the Adders, are they carved on it?'

After breakfast, I had an appointment with one of the City Waits outside the Minster, that great white confection that can be seen from afar across the Vale of York, gleaming like a Gothic gateau. The Wait was not there, but everybody else was, for I discovered the House of God under siege from mankind, protected only by a marshall in a gown of royal blue and a verger in black. They looked so heraldic that, in my own mind, I immediately christened them Blue Dragon and Black Dragon – though in fact they were more like eggs going up and down in a saucepan. They dodged in and out of the little door inset in the great one on their own shift system – and as one boiled to the top under the strain of passing in worshippers while turning back tourists, the other was already preparing to bubble up in his place.

'Service only: there is no sightseeing *at all*: sightseeing at one o'clock,' was their canticle, with an antiphon of 'Sightseeing no, service yes – choral matins at 11.30'. The throng at the door was made up of people who might believe in religion, but were sceptical about everything else in quick succession.

'It is *choral* matins?' questioned a consumerist Christian, severely.

'I try to be diplomatic, but I'm not much of a diplomat . . .' said Black Dragon, aside to me.

'Aren't they coming out yet? I've got two old girls in there,' complained a bored chauffeur.

'. . . I'm far too earthy, far too basic.'

'Are we all right like this?' asked a young woman wearing a dress in which the hemline and neckline were doing their best to crowd out the rest of the garment.

'The Almighty doesn't mind: come in your bathing suit as far as I'm concerned, my dear,' hrummphed Black Dragon genially. He told me that, after starting in the pits as a Bevin Boy, he had spent most of his life working with handicapped people, but had treasured an ambition to be a verger in a cathedral.

'There's an old saying that you can't get near the fire of hell for parsons, because they prefer a warm place,' said Black Dragon. 'On the other hand, "It is Better to be a Doorkeeper in the House of the Lord than to Dwell in the Tents of the Ungodly".'

'If God frowns on doorkeepers, St Peter's in trouble,' I suggested.

'I'm afraid I shall never get there,' said Black Dragon, alarming me with a sudden and quite unprovoked excess of seriousness. Being unaccustomed to conversations about salvation, let alone with people convinced they are already damned, I felt at a loss for words.

'Never get to St Peter,' Black Dragon prompted me, mournfully. I laughed a weak sort of laugh, which I immediately felt was a mistake. He came through with a spiritual uppercut. 'I've not much hope of that.'

'No,' I said giving in. He cheered up immediately, and passed in a couple of religious Germans while excluding a family of irreverent French with great dexterity.

'Sometimes I feel like tearing my hair when I see the great mass of people totally unaware of what this church is for. Their timetable says "Eight minutes in York Minster", which to me is an insult – but at other times when this great cathedral is rocking with noise and bursting at the seams with humanity, I think it is really worth it. When I come in, it's early morning, very peaceful and quiet, with the sun coming through the medieval stained glass – it brings us all down to size. It lifts you up. No sightseeing *at all*,' said Black Dragon, falling into religious paradox on his way back to the job in hand.

'What do you mean about that?' asked a fair-haired young man in one of those continental accents that sounds as if it is produced without the intervention of the tongue, but wobbling the back of the throat. 'I come from Holland.'

'We-are-singing-a-service: it-is-a-church,' said Black Dragon, nicely but with precision. 'I have friends in Delft, Utrecht, Gouda, Amsterdam, Harlem.'

'Bessom?' inquired the youth.

'Bishop? No, I'm not a bishop.'

'No Bessom?'

'Not in Bessom – Vissinger and Shavingen, yes.'

'OK. I'm not going to sing,' the youth decided, giving up on international communication, and rejoined his party.

'Wouldn't it be easier to have a notice in a few languages?' I asked.

'Sir, I can assure you that the great mass of people totally ignore notices – especially if it tells them something they don't want to know,' said Black Dragon.

'Well, I read notices,' I said. Black Dragon gestured with Christian forbearance. My gaze followed his. There, was a notice. I had failed to notice it.

'Oh?' said Black Dragon (or possibly, 'Lo!'). He darted inside the Minster, and Blue Dragon popped out to deal with the next tourist in the mob, an indignant and impatient Italian.

'*Questa matina sempre chiusa! Modo bruto, questo, modo bruto!*' said the Italian in the manner of Lucrezia Borgia confronting an apothecary out of stock in arsenic. He went on to say that he had been once, he had been twice: the church was still closed, it was ridiculous. '*Non disturbo!*' he finished in a shout, waving his camera with flash unit attached.

Not speaking Italian, Blue Dragon was unmoved, remarking only: 'One o'clock.' The Italian remarked pointedly that St Peter's was a much more important church than any old Minster, but you could go in there and wander round whenever you fancied, and huffed off.

'Can we sheet down?' asked the next in line.

In between tourists, Blue Dragon told me he was a joiner retired from the Minster maintenance staff of about sixty workmen, all one friendly band in one big workshop. 'All dovetail together,' said Blue Dragon. 'There's the Minster, the Song School, St William's College, the Deanery and so on to look after – you're never out of work. Next service at half-past eleven.'

'Were they good, the old craftsmen?' I asked.

'When you go to do a repair, you sometimes wonder how they managed with their primitive tools – though my own tools go back a hundred years: they were my grandfather's. If you've been trained with modern-day machinery, it taxes you a little bit at first to go back to – caveman ideas, shall we say? Drawknives for curves that are too long for the bandsaw, oak pegs to hold the mortice and tenon joints – you think it's primitive, but by golly, it's strong! We're a bit more critical about joints, but they did it very well, in their own particular way.'

'Satisfying thing to do, I expect?'

'Your work's there for all time – that's a reward in itself. You know somebody else is going to see it, even though they don't know who's done it. Sightseeing at one o'clock.'

'Less trying than the present job, anyway.'

'We have to watch for people eating ice creams, smoking, sucking ice lollies, coming in without tops on. Service only. My skin's gone from that thickness' (indicating a veneer) 'to that' (something about the size of a railway sleeper). 'An American gentleman came in and said, "What is this place? Why don't you put a bloody notice outside?" And then you get those who ask, "Was this ever the capital of England?" You get all sorts of questions, believe you me.'

'No posseeeble to prrray?' asked a short, cunning tourist with a vague-looking blonde next to him.

'Yes, oh yes.' Blue Dragon opened the door, and the tourist hopped in, but the blonde hung back. 'Go in, dear.' He shut the door behind her, and turned his gaze to the bottom of the steps. 'There's somebody making faces at us down there.'

I looked: it was a tall young man, smiling. 'It's for me,' I said. 'He plays the sackbut, or something.'

There was a scrabbling noise from the other side of the door. It opened, and out came the vague-looking blonde.

'I don't want to go in,' said the blonde, retreating to a safe distance from Blue Dragon. 'I'm just waiting for my husband.'

Tony Barton, the tall young man, turned out to bang the drum rather than to wind the sackbut – although, like most early musicians, he played a number of instruments. We sat on the Minster grass, well away from the tourists, and he told me how the six City Waits had come together in 1977 out of the simple necessity of having somebody else to play early music with, and had found themselves moving ever closer to the original idea of a town band wearing the city livery – a privilege granted to them in 1980. Thus was revived a tradition that had been officially abolished almost a century and a half before by the Municipal Corporations Act of 1835, but which had survived into the twentieth century in such activities as playing in the streets at Christmas.

'What we're doing is basically a form of early wallpaper music, mostly sixteenth-century, which is when the York Waits were coming up to their heyday,' Tony Barton told me. 'It's music that needs a context, so first we became the Waits; then we said, "Let's play out of doors", and went to little fêtes here and there. Then we dressed up: I made the costumes – straight copies of period clothes – and ensured they worked, with breeches that stayed up, buttons that fastened.'

'I know about funny clothes,' I said. 'I used to work as a minstrel in an Elizabethan restaurant. It doesn't half hold up the demi-semi-quavers when the hose starts slipping.'

The York Waits began in the thirteenth century as a cross between a guard dog and a fire alarm, blowing horns to warn the townspeople of anything unusual – from the arrival of strangers, to a conflagration, to a particularly interesting public execution. As time went on, municipalities grew in riches and dignity, and the Waits became town bands as a counterblast of civic self-importance to the musicians at the courts of royalty and aristocracy. In the 1600s, London had a band of twenty-four – four times the size of York's, but with the same sort of duties, playing in processions, on public holidays and on state occasions.

'We play at banquets,' said Tony Barton, 'but for outdoors we have to learn all the pieces. We can't have music stands at the head of a procession – and even if we're stationary, the music blows off on the calmest day imaginable. Now we can play from memory for two hours continuously to almost any audience. I don't suppose everybody likes us and our shawms and crumhorns, but most people seem to: they crowd round and listen – though sometimes we have problems with traffic noise. Medieval instruments are supposed to be loud, but they won't stand up to that.'

'And you play all the stuff the original York Waits used to?'

'Well, at maximum strength, there were six of them, like us, and by good chance we happen to have all the instruments they had – cornetts, sackbuts, bagpipes (the English bagpipe, which is an open-air instrument like the Scottish pipes, but softer and in a lower key). We know they played early in the morning round the town – people would pay them to wake them up – and almost every day in the market place, and we know that they were reprimanded for wandering round the countryside drunk with their hose round their heels after some rural debauch. On one occasion the whole lot were sacked; on another, one had to go because he was so old that he'd gone quite deaf, and the rest of the band couldn't stand it any longer. Generally, they were competent musicians – unlike the famous piper of Carlisle.'

'He's not famous to me,' I said.

'They say that he had three tunes – one of which everyone knows; one of which nobody knows; and the third of which he doesn't know himself.'

'But do you play the same tunes that they did?'

'Well, we know who they were, how much they were paid, and when – it's all in the civic records. But what they actually played, goodness only knows,' said the City Wait. 'Arrangements of popular tunes I think – and processional music.'

'Middle-of-the-road, I expect,' I said.

'Anyway, it's more immediate than wandering round with a set of headphones clamped to your head. We listen to too much music nowadays – we don't appreciate the good, we don't distinguish it from the indifferent. There's this huge industry turning out things that go in one ear and out the other, removing brain-waves. I've given up listening to music so much: I find if I'm more selective, I enjoy it more.'

We went off together to a snack lunch in a bar which purported to put on a good spread.

'Sorry, no food today,' said the barman.

'Is the anatomy of the British not peculiar?' I said: 'that they have stomachs the rest of the week, but none at Sunday lunchtime?'

The barman was a lad, and keen: so he left his bar, and made us beef sandwiches. I wished him well for that little bit of service, and hoped it would not be too soon before a greater experience of British catering cultivated in him a proper professional indifference to his customers.

Though he was a Wait, and sometimes busked, Tony Barton's living was making models – mostly for museums.

'When I was about two, I was given a lump of plasticine, and I made it into something,' he told me. 'It's not a job to have training for – you can either do it, or you can't. The sort of

thing I do is based mostly on the traditions of illusionism in
stage work, using flimsy materials like canvas, plaster, bits of
wood and rolled-up newspaper – though nowadays you can
carve a lot out of a slab of expanded polystyrene.'

'Thinking great thoughts the while?' I said.

'Craftsmen don't, generally: brainlessness sets in. You get
some silly word that goes over and over in your head, you
worry about this little bit of balsa wood, or that little bit of
plaster. The work is sometimes rather tedious: I'm kept going
by my idea of what it's going to look like at the end – although
of course no model is ever finished. It's finished when they
come to collect it.

'Problem solving is a lot of the fun. What do you do if you
want a field of wheat on a scale on which people are about the
size of a fingernail? I ended up with a sort of fur fabric I could
crop about in various ways to show the reapers going through
the field. For water, people used to lay in plates of glass – but
they're far too flat. I cut away the model and paint it carefully
underneath to give it depth, lay perspex over the top, and
work up the surface into ripples with resins.'

I told him that when I was a child with a father doting on
model railways to support, the problem I had always had was
vegetation, and had noted in particular that only God could
make a tree. Tony said that contemporary imitation grass was
not too bad (although God was still winning on the weeds
problem – what to do for a scrubby strip of road verge, with
dock-plants and fireweed growing?). The best trees were no
longer the plain sponge rubber I had known: there was sponge
rubber chopped about and stuck together with various sorts
of fibre to give a more realistic effect – but the ultimate in
realism was brass foliage, etched from photographs and
microscopically correct within the limits of the brass falling
to bits.

'I made a model of Queen Victoria for the Castle Museum
last year,' he told me. 'Full size.'

I was fully impressed.

'Four foot nine tall, and forty-eight inches round the middle, poor dear – which is almost as broad as it's long, if you see
what I mean. Unusual job since most of the stuff I do is fairly
small. The museum had a fine black silk dress she wore when
she was terribly old and spherical. We measured the inside of

the dress, made a shift to fit it, and made the model to fit the shift.'

'And with what did you stuff Queen Victoria, if I may make so bold?'

'Some spongy stuff – nothing pejorative. She wasn't a stuffy old thing, you know: there's a picture of her at the end of her life, in her carriage roaring with laughter like some immense, chortling baby – so I gave her the beginnings of a smile. It was an extraordinary feeling as she grew. I had her in the front room and, after a while, I found I would come down to breakfast, give a quick bow, and say "Morning Ma'am" before getting on with the daily round. My friends got rather fond of her – several parties came to visit her: later I put her in the front window peering down the street through the lace curtains.'

After lunch, I unlocked The Roman Philosopher, for I was going into the country to visit a man who had seen ghosts, and set out through the city on logical principles. But the grid pattern of the streets turned out to be subtly at variance with right angles, and when I came to a side of the city I had not been hoping to see, I judged it quickest to ride all round the outside and start again.

The walls of York are the city's surest means of navigation, apart from having kept development compact enough for the town centre to be of pedestrian size. The cream-coloured limestone of which they are made gives them a picture-book quality: a shade unworldly, like a man in a white suit. They have more than once been threatened with destruction by development, but York fell upon relatively poor times in the eighteenth and nineteenth centuries when the lack of local industry inhibited too much improvement. And when there was a serious danger, the walls were preserved (apart from one short stretch and all but one of the barbicans) through the efforts of an early nineteenth-century pressure group starring Sir Walter Scott, among others, who promised to walk between Edinburgh and London if they might thereby be saved.

The past is preserved in mysterious ways: no new culture works on a clean table, and one of the great fascinations of

Britain is the complicated build-up of bits and pieces of history, like leaf-mould in a forest. Not only did York keep its walls, but it kept its underground, being spared the building of big Victorian blocks whose deep basements destroyed the archaeological levels in other cities. There is a Viking capital below it: the rich and powerful city of Jorvig, from which York gets its name, and whose latter-day ruler, Peter Addyman, Director of the York Archaeological Trust, told me how excavations for a bank vault in 1972 had uncovered the first part of a timber town whose wood had survived through being waterlogged, even remains of wattle fences being visible after a thousand years.

But then there are the less straightforward survivals: Scandinavian words in names – 'Coopersgate' is not a gate but a 'gut', a street; elements of the original town-plan; the church as a centre of influence over the centuries. A Viking sock survived – not knitted, but made by nol-binding, a technique of looped sewing still used in parts of Scandinavia. Peter Addyman told me that it was rather knobbly, and not a very long sock but, as befitted the oldest sock in Britain, it had a hole in it. Still less tangible was the apparent endurance of a Scandinavian sense of humour: he had Danish friends, he said, who always liked coming to York because they found that the people laughed at the same sort of jokes.

Of course, what we hardly notice ourselves is that the past continues to build up its layers around us. Factory sites are cleared, and the processes that went on there become a mystery: the magnetism on a computer tape ebbs away, and the record of how something else was made is lost. Peter Addyman told me that if he had been born a century later, he would have had his eye on a site in Southampton which had just gone underground with the building of a superstore on top of it. The site was, he said, of a magnificent gasworks.

At last I came round the walls to the south of the city, and cycled off into the country to meet the man who had seen the Roman ghosts – Harry Martindale, a policeman living, appropriately, in the village of Copmanthorpe.

Harry had a feeling of substance about him, being a broad, open-faced man with a measured way of speaking as if he were still in the crown court, where he worked. He moved with the practised calm of a big man with heart trouble – and, following a cartilage operation, all the more carefully. The sitting-room of his bungalow had armchairs in trim chintz suitable for substantial people; and a white china copper's boot filled with pink plastic polyanthus stood in the fireplace next to a crimson rose in a copper vase. He told me his tale as I questioned him for an hour, for although I keep an open mind on such things as ghosts and God, it will take some personal experience to make me close it in favour of either. I still have the open mind, but there were no inconsistencies in his story that I could see – though it was plain he had given that evidence many times – and only one minor uncertainty, pardonable after almost thirty years.

It was in Treasurer's House, just behind the Minster, that Harry Martindale saw the men of the Ninth Legion. It was February 1953: he was eighteen, an apprentice plumber told off to knock a hole for a central-heating pipe through the ceiling of one of the cellars.

The cellar was about fourteen feet square, reached by two tunnels, the second of them so low Harry had to bend almost double to get through, pulling behind him a ladder borrowed from the old curator. There was a dirt floor, and the middle part had been dug out about eighteen inches, down to the surface of the Roman road that ran beneath the house: to Harry, it was just a hole down to something old – he had not been taught Roman history at school. The ceiling turned out to be stone several feet thick: by the light of the extension lamp in his toolkit he knocked all one day and half of another, until just before lunchtime. He told me that he was bashing away, three rungs up the ladder, when at about ten to twelve he started to hear a sound like music in another part of the building – someone with a trumpet who couldn't do more than make a noise on it. He ignored it at first, but the noise – musical or not – got louder, and with that he realised that it was coming from the wall supporting his ladder. He glanced down to his right, and was very soon off the ladder and scrambling into the corner of the cellar for safety – because what he had looked down on was the top of a helmet that came out of the wall next to him on a level with his waist.

'When I looked back, I saw the figure of a Roman soldier. The wall didn't exist as far as he was concerned – he came straight out of it and walked across the cellar. Then a great big cart-horse with a Roman soldier sat astride it; then a complete column of soldiers in twos behind the horse, going across the cellar and out through the far wall. It's since been discovered that the spot where they disappeared was the exact entrance to the Roman garrison.'

Harry told me that the sounds he heard were the trumpeting, a mumbling of voices without distinguishable words, and the noise of the horse passing across the surface of the Roman road. This was the minor uncertainty – though I am not even sure it was that – at the sort of question only someone using sound effects professionally would be likely to ask: 'What was the sound of the horse? On paving?'

'Well, it was on stone. Obviously. It was on the surface of the Roman road – just the sound of the horse passing you. I'm not going to say "clip-clop", because it wasn't.'

'I was just wondering whether it was on grass or stone,' I said, innocently.

'Well, when I saw it walking in the centre where the excavation had been done, obviously it was walking on the surface of the Roman road, which was stone.'

It could have been that he was reasoning back to the sound from the situation, or it could have been simply a restatement of his point, but there is no reason to suppose that he would have taken in that sort of information in the first place, not being a professional pair of ears, as I am. Nor did he have long – just the time it took for the column to cross the cellar. During it, he absorbed a number of details which he said he could not have known at the time, and some which nobody could have known.

'It was only seconds, but once it's imprinted into your mind, it's *there*, it's a thing you can never forget. The helmet I looked down on was beautiful –all different coloured plumes out of the back. The soldiers carried a short sword like an over-sized dagger on the right-hand side. They wore what I can only describe as broad bands of leather all joined together to form a jerkin on the top and, below, a skirt, which was all different shades of green as though it had been hand-dyed. You must appreciate I've never studied any of this because I think that if I did, I wouldn't have the same interest in it. But there was a meeting where people knowledgeable about Roman history and ghost stories came from all over the world to interview me, and they put a date on the soldiers from my description of the uniform – 390AD. I've been told that they were part of a forgotten army who stayed in the area so long that they became mercenaries; and that they dyed their skirts green, where a regular Roman soldier in this country wore red.'

He could see little more of the faces under the helmets than eyes, cheekbones, and the beards that most of them wore. They were dark-skinned, of some different nationality to his own.

'One of the things that struck me about them was that they were all extremely scruffy, as if they'd been out wherever they'd been for a long time. There was nothing smart about them: they didn't come marching through the cellar – their heads were down.

'I could have put my hand out and touched them, I was that close. What I'm describing is not like wisps of smoke, you see, or ghostly figures in the middle of the night. They were human beings – as you or me. That's when the biggest fear came in – because I thought that if I could see *them* as human beings, all they had to do was to glance slightly to their right to see me. Not one did so, but I was absolutely terrified and I can assure you that your hair does actually stand on end, because I could feel it on the back of my neck.

'When the last of them had gone, there was nothing else in the cellar to keep me there. I made my escape to the ground floor, and sat on some stairs for a while. The old curator came up and said, "Well, by the look of you, you've seen the Roman soldiers" – and I knew it hadn't been a dreadful nightmare. I went back to the firm I worked for and told them what I'd seen, and what they could do with the building – and I didn't go back there for twenty years. I was off work suffering from shock, and went to see my doctor, I was in such a state: years later, when I'd forgotten the date when it happened, he had it down on my records.

'One of the people who came to see me afterwards was a Professor of Roman History: he told me that I was the third person known to have seen the soldiers though I'm told they have been seen since. The only difference between my account and other people's was that I saw them walking on the excavated stone surface of the Roman road which had only been done six months previously – although I didn't know that then. Where the ground was not excavated, they could only be seen down to their knees.'

He had never given the supernatural a thought before, he said: and when all the fuss and interviewing had died down afterwards, he was glad to keep quiet.

'Being only eighteen, I was somewhat dazed, I think. When it became public again, a few years ago, I was quite happy because all I was doing was relating my story, not trying to convince anybody.'

'It must set you apart, though, having such an experience?' I suggested.

'I was quite happy to let it lie dormant – as it did for years; but, realising the interest people have in it, I'm also happy to tell my story to people such as yourself, because never once has anyone made fun of me. I am a personality because of the story: but my wife knows me as a husband, a father and a policeman. My son doesn't bother – it's just something that happened to his dad.'

Having talked to Harry, I could not tell you whether you will see Roman soldiers walking through the walls of Treasurer's House if you go into the cellars at the right time, but I was convinced that he had told me as truthfully as he could what he believed.

'The greatest thing that ever happened in my life was when I became a born-again Christian ten years ago: I gave my life to the Lord, and I'm happy,' Harry told me, looking happy. 'I thought then: "Am I doing wrong in telling people what I've seen?" – and I feel I'm not, because I'm not trying to convince anyone, all I'm doing is relating. I like to meet people, and I take out ghost walks – in Treasurer's House, it's nice to see the look on their faces when I tell them my story.'

Harry's wife came in with tea: her own Swiss Roll, moist with raspberry jam, chocolate biscuits, cherry and walnut slices topped with a breath of meringue. They were going to a tent and caravan service that night, they told me, five and a half hours of 'singing and dancing in the spirit'. They were taking children with them, they said, who had asked to come specially, having only had five and a half hours the night before. I felt as if I had suddenly become a character in *The Vicar of Wakefield*.

'Come again,' they said, 'come and stay.' They asked me about my journey as if they wanted to know the answer, they wished me well, and when I was a couple of miles down the road back to York, their car passed me on the way to the service, tooting cheerfully, loaded with people looking happy. Its paintwork was angelic white.

At Bishopsthorpe, where the Archbishop's palace is only one room deep because someone thought it ought to really look like a palace and built it as a façade, I stopped at a little market garden by the railway bridge. It was more garden than market: an old green railway carriage stood in one corner as a substitute for a caravan, and flowers edged the front beds. There was fennel, herb, marjoram in flower, parsley, apple-mint, asters, dahlias, feathery summer carrots, rows of bush tomatoes with star yellow flowers.

A girl all smile and glasses beneath a bee-keeper's veil told me she was one of a co-operative of four, and was just off to take the bees to the heather. 'You take up bees and hive; and bring back bees, hive and heather honey,' she said. She had a gentle voice to go with the smile, and picked me bunches of sweet peas and basil (which confirmed my opinion of York as a place worth living in – possibly even in February, when the damps come down).

As I rode off, a brisk soft wind sprang up and began blowing the sky about, making patches of blue so that even the greyest clouds silvered up their edges. With the sweet peas blossoming and the basil spicing in my handlebar bag, I rode back to York past the race-course as green as Ireland and the chocolate-coloured chocolate factory, to find Jenny back from London with fresh supplies of tape, but now the reels of the recorder refused to go round, as though the ghosts of the Ninth Legion had got into the works.

VIII

THE DOBSONS
OF BRANCEPETH CASTLE

TO DURHAM via NORTHALLERTON and SEDGEFIELD

On the Monday morning, the abscess on my jaw was about half the size of a lemon – which, since it didn't hurt much, I regarded more in the light of an achievement than an inconvenience – and it was plain that £3000 worth of new tape-recorder had indeed given up the ghost, shortly after having been confronted with the spectres of the Ninth Legion. I looked at the outside of the machine with great concentration and firmness: then I took it apart and looked at the inside with great concentration and firmness. There was no sign of any of the simpler sort of electronic fault I had hoped to find, such as a jackdaw's nest, a pickled onion in the works, or a colony of wire-eating voles: within the box, rows of yet smaller boxes looked at me, inscrutable as the Dalai Lama, and dared me to lay a finger on them. I put it back together, and the wheels still refused to go round.

'It is definitely up the drainpipe,' I told Jenny, in tones of authority marred only by a speech impediment about half the size of a lemon. Jenny phoned the agent: the agent said that if the fault did not lie within the second smaller box from the left (lying on the carpet with your head in the fireplace looking upwards towards a hypothetical tape-recorder normally orientated on a transparent mantelpiece), it was probably in the third, but that he would send a whole set of small boxes up on the train to Durham, to be on the safe side.

'And there is another slight difficulty,' said Jenny. 'We seem to have lost the Roman road.' I looked at the map: it was true. While Dere Street went off to the west and became an unpleasantly main road to Scotland, there was a gap of some twenty-five miles between York and the smaller eastern route northwards.

'It'll turn up, sooner or later,' I said, indistinctly, and set off up the main road to Northallerton.

I had not gone far before I met the picket; nor much farther before I met the second. I decided to stop at the drive to a psychiatric hospital where a little band of health workers were eating fish and chips and reading *Men Only*, a copy of which had been passed out to them with lunch – superfluously, to my mind, in view of the presence among them of a strawberry blonde social activist displaying a most interesting solidarity.

The organiser wore green, like Robin Hood, and had a larger beard than Lenin. His name was Roger, he told me: he had been picketing for three months, and he found it exhilarating to show what he had been feeling for a long time before. 'I was nervous at first, asking people to do things, but once you've done it you're committed, and all the exhortation in the world won't take you back.'

A motherly woman next to him said she had been a nursing auxiliary for eighteen years, and had never done anything like it before, but she'd tell Margaret Thatcher what to do. 'She ought to be shot!' said the motherly woman, with unmatriarchal vigour. A lorry tooted approval as it went past, and they all laughed.

'It's a matter of whether the principle of free medical service survives at all. We need the sort of massive cash injection that's been put into nuclear weapons,' said Roger, and went on to tell me that I would be horrified to see the geriatric wards under-staffed and silting up with helpless old people.

We swapped horror stories about countries dependent on private medicine: of the Canadian family who had had to mortgage their house to pay for treatment when their little boy was badly burned: of poor Americans lying in hospital corri-dors until the registry could check that they could afford to have their accidents. We convinced each other very well that everyone had an equal right to good health care. It would have been nice if we could also have convinced someone who disagreed with us, but of course none of them stopped. Since it was a psychiatric hospital, there was not even much point in consulting the strawberry blonde about the lump on my jaw, but it seemed to be shrinking anyway. So I left them eating their chips, and cycled on.

It was a domestic and unpretentious sort of day. Someone was baking apple pie on the housing estate at Fairfield, because the fragrance came wafting on to the road, making a passing cyclist's mouth water; and by the Blacksmith's Arms at Skelton, which bears a motto as well as a sign, 'By hammer and hand, all arts do stand', a gentleman in shirt-sleeves with a dome of a head had taken the sentiment to heart, and was clipping his front hedge very seriously – as he had reason to, for he was rounding off all the corners in the most appalling manner, and the more he rounded them the more serious he looked, and the more serious . . .

I was leaning over a field gate admiring a monster combine harvester with red turners at the bottom and a long green snout like a child's model of a dinosaur which clanked and clattered and snorted out clouds of chaff in haloes of dusty sunshine, when the nearest thing I had to domesticity came past – Jenny in the Alfa with a small kitchen garden of basil on the dashboard. It was time for lunch.

As usual in the real country, there was nowhere to picnic, so we laid out a tartan blanket on the edge of Bohemia – I was inclined not to believe it, but it was what the map said. In physical terms, it was the corner of a pasture beneath the fringes of a modest wood of larch and alder, birch and sycamore, whose branches just extended far enough over the fence to keep off most of the sprinkling of rain which now began to fall. There were thick slices of home-cooked ham and blue Brie from the proper grocer in Bootham, tomatoes which could not escape being English tomatoes but were better because of the basil to go with them, good red Leicester cheese and wholemeal bread which was still hot from the baker. The light rain blipped on our legs and on the leaves over our heads: it was odd, I thought, that the sound of rain on alder leaves should be a dry pattering.

'It's a peculiarly English entertainment, picnicking in the rain,' I said. 'Why on earth do we do it?'

'When else would we be able to do it?' asked Jenny, wriggling her legs. 'Look, goose pimples.'

I cycled off slightly fuzzy from the effect of a quart of strong lager, or so I judge from the entry in my notebook immediately afterwards, which reads: 'I am conscious of what it is like to be a triangle on a bicycle: if one is a triangle, do one's bottom corners push outwards, or inwards, or both?' The fact that I had run out of Ordnance Survey at this point completed the feeling of disorientation: if I had no map, how could I be certain that I was anywhere at all? I focussed on a cottage by the roadside – it was so perfectly cottagey that it would have done for any part of England, with an orchard of lichened trees so old their branches had to be propped up on sticks, a pallisade of roses and beans growing up wiggly poles: only the walls suggested Yorkshire to me.

The brick in this part of Yorkshire is pale, almost Italian in colour, and variously mottled so that no building made of it can possibly appear daunting, for it is the constructional equivalent of a patchwork quilt, and has more or less similar connotations. One of the more spectacular examples of the English sinking their aesthetic principles as soon as money is mentioned has been the widespread adoption of standardised brick without life or lustre: anyone who puts up a wall in it creates a plane of drabness to depress people for decades thereafter – and this is on top of the egg-box architecture which has neither the eccentricity of the individual builder, nor the adventure of the good architect. We pride ourselves on our planning regulations that cost us so much to maintain (and it is true that crass and greedy people have to be stopped from pulling nice things down), but would building be less competent, would it not certainly be more interesting, and would the public not have developed their own ad hoc safeguards against the jerry-builder if Parker-Morris and all the rest of the regulators had never existed? But it is the way of twentieth-century England to make everything either socially unjust or universally mediocre: our national celebration of individual separateness has been democratically extended to award respect to the work and opinions of the boring, lazy and incompetent, who have no right to such consideration – and the result is dullness.

If anyone ever preaches a Sermon on an English Mount – which mount, I don't know, possibly Tower Hill, so that their head can be cut off immediately afterwards for being traitorous to the national character – they ought to include a new adage: 'Blessed are those who love excellence, for they shall sometimes obtain it so long as they try hard enough, and are not beset by too many twits (the term to include twits *per se*, and also a tidy proportion of those who think that they are good at managing other people).'

It was only spotting with rain as I rode over the vale to Easingwold, which eases in the other direction, and is a long, wide street of low houses with a stone trough at either end – such things being often to be found as boundary markers in the North Riding. Beyond the little town, a range of hills began to creep in towards my road: the grey skies darkened them, dulling the green, turning the corn from straw to hessian. But from the sombre colourings stood out all the more the white horse cut into the chalk of the hillside.

He had a primitive quality about him, the White Horse of Kilburn, for he was all deep chest, with a very slim belly, an improbably small head and rather short legs. I travelled below him for a long way and he was as good as a fertility ritual to my sense of cultural anthropology, for he was totally unexpected, and I did not know that he was cut in 1857 by good Victorians to whom fertility rituals were among the less fashionable ways of passing the time. Below him on my road was also a Black Bull, which I thought might reveal something of the history of primitive man in the area, but it was not yet open.

In fact, all the animals of the North Riding seemed to be of a rather peculiar temperament. I observed it first with sheep. I had noticed one animal which had come to the conclusion that to stand on four legs was an inefficient way of grazing, in that the head was thereby further from the ground, and the neck muscles liable to needless strain: it had therefore decided to eat upon its front knees – not in the sense in which people consume TV dinners, but front kneeling. I stopped next to it. My intention was to decide whether it was particularly indolent, or particularly intelligent, or both (since the qualities often go together). Granted, it was none of my business, but the over-reaction of the others was quite unwarranted: the whole flock stopped munching, glared furiously, galloped up with an intent to surround me (in which, fortunately, they were defeated by the hedge), and set up a bleating like Prime Minister's Question Time. While this manifestation of Sheep Lib was not actually alarming (though on the Mendips I had met a farmer bigger and stronger than I am who twice had had his leg broken by an angry sheep, and never felt the same about them afterwards), it was – like most protest demonstrations – embarrassing. The only sheep that remained indifferent was the one I had stopped to look at, which remained munching – either through extreme intelligence or extreme indolence. Nor would they stop demonstrating until I had gone away again, at which point another member of Animal Solidarity took over, a very angry red setter in a garden across the road, so that the housewife came out to see what I was doing to the animals. Shortly afterwards I came to a field in which there was a bonfire, and an entire herd of cattle was clustered round it, warming themselves: and, taken together, these two instances of peculiar behaviour convinced me that all Yorkshire animals are stark mad and ought to be avoided by all but James Herriot, who lives nearby – unless he is the person responsible for giving them ideas above their station.

Thirsk was a rather squat town, with one of the shortest clock-towers in the world in its market-square, and had a down-to-earth feeling about it generally, a no-nonsense approach to life which was exemplified in the jam puff I bought there: pastry full of salt, in case some self-indulgent soul might revel in it, and an extremely thin spreading of jam. The country became increasingly pastoral as I cycled along the slopes above Cod Beck (optimistically named for a stream that size), but the puff rankled.

'Somebody ought to do something about jam puffs,' I said

to Jenny, when she stopped the car by me on the outskirts of Northallerton in a cloud of spiciness since the basil was still waving on the dashboard. 'They are one of the Great Disappointments in life.'

'You never mind about jam puffs,' Jenny replied. 'You wait and see where we're staying.'

'Some sort of pub, isn't it?'

'The sort of place that was Egon Ronay Number One a couple of years ago, that's all.'

'You are sighing like the Lady of Shalott with stomach-ache,' I said. 'We'd better get there before you swoon all over Northallerton: this is jam-puff country, and honest folk don't like it.'

The Cleveland Tontine Inn sat below the Hambleton Hills in company with a stone quadrangle which was the stable-block, and its contemporary equivalent, a car park. A 'tontine' was the opposite to normal business ventures which, from being private, go public, since it begins with a number of people who have a stake in it and, as each dies off, that share passes to the others, so that the surviving partner inherits the lot. This practical, but rather dangerous arrangement was named after an Italian banker, Lorenzo Tonti, and, until it was made illegal, was one of the best inducements to murdering your friends ever invented. However, I found the inn that began in multiple ownership still run co-operatively by the three brothers McCoy – although, as I only ever saw one of them at once, I decided that it was most convenient to think of them as a single entity, whom I named the Real McCoy.

The inn was guarded by an old black dog, extremely fat and prudent, and which was very fierce to us from a safe distance. There was a front door, but we went in at the back, which the Real McCoy had chosen as the main entrance because he liked people to make themselves at home while he was busy with really important things in the kitchen – one-third of him doing main dishes and sauces; another starters and desserts; the rest looking after the cellar.

The decor was anything but traditional Yorkshire. The bar ceiling was mauve, and the walls green with an exotic tracery of golden branches with flowers of pink and pale blue. The bar itself was a shiny wood temple crowned with a bulging art-noveau vase with decorations like a floral Rorschach test, and a prim art-deco jug in primrose yellow. In the restaurant, there were palm trees big enough to hide a minor romantic indiscretion, ferns that hung and ferns that sat in vases on Empire pot stands, as formal as if they contained someone's ashes. The table cloths were dusky rose-pink, the heavy napkins folded with Japanese delicacy. Above the tables were great umbrellas of painted paper and bamboo.

'Old chap used to make 'em, can't get 'em now,' said the Real McCoy as he handed the menus at dinner. 'Man snuffed it, no more umbrellas. Some of the stuff is good — the jardiniéres, some of the lamp fittings — the rest of it's rubbish, but it's nice rubbish that looks good at night-time. No particular style: if something looks nice, we stick it in.'

Dinner began with a mousse of salmon and spinach, and slices of beef fillet marinaded in oil, wine and herbs — a dish I had not seen since a lady who made lark pie surprised me with it one lunchtime in a turretted farm near Pithiviers, when I was cycling to the Mediterranean three years before. Duck with a wine and blackcurrant sauce showed the meat rosy and perfect in texture, a sauce velvety and not too sweet. We drank Gewurztraminer and Beaune, and ended with Cointreau ice-cream with prunes soaked in cognac and a concoction of raspberries and insubstantial pastry that came in ethereal slices like an angel cake really for angels.

It was a pleasant change from the orgiastic British sweet trolley, which is the gastronomic equivalent of plastic flowers — a lot of colour and little to enjoy when you poke your snout into them — typically consisting of: Black Forest Gâteau with lots of chocolate, glacé cherries and cream; Bowl of Very Sweet Figs, available with sugar and cream; Catering Apple Pulp Pie, to be eaten with sugar and cream; Yellow Gâteau with Tinned Sweetened Mandarin Segments and a cardboard-like substructure bulging and oozing with sugar and cream; bland Fruit Salad, to be taken with cream; blander Trifle hiding behind the cream jug; Crème Caramel; and Ice Cream (made out of seaweed).

The Real McCoy said that he had recently taken his first holiday for fifteen years, covering 2,300 miles in five days just to go to three restaurants – in one of which, in a little village just outside Lausanne, he had ordered a sorbet, only to be presented with sixteen from silver thermos-flasks on a little trolley and put out on the plate in a leaf design in less than a minute. That was the sort of refinement he admired.

'There isn't a restaurant like that in England,' he said. 'When we were there, a helicopter arrived with four businessmen who'd come from Paris just for lunch; there was such a welcome. One dish we re-created here – langoustine cooked inside a Savoy cabbage leaf with just a bit of *beurre blanc*. Beautiful! – though they had the big, pink langoustines that we can't get.'

There was not enough care put into British catering, he said, nor in the looking after of people, although things were getting better. He had noticed how more people had begun to say they liked small portions – and no longer complained that the vegetables were undercooked.

'We like a mixture,' said the Real McCoy. 'Different types of food, furniture, people from all walks of life. Your restaurant can get very cold if you're serving only the sophisticated. I like to get a really ordinary couple mixed in with them – persuade them to have a glass of champagne with a little bit of framboise in it before the meal, instead of beer – and to have salad after the meal instead of with it; separate dishes instead of everything on the same plate – that's dreadful. It's great if you can persuade people to do things like this, so that next time they come, they do it themselves. I've stopped serving draught beer in the restaurant. I don't like to see pints on the tables to swill down sauces that have taken days to prepare. One chap last night had four pints of lager with his dinner – Australian.'

He shook his head sadly. I knew what he meant, since in another restaurant I had recently seen a man eating such a large plateful of duck and chips that he had had great difficulty fitting his boiled carrots, fried onions and mushy cauliflower on to the top, and when he had poured his green salad over the top of that, quite a lot had fallen off the side.

Next morning, the Real McCoy appeared in a white open-necked shirt to serve breakfast and chat in his soft voice and easy manner. He had gone to bed at half-past two, and had been up at half-past seven, he said, but he liked doing breakfasts, and would we like fresh mango to start with?

We ate in the company of a tumbling black-and-white kitten called Ginger, which wound itself up in my microphone cables, went on to weave a harness out of the camera straps, and – having found there was not enough room for it to disappear entirely within my handlebar bag – finally got into a copy of *The Times*, and made something between a house and a sari out of it.

The Real McCoy was some time coming back. When he returned, he said he had had to fight the chickens for the eggs, and would we like the local honey? When he opened the pot, for the first time in my life I totally understood Pooh Bear – a fragrance instantly spread through the entire room.

'Just like the car yesterday,' I said. 'You can smell it coming, until your nose gets fatigued: Jenny's got it full of sweet peas and fresh basil,' I explained to the Real McCoy.

'But it's wilting a bit,' said Jenny: 'needs a head's start, basil.'

At Northallerton, I came back on to a Roman road. It was all the more welcome because it was a lane, because above me fleecy clouds were luminous in a blue sky, and because the breeze had taken the unprecedented course of turning itself round and blowing at me from behind, though hardly enough to cool the sun on my back. Whether it was that country looks different seen from a little road, or whether it actually was so, the hedges seemed wilder – bearing honeysuckle and haws turning russet – and the verges were full of the bright but absent-minded flicker of the wings of butterflies – fiery orange, and white. I saw a greenfinch, even brighter.

'Long Lane' named the road – a sign on a tiny signal-box, with the signalman hunched over rows of shining levers, but one of the best things about it was that it was anything but long, for it was continually turning into a hedge boundary, a tunnel of nettly green road, or a darker line through a field of grass, while the lane and I went on detours so inconsequential that I could not imagine how the change ever furthered the territorial ambitions of some long-dead farmer – unless that farmer had been a happy anarchist devoted to making people take their time, and not spoil a good summer's day by using it to rush somewhere.

It was while I was tacking across the landscape in this manner that I came full-tilt round a bend and stopped dead, trying not to breathe too hard, next to the Astonishing Extraordinary Object. The Object was neither large nor interestingly coloured, being about nine inches tall and brownish; nor was it doing anything but sit aimlessly by the side of the road. However, I had never been within half-a-dozen feet of a baby owl before, and certainly had not expected to find one out in the noonday sun – or, rather, just out of it, for it was in the shade of a stout-trunked ash tree. I stared at the owl, and the owl stared at me, and although the owl had the advantage in terms of eyes, for his were big and yellow, with dark vertical slits for pupils in the most inscrutable manner, there was no telling which of us was the most surprised. There we stood, stock-still both of us, for a minute or more; and we might have stood there longer except that I fumbled in the bag for my camera, and the lens flashed in the sunlight as it came out, whereupon the owl – which could not fly very well as yet – flapped heavily up into the ash tree. When I got round to the other side, the bird had vanished through a hole in the trunk back to the owlish bed it should have been in in the first place.

At Deighton, I left the light dancing in the fields and entered the village beneath the shade of horse chestnut trees, beneath which stood a red telephone box. There are few things to say 'village' to us now; the school is closed, there are strangers at the manor, the post office has been shut down for reasons of the soundest economy while the rest of the village shop died of a broken heart when the grocery customers committed adultery with the nearest supermarket. Perhaps the pub may survive and the old cast-iron finger-posts which were made to last in the days when all village communities were going to last, and work, and play – which many of them do much less now that so many of the children are gone (for the retired people had their families somewhere else, many years ago) and there are now weekenders and commuters in the cottages. But one of the things that for me still has villageness and solidity about it is the red telephone box: not that it has antiquity, of course, but it speaks of a coherent social structure with the royal family at the top (EIIR on the Deighton box), and a quality of due respect paid to traditional architecture in the mouldings round the window-frames which remind me of the reveals in a Georgian country house. (It is also nice that village telephone boxes are rarely vandalised, although that is a different point.) The red telephone box is formal, and it is friendly (which is how the English like things) and is built with great solidity: the idea that any *yellow* telephone box might ever adequately substitute for it is, by law of nature, absurd.

From the rise north of Deighton is one of the three best views of a Roman road that I saw: the Fosse Way to or from Wraxall Hill is impressive and Dere Street from Beukley Hill in Northumbria even more so, but both are A roads and rather too large and modern for the sense of the minor march of history you get at Long Lane before you zig-zag down over the river to Appleton Wiske.

Appleton Wiske was a jumbly sort of village, architecturally speaking – there was a beautifully modest Georgian brick chapel like a private house, but otherwise the place had the haphazard and undistinguished charm that comes from centuries of make-do, fiddle-around, and do-it-yourself. It made me wonder whether there was a time when traditionalists deplored such things as the Regency bay window added on to the cottage in the same way that we complain of the ludicrously-proportioned picture windows dominating little walls today – and whether those windows, the fake bottle-glass, carriage lanterns and all the rest of it may not seem charming, instead of in bad taste, when enough time has gone by.

I lost the Roman road a mile or so out of the village – although a straight hedge line continued as far as the eye could see – and took to rambling lanes for the country around the Tees (which rambles disgracefully itself here, in the manner of a river unable to make up its mind to have a proper valley). A little beyond Hornby, I met the mower who was scything hay on the roadside and pitchforking it into a car on the back of an old blue tractor such as I used to pretend to drive when I was small, covering myself with a mixture of oil and chaff-dust until it looked as if I had been rolling in black treacle-pudding.

'It's a '57 model, that,' said the mower proudly, after he had asked me the time. 'A good 'un – there's solid stuff in there,

like. Five hundred pound by the time purchase tax were on it –
I had a house I sold to buy it – twenty odd thousand they are
now. But I had a 'oss up to three year ago: we used 'osses all the
time up to 1962, when me feyther died.'

It took me back, for I am old enough to remember being a
little boy in a stable full of gently-snorting, heavily-fidgeting
Shire horses with hair flowing over their great hooves like a
guardsman in his shako turned upside down, and mighty
heads and chests too far-off to see properly in the gloom above
me. The Welsh farm where I lived had a ploughman then,
Ivor, who was very strong, very brown and very loud, for he
laughed in the farm kitchen the sort of laugh he was used to
laughing out in the open. Once when I went to the fair, I went
on horseback, but the horse bent its head to drink as it was
crossing the ford so that it pulled the reins out of my hands:
I was too small to reach them back, and was extremely
frightened.

'She didn't do owt much at all, but she were getting about
thirty when she died.' He had been out with the mare in the
fields one night, he said, and the morning after she was dead –
and the thing that rankled was that a young vet – 'He were only
a lad, twenty-one or two' – had accused him by implication of
neglecting her, the last of his horses.

' "She'll have been down more than one night – she'll have
been down a week," he says. "Ruddy 'ell," I says, "have a
look at the bloody 'oss." 'Cos you know when somethin's
down, they get sore, really sore, and she'd bashed her heels
with flickin' (you know how they flick when they're sort of
dyin', like?) but there was no other sores on her body. "She'd
'ave gone bloody rotten in a week," I says. And that's how
much he knew: buggers went bust just after.'

The light moved in stripes over the grain, the wind in
ripples across the clover.

'A tractor workin' on the fields, to me they're nowt: 'osses
like, you can talk to them like they're company. And with a
couple of 'osses, it were surprising what you could get goin'.
Years ago we had an eighteen-acre field – I were telling my
lasses the other day – there'd be about five of us forkin',
sweepin' it up to the stack and stackin'. We started to sweep
about two o'clock, and at half past seven, we had three-
quarters of it done. We used to enjoy ourselves, like: I think

they've gone too far, too mechanised – and a lot of them today, of course, they don't want to work.'

I said I wasn't really one to talk, since I didn't want to break my back all day either, and told him about my owl, which was not at all astonishing to him.

'Oh, we often see them, like,' said the mower.

'Often?'

'Often: hawks, weasels, terrible rabbits – one in my greens just before I come away from hoome, having dinner – white owls, like, and brown . . .' In this part of the world, there was plainly no social distinction to be gained by owl-dropping, so we started a joint admiration society for the countryside of the North Riding, with the mower taking every compliment as graciously as if he had been Chinese royalty, as much as to say, 'Of course it is – but do you, a foreigner, really think so too? Because if so, the whole world must be agreed on it.'

'But you haven't been to Swaledale, like? You'd enjoy that: they're friendly people. My grandmother used to live up there in a valley down by the river Swale – she never had much money, but anyone callin', visitin', they'd never goo without a cup of tea and somethin' to eat, like. Even a tramp: there was one used to coom for years – and a woman with him as well – except one morning, there was nobody oop, it were about six, and she's gone down (she'd be about eighty), and he played bloody hell with her 'cos she wasn't up. So her son Tommy says, "That's it, he gets no more like." But they're Vikin' folk, aren't they, in Swaledale? Blue eyes, sons and daughters of Vikin's, supposed to be – used to have the double-bladed axes and all this and t'other, but civilised today, like.' I was glad to hear it, for fear his grandmother had taken her double-headed axe to the tramp.

I left him mowing with dignity and wound through the bright afternoon, for what had seemed flat country dipped and curved in hill and dale, and the lane with it, revealing a different prospect at every bend: two flocks together in a green field, black-faced sheep with crows among them, so that it looked as if some of their faces had fallen off and were strutting along the ground in search of worms; an avenue of elms not yet fallen to disease, though a few yellowing boughs suggested that they would not last for long; a tumbledown farm; a spick and span estate; and the greatest surprise, a narrow bridge over a wide and deep-set river waving bright green weed in clear water above a dusky orange bed.

With my crossing of the Tees, I was in County Durham, and I climbed away from the river through Middleton St George until the Roman road and I met up again in the company of nondescript terraces, the forlorn and gateless line of the York North-Eastern railway, and The Fighting Cocks pub with two fine birds very angry on its sign. Suddenly the country began to feel less prosperous, as if every life had one fewer comfort, every house one fewer room and six inches less to its chimney. It was not simply the county boundary (although old boundaries, unlike new ones, often mean more of a real division than we give them credit for, if only because many of them were based on such divisions to start with and, even where they were not, have had some centuries to make their mark): the difference was that I was coming to the uplands.

The rise was stealthy, hidden in ups and downs, through Sadberge (was there ever a name more soggy with self-pity?). It was a proud royal manor once, and there is a boulder on the green to prove it, inscribed to its countess, Queen Victoria, in celebration of her Golden Jubilee; but the only proud thing I saw was a little stone turret on the reservoir, with battlements to which officials of the Water Board might repair with culverin, cross-bow and pots of molten lead, in case of siege. At Petty's Nook, which is no more than a corner, the sight of a tree-lined green lane stretching very straight into the distance made me stop and consult my map to make sure the Roman road did not take that course. Certainly, it made an extremely direct route – though broken now – to Bishops Auckland and Dere Street, but neither the twentieth-century nor the Roman Ordnance Surveys attributed it to the Romans, so I went straight on.

At Great Stainton (which – as usual with Great places – is extremely small, with a tiny, tumbling brook below it and a lawn walk from the road to its hilltop church) I came out on to an open plateau where the few farms kept their heads close to the earth, out of the elements. The hedges and what trees there were seemed to be a blacker green – perhaps the effect was caused by the greying sky, or the contrast with the grain (for the harvest that I had seen accomplished south of the Humber, and in progress in Yorkshire, was here not yet begun), but away on the eastern horizon was Stockton – all cooling towers smoking and steaming, and many chimneys, like a forest of brick and concrete trees whose tops had been cut off – and the wind that blew across the rye like the wake of an invisible ship had the tars of industry on its breath.

The road, which was far from straight generally, skirted Sedgefield and went round Hardwick Hall which is rather long on gardens and short on Hall, and apparently has always been so, as if the country is too poor to maintain the pretension. Hardwick had fine trees and a notice saying that it was a Country Park, but the parkland on the other side of the road was down to grain, and its trees looked like poverty-stricken aristocrats lost in a commercial world. Then the landscape became yet barer, the fields sometimes began to sprout chimneys, tips, old workings; at the top of the weary hill up to the Hare and Hounds, I saw the slate roofs of Coxhoe with a sheen on them from the evening sky, the white cliffs of a big quarry, and a sign to Trimdon.

As the Peleponese must do to the Greek scholar who makes his own first odyssey to them, so Trimdon and its pit disaster ring in the head of anyone who knows folksongs – and everyone in the British Isles ought to because there is no better poetry made for ordinary people by ordinary people; and the long broadside of their loves, jokes and disasters, their history of struggles that are past (some of them) but ought not to be forgotten, produce a sympathy which allows all our past to belong to us. Too many restrict themselves to the official history of the wealthy, and those who scorn folksong and the petty record of social history, scorn the common heritage. In County Durham, there is music in the voices of the people: I passed a group of women chatting near the back-to-backs of Coxhoe and it sounded like Old Norse – not a word could I catch, but I heard the tune.

Many of the pits are closed and most of the tips levelled now, but the back-to-backs (those pens for factory-farmed people), the mining villages, the small, solid farmhouses that hug the high lands to keep out the wind, mark Durham as a county that wears its economy and its class-structure on its sleeve. When I came into the city that evening, the clouds had gone and the late sun was golden on the tower of the cathedral, a building even more solid and obstinate than the castle with which it shares the crest of the almost-island in the river's bend. It is set so high just as much to dominate the city as to reach to God – a palace for the Bishop Princes who were the power in that land for centuries, before wealth passed to the coal-owners – but wherever the power was, the strength of Durham County was in the hands of its people.

There was classical music wafting on the bacon-scented breeze into the dining-room next morning, because the couple who ran the Kylesku Hotel – which they said was named after something Scots, and not something from the history of Serbo-Croatian grammar as, in my ignorance, I feared it might be – were retired music teachers. They had given up, they said, from lack of stamina, being unable to bear the sound of pupils playing badly all day long. Their baby was also deficient in true grit in that it bawled loudly when put into my arms, and refused to be comforted. (I am not good with babies, which I regard in the same light as Capo di Monte and other china figurines – something you would like to drop, if you dared.)

'Teething,' said its father.

'Sixth sense,' said Jenny.'

I abandoned the baby but continued with the music, for just round the back was a noted firm of organ-builders, Harrison's, and the last Harrison to run the firm came willingly out of retirement to show me round for he loved to get back into the works even though he had begun reluctantly as an apprentice who had never got on with his uncle, the boss, and who quit to join the army after a couple of years.

'When my uncle died in '37, my father wrote to me in India and said I must come home and carry on the business,' Mr Harrison told me. 'I wrote back and said, "No I won't: let my brother do it – he's the eldest", but then I got a letter from my mother which said, "You'll do what you're jolly well told". I didn't dare say no to her – she was that sort of lady. My father founded the firm in 1871.'

'A time of great expansion in the organ business?' I asked.

'Oh enormous. Non-conformist churches were being built,

and they all wanted organs. It was a boom business. It's had one or two booms since, and one or two dreadful flats. It's rather flat at the moment. We've just finished in Peterborough Cathedral – a good old English cathedral organ, nothing much altered since it was built a century ago. A lot of organs being built now are classical and copied from continental practice – no good really for the Anglican service which demands a straightforward organ tone, a homogeneity of sound.'

The organ-builder's smelt of the shavings of good timber, of paints, glues, varnishes, and a hint of metal. In the middle of the largest workshop, a man was working on an organ-case – from the inside.

'We take the man out when we put the pipes in,' Mr Harrison explained kindly, but as far as I could see, they might just as well have left him in as a sort of caretaker, since it was the size of a small house. Organs are the most monolithic of instruments, like musical shrines to those who love them: you have to make a pilgrimage to encounter an organ, and it has its own fixed servant, the organist, and a whole gamut of local institutions and traditions that flourish round it.

'Is there any sort of topping-out ceremony for organs?' I asked. Mr Harrison said that there wasn't. It seemed rather parsimonious to me, not to empty a half-bottle of champagne down the diapason, at least. I wondered whether things got left inside, to be found by future generations or organ-builders.

'Occasionally men's names – the pipe-makers always sign the bottom note of every rank of pipes they make.'

'Why the bottom note?'

'Where else would you sign it?'

'The top note?'

'The top note's like that.' He held up his little finger. 'It's difficult to get the note stamped on it, let alone anything else.'

In the gallery, a keen cyclist was making a manual: I could tell he was keen because he was extremely lithe, and dressed in a track suit and cycling shoes. In the metal shop, a pair of pipe-makers sat placidly at work. One was shaving shiny curls of alloy from the edge of a sheet with an old wooden block-plane. The other, who had a rank of treble pipes almost completed told me that they were a flute stop for Westminster

Abbey, and that he had three sixteen-foot stops in Coventry Cathedral.

'It's like a finger,' he said. 'Every organ has its own person-ality, every pipe is an individual thing, every pipe has a name. And if you go and look at an organ built since the war, you might well find my name on it. Ron Greenwood's pipe. I'm as proud of that as I could be of anything.'

I wondered whether master-plumbers did anything similar on water-mains.

I had not heard the last of pipes for that day, although I did not realise it when we left the organ-builders and went out into the city to look for lunch. It seemed that Durham consisted of hills and holiness, and was rather better supplied with saints (St Cuthbert and the Venerable Bede) than it was with cater-ing, which was cheap enough but relied heavily on beefbur-gers. Doubtless there was good local food somewhere, but the nearest we came to anything interesting was the sight of an extraordinary looking bun in the baker's windows – flat, large and circular with what looked like a thumb-hole in one side like an artist's palette. I asked a passer-by what it was, but chose one with such a thick accent that it was impossible to distinguish much more than the words 'stomach ache', which recurred several times in the course of an immensely friendly, but extremely one-sided, conversation.

In the afternoon, we took the car and went off into the country for we had an appointment with a castle. There were people living in it, and we expected to meet them too, but we thought that on sheer weight and volume, the castle was likely to prove the more remarkable, in the same way that the organ may dwarf the organist.

'But they'll probably have finely-cut cucumber sandwiches for tea,' I said, the taste of the beefburger still greasing my mouth. 'People in castles do. It keeps the butler occupied cutting them.'

Brancepeth Castle was occupied by a family/commune/pub-lishing company mostly called the Dobsons, for the extent of the Dobsons was almost as difficult to define as the ramblings of the castle – which looked deceptively simple from outside the fairly blank face of the medieval curtain wall, but was all halls, holes, rooms, passages, and stairways within, as if it were a cliff honeycombed by a rock-eating variety of Super-Woodworm.

There seemed to be students lodging in the castle at times, and a handloom weaver, a woodworker, a picture-framer and fudge-makers in the workshops, but the Dobson sons and daughters and Mrs D. herself were the kernel of the establishment. There was also a White Lady (thought rather dull by the family and seldom seen), and a more interesting ghost who lived in the gatehouse clock and turned the cast-iron hands to all sorts of peculiar times without any provocation at all, and without any works to help him. It was just after two when I arrived, and the ghost said half-past four.

In the gatehouse was: Mrs D., the portcullis, a notice which said that the castle was the local post office, and various signs of familial occupation including the morning milk, waiting to be carried a quarter of a mile or so and put in the fridge.

'It's a very *domestic* sort of castle,' I said.

'Now perhaps, but we were under siege in 1341,' said Mrs D. 'I discovered that only the other day. Sorry about the dustbins.' She had a breezy air, which blew her conversation in gusts, from various directions.

The castle was guarded, not by old baronial boarhounds, but by far more consumable and rather louder sentinels – geese which lined up like a parade of soldiers to welcome me with both ends: the front cackling at tremendous volume, and the back adding to the already not inconsiderable layer of droppings which carpeted the lawn, the paths, and were trodden a little distance into the halls.

'I suppose that means they've accepted me,' I said, as they stood in perfect stereo – one goose to the right, one goose to the left and three in the middle. 'But I would have thought you might have fancied a more aristocratic bird.'

'Peacocks aren't much use,' Mrs D. replied, 'so I decided we'd have geese, which bear fruit as it were.'

'I see them doing it,' I said. Remembering that the Romans used a similar early-warning system to look after the Capitoline Hill, it made one seriously concerned that the feet of the Vestal Virgins might have failed to match up to the rest of them, as far as purity was concerned.

We entered the castle which had a well-established air of just-having-been-moved-out-of. The Dobsons had moved in four years previously, but four years is an exceedingly short time-span to a castle of medieval origin, and it did not appear to have got round to noticing them yet. They were adjusting, however: the Long Gallery had its name up on a notice to help visiting parties find their bearings, but Mrs D. said that all the family knew where they were quite well now, and rattled easily through the Billiard Room into the Chapel to prove it.

'But how splendid to have your very own chapel,' I said. 'I do hope you're extra-specially religious.' Mrs D. was not quite sure, but showed me a monument to the man who had made it extra-specially ancient, at the start of the nineteenth century. He was a banker and coal-owner: it appeared that the castle had been medieval before he got at it, but not as much as it ought to have been. Before the coal-owners, who were Russells, the castle had belonged to the Nevilles, and before that to the Bulmers who had built it. Before that, it was the Dark Ages.

More recently, the Dobsons had been preceded by the Durham Light Infantry who had the place in the 40s and 50s, and a glass manufacturer who used the place as a research laboratory, leaving behind a legacy of grey vinyl floor-tiles, enough electric storage-heaters to bankrupt a minor principality, and a new telephone switch-room abandoned half-completed, as if the staff had fled from a ghost that had come down the fractional distillation column and groaned at them from the test-tubes. The last family in the castle had been the Boynes, who had departed for some other stately home more than half a century before. I wondered how the family had ever been able to move from a place so huge, how many pantechnicons they had needed, and how they could ever have been confident that the only really sharp kitchen knife had not been left behind in the fifteenth drawer of the kitchen dresser in the two hundred and twenty-fifth room. Mrs D. said she had discovered a recipe for peach shortcake below stairs in the Housekeeper's Room: it was a very good recipe, but it did not seem much in comparison with the rest of the castle's literary heritage.

'Of course, Russell's wife was Tennyson's aunt,' Mrs D. told me as we swept over a badminton court somewhere in the middle of the Hall. 'She made him an allowance, and he spent quite a lot of time here. He wrote "Maud" here: "Come into the garden, Maud" is our garden.'

'As a garden, do you think that Maud would have been keen to come into it?'

'The gardens were tremendous once, but Maud's rose garden is just grass now, not even part of the estate. It's quite a way off, over the other side of the medieval road.'

'So it wasn't just a matter of Maud opening the French windows?'

'Oh no. Poor Maud had to go right out through the Postern Gate. If you'll just come round the badminton net . . .' We crossed the court, and Mrs D. said something about the game playing better in the ballroom.

'You have two badminton courts in one castle?'

'Oh no. My friends say in a snooty way, "Of course, she only has room for one full-sized badminton court." It's amazing how one adjusts to the space: it seems quite natural now,' remarked Mrs D., doing her best to peer down to the far end of the Hall. 'Nobody wanted the place, you know: we paid infinitely less than they're asking for the little pseudo-Georgian houses on the new estate.' It struck me that pseudo-Georgian was probably warmer in winter than Victorian Gothic, but Mrs D. said the Hall heated up very nicely with log fires at either end, which only consumed about a tree a night.

I learned that the duties of the laboratory caretaker had included going round the castle opening the door to every room and taking a quick glance inside: it had taken him two and a half hours at top speed. The Dobsons were slightly but seriously worried that one of them might have an accident in a remote part of the castle, and not be discovered before it was too late. If one of them were elsewhere indoors when a phone call came, it was no use the caller asking for them to be fetched: the answer was always no, because it was impossible. In extreme emergency, they could always go up on the roof and shout: it was a process rather like casting your bread upon the waters and hoping for it to return to you again as a sardine sandwich.

Mrs D. told me that she had bought the castle almost on impulse: previously, family and publishing company had co-habited in Kensington, a few hundred yards down the road from their warehouse, whose lease was running out. She happened to be in Durham on a sales trip, and came upon the empty castle one January morning when snow was on the ground; she was taking a walk to pass the time before her train came. By the time she was back in London, she had come to the conclusion that there was no reason why the family shouldn't live and publish from a castle, where at least there would be room for the books.

We came to the Grand Staircase. It was so Grand and dusty that it was rather lonely on it with just two people, but the Dobsons kept their 'No Parking' signs at the bottom, which made it feel more lived in. On the walls, the Boynes had left the patterns of a grander existence – pink faded ovals, rectangles – the shadows of their family portraits in the dust. At the top, at the very far end of a corridor, was a tiny and even dustier stair leading to a servants' attic and then to the roof.

'I apologise for these stairs: we never quite got round to sweeping them down,' said Mrs D., clicking the latch. 'Cleaning the main corridor even, you start at one end, and you're still at it a week later.'

We went up on to the leads, which were partly felts where a previous tenant had succumbed to financial temptation just after the war, but the original lead chimney-pots were still there.

'They're rather beautiful, aren't they?, said Mrs D., reflectively. 'I suppose in extremity we could . . .'

'Flog them, yes . . .'

'. . . probably . . . Oh dear, no: I don't think that's really on!' said Mrs D., returning to her decisive mode, and told me of the marvellous plumbing of lead tanks and gutterings within the cavernous roof designed to catch rainwater to feed the upstairs baths, and how the family always went in there two at a time, for fear of accidents, for behind the lath and plaster walls were chimneys of emptiness stretching from top to bottom of the castle.

There were old towers and battlements on the roof, the Dobson's washing line, and a view of anything worth seeing – over the dale, towards the sea, to Durham cathedral. There was brilliant silver cloud overhead, sun on the wheatfields and the hedges that squared them out in dusky green: the leads stretched out like a seascape, taking a grey sheen from the sky.

'Practically everything you can see from here was Russell estates in their heyday: they were the richest commoners in England in their time, I think.'

'Just as well, isn't it?' I asked. 'A bottomless pit for money, this place, I imagine.'

'Oh, absolutely, but *we* don't have anything to put into it, so it's fairly simple from that point of view. We do up a room, let it to students, collect enough rent to get the cable to wire up the next room. It's a Grade One building, so we hope to get some grants one day.'

'You could turn it into a Stately Castle, and open it to the public.'

'But there's no furnishing, you see: nothing to show the many who like to come and look at how the other half live. I'm afraid I'm the wrong half. And it takes such a long time, even to do a small tour – as you see.'

I looked at my watch: it was getting on towards four o'clock; or half-past six, ghost time.

'That was the Boyne Park, which is now the golf course – very nice for us, because the golf club keep it up. You see the lines in the ground near the first holes? Medieval field ridges – it was obviously the home farm then. Looking from here, straight across, were the Shafto's estates: it was from these battlements that Lady Mary Bellasis is supposed to have pined for Bobby Shafto towards the end of the eighteenth century. It's the local song. He didn't come back and marry her, I'm afraid: she died a spinster.'

We walked across the roof to a turret, and down the medieval stair of the Neville Tower which no longer reached quite to the bottom, because the Victorian maids could not get the breakfast trays round the spiral staircases, and the Russells had had them sheared off and replaced with straight ones.

Mrs D. said that there were so many more things she could show me, she really didn't know where to start: so we began with Lord Russell's lavatory which was exceedingly advanced for its time, and built like an oast-house, with a conical chimney leading up to the roof through several feet of medieval stone, to bring the sun to his lordship as he sat in state. It was like being inside a witch's hat, or an oubliette.

'It's rather good, isn't it?' said Mrs D. with some pride.

'Such a shame the mahogany and what must have been a beautiful blue-flowered bowl have gone.' She gave a disconsolate glance down the horrifying stone shaft that conducted a colonnade of pipes the size of tree trunks darkly into the stone bowels of the building. I peered down with her, and it gave me vertigo immediately.

'There's lots of drainpipes: they take an incredible weight of water off the roof, but they're built into the buttresses so we can't get to them if the cast-iron splits or anything – and if they get blocked, we get a veritable Niagara downstairs. It's a very alarming situation.'

'Very,' I said, wondering if my own, smaller-scale plumbing was getting on all right while I was away.

For anyone keen on privies, the castle was an Eldorado: there had been medieval ones; there were modern ones; relics of Victorian ones: and if the Durham Light Infantry had ever made a practice of marching upon its stomach, that stomach had been exceedingly disturbed, to judge by the vast quantity of water closets provided for its relief. They were laid out in rows with military precision: did the infantry sit at attention, I wondered?

'The army did quite a bit of damage,' Mrs D. told me. 'They weren't entirely worried about the perfection of the building, so when the officers were quartered in rooms far away from the natural plumbing, holes were knocked through the vast outside walls – anywhere they needed a tank of water and a basin. Which is very useful for us, because we'd never be allowed to knock them now.'

The army had painted enthusiastically in weak green: fortunately, the size of the castle had prevented them from having much of an overall effect. As a special contribution to aesthetics, they had taken one stone fireplace, covered it in brown varnish, and wood-grained it.

'Such a lovely idea,' said Mrs D., grimly. 'And you see how they knocked out this piece of nice stone stair – just banged it, instead of saving the balustrades and things. It's all rubble down in the basement.'

There was a notice on the wall saying 'Officers' Bar' and another, 'Ring for Batman', which Mrs D. told me was a favourite with little boy visitors. We saw Lord Boyne's bathroom, which the army had allowed to retain a bath the size and shape of an Egyptian sarcophagus, and the Other Ranks' Showers.

'They were very serious about their plumbing, the army,' I reflected.

'Oh, very. We've saved lots of useful things. We walked the officers' baths down the Grand Staircase. Be careful here – there's no wall, you see.'

'All right,' I said, sincerely.

'We'll be in the more homely parts in a minute. We'll have a cup of coffee with my daughter Alison, and then I'll take you down to the dungeons.'

'Thank you.'

There was a horrible smell in Baron Bulmer Tower, which was nothing to do with Baron Bulmer, but the stuff they were putting on to stop the distemper flaking off. Then we came to a room fit for a Capulet, with a ceiling swooping down in graceful vaults, a tall Gothic window with a top like sham-rocks, and a fireplace in the shape of a Norman arch, as if it continued down through the floor as a gateway, and most likely still had columns of Norman men-at-arms walking through it at the bottom.

'It's like "The Eve of St. Agnes",' I said.

'It's going to be mine,' said Mrs D. with satisfaction. 'It was the Lord's room, I think. The vaulting is 1398, certainly not later: the Russells found it when they took down a false ceiling which had been there for generations, and there was medieval painting all over it. We're not sure what may still be there underneath.'

Fluorescent tubes dangled among the vaulting, relics of the laboratory, which had also cut a ventilator into the window. It was difficult to see how the pane would be easily replaced so high above the ground. I asked how they cleaned the windows (which, being in proportion to the rooms, were enormous), and Mrs D. said she couldn't imagine. As far as I could see, the best way would have been to construct a hoist on the battle-ments, hang out an under-gardener dressed in sheepskin and annointed with Windowlene, and rub him round a bit.

Alison's flat, which – as the estate agents say – comprised of being self-contained and two floors, was constructed entirely within a single castle-size room. It struck me that on that principle, it should be possible to develop the castle internally as a whole housing estate, if not a village or two. The rafters and stud partitions seemed like a balsa model beside the solidity of the rest of the fabric.

Alison was relaxation where her mother was angular energy – a smiling blonde in sandals, red shirt and jeans – her flat full of art, with her boyfriend's first do-it-yourself stained glass taking the sun against the windowpane.

She told me how the castle over-awed her at first. 'I was amazingly frightened to go up the outer stair. I kept very much to the caretaker's flat, which is like a little suburban house. On the first night, we had terrible rainstorms, and the roof above us started to leak: I had to get up at four in the morning to see whether the leaks were still dripping badly.'

'It was a fearful December,' said her mother. 'The first of us came two weeks before Christmas, and we moved in as a family on Christmas Eve. The rains poured and poured, and of course we knew where nothing was – downpipes or drainpipes or anything. Then we had terrific snows and frosts. We said nothing worse can befall – but we weren't prepared for last winter. It was diabolical. The water comes off the old cast-iron main that runs right up to the roof and all the way round the castle: there's no way of draining it at all – we just had to watch it freeze, and wait for it to open up when the thaw came. I don't know how many leaks there were: it was ghastly.'

'It sounds like Dante's Inferno,' I said. 'The last circles of ice, and hell with a blowlamp. Did you say we were going down the dungeons?'

We collected torches and descended a staircase covered with a Great Antiquity of dust and cobwebs. Past the strongroom, with the heavy metal jambs still in place but the safe door gone and the interior indecently empty and exposed, we came to a heavy wooden door, which turned out not to be for restraining prisoners in, but for stopping the menials getting at the booze in the adjacent wine-cellar.

'They call this bit "Dungeons" on the Boyne maps – though it's miles above ground, with perfectly good windows. Ralph Neville knocked them through in 1398. But we know people *were* in dungeons here – we have a record of someone being let out just before the Conquest.

'This is a medieval loo,' continued Mrs D. in a sudden

reversion to plumbing, indicating a stone window-seat showing a circle of new masonry put in with consummate craftsmanship sometime since the fourteenth century. There was a jackdaw in the loo, and a shaft of sunlight that came in through the bars, but not a gyve or fetter to be seen.

The only prisoners in the dungeons were the stocks of books lying in the wine-cellars. There was not a single case of wine to be seen: if there had been, nobody would have seen it. In such vaults, anything much less than an entire vintage was unnoticeable. The books seemed to be maturing well, however.

Next door, a Brobdinagian stone bench was empty of its original occupants, the castle beer barrels, tuns as tall as a man, wide at the bottom, narrow at the top. A dozen of them lay scattered drunkenly about, too heavy to lift back to their seats: they had been sold once, but it had proved impossible to remove them. Great lumps of dressed stone were neatly piled, ready to refurbish the castle walls when they needed it, some time in the next two or three millenia.

'That's the sort of foresight you don't get nowadays,' I remarked. 'They had a good class of menial in early Victorian days, and a good number of them I should imagine.'

'There were fifty indoor servants, I believe. After all, there must be well over a hundred and fifty fireplaces to be serviced with coal all day, and before the proper plumbing went in, all the hot water to be carried upstairs.'

'I don't think I can quite imagine this place without the plumbing,' I said. 'And to have to do the housework in it! One can only hope they were happy in their place,' I said.

'I think they probably were – one gets the impression that it was a very good community. The entire village was estate of course: there used to be the village of Stockley, the other side of the Beck, but it's said that the Russells didn't like having the *hoi polloi* so near, so they erased it. There's Stockley Farm left, but no other village at all. It was very feudal: maids turning their faces to the wall in the corridors when a member of the family went by; and the old people who worked on the estate say that when their parents were there in its heyday, women and children and everybody had to be inside from about ten o'clock in the morning so that the carriage could drive out into a clear village street.'

The servants seemed to have lived in passages – long,

stone-flagged and gloomy, with gigantic pipes from the central heating hanging overhead like the works of some great liner. I came across a boiler, but it would hardly have heated a small hospital: I think it used to do the kitchen hot water. The real boilers, two of them, seemed to be converted tank-engines (except that they were perhaps a little big for tank-engines). They were almost a little big for the castle, for they had had to be sunk in deep pits – shadowy monsters back-to-back as if condemned to pull each other and get nowhere for eternity.

'They take up most of the area under the Armour Gallery, and that's one hundred and sixteen feet long,' said Mrs D. 'The pipes run right round the castle, including the servants' quarters – that's good, isn't it?'

A cunning arrangement of wooden shutters and chuting folded out across the corridor to allow coal to be shot from outside and straight into the bunkers, and then folded up afterwards so that the maids could get past with the trays with a minimum of delay.

'It's all so professional,' I said.

'I don't think the Victorians liked things that didn't work,' said Mrs D., and went on to remark that it had been the permanent job of one man to trot his horse and cart the quarter of a mile or so to the old railway station, fill up with coal for the central heating, and shoot it into the castle cellars – one man, all the year round.

We went back upstairs to have more mugs of coffee in the Drawing Room, which was big enough for a cricket pitch, and made the Dobsons' own normal-sized furniture look as if it had come out of a doll's house. Castle scale had entered the catering, for the Golden Crunch which accompanied the coffee came in several catering-size baking trays so that it looked like something intended for repairing the castle walls.

The family was even putting down its own layers of domestic archaeology – for throughout my tour, I had come upon relics of Mr Dobson, in the shape of hi-fi equipment from every possible period. He had worked constantly, and never stopped recording contemporary and classical music to lighten his labours in the small hours during which he considerately wore headphones. At his death, it was estimated that he had amassed three years of music on tape, although it was difficult to be precise, because – though he usually had half a dozen or so tape recorders and banks of time-switches – his recording technique depended on three principal machines, one of which ran too fast, one too slow, and the third just right. His recordings of many works and performances were unique – and of what sounded like uniquely poor quality since he habitually used the lowest possible speed, the largest number of tracks, and the cheapest possible tape.

'He wasn't one for labelling things, either,' said his son, Oliver, reflectively. 'And he used to cut out the announcements to save tape.'

His personality has lived on. His family spoke of him as if he were still alive: and even his obsession with electronics survived, for they found his tape machines still running a week after his death. He sounded as if he would have been able to cope with the castle, too – though I had my doubts as to whether I could.

'Well, I sort of envy you,' I said. 'I think. How many rooms did you say there were?'

'We've never succeeded in counting,' answered Mrs D. 'The question is, when is a room not a room, but a walk-in cupboard, or a window or something? I say well over a hundred perfectly good rooms, Oliver says he's counted two hundred and twenty-five. But only a few months ago, we discovered a room we simply didn't know existed, even though it had a window looking out on to the courtyard. We only found out because the man who came to read the meter used to read it for the laboratory and he showed it to us.'

I though to myself that to be a Dobson having a relationship with Brancepeth Castle was like being a David facing an architectural Goliath who had previously obtained the concession that he should be allowed to eat his opponent before the contest began. Do-it-yourself is often a heroic struggle: but this was epic.

Mrs D. went on: 'When we first arrived, I was left on my own after the initial family Christmas party. I remember looking out of the window of the caretaker's sitting-room over the courtyard, seeing a light and thinking, "Oh, I wonder who our neighbours are?", then realising it was part of us, at the other end of the castle; it was a funny feeling.'

Massive as the castle was, and little though the Dobsons

were, they were not dwarfed by it. They were making an impression from inside. It was being grand, they were being friendly: it was being imposing, they were laughing at it: it was demanding respect, they were being fond of it, where it deserved.

In their ancient, untidy, uncomfortable, leaky, beautiful, rambling castle, the Dobsons were like Britain itself. The ability to value the past while not taking it too seriously, the prosaic eccentricity, the trading-off of comfort against character, the practical coping with an impractical fantasy were, I thought, very British: and the best British thing of all was that they could afford none of it, and refused to allow shortage of money to harm their values. In that unprosperous time, it was a moral to remember for a nation which had taken to putting economic success above everything else.

'It *is* a domestic castle,' I said to the Dobsons, who had come out in a band to see me off, crunching my way over the gravel and goose-droppings towards the outside world (or, possibly, out of the inside world). The massive towers of the barbican made me feel rather like a flea in the corner of a chessboard, but the afternoon sun was warming the stone and reddening the ends of the Virginia creeper, and the milk and the dustbins were still waiting at the portcullis. The ghost in the gatehouse clock said five o'clock.

IX

THE COUNTRY
OF MANY WEATHERS

TO OTTERBURN via HADRIAN'S WALL

Durham is not only a place of saints and castles, but of fabled animals: the Brawn of Brancepeth – a prodigious boar, nobly and knightly slain; the Lambton Worm of the song; and now Jenny and I headed to Bearpark for the evening. The name of this colliery village – one of the few with a pit open – actually comes from Beau Repaire (for in the Middle Ages it was the country retreat of the priors of Durham). For at least one of the local men, however, it meant 'Home of the Bear', even if the bears had gone to the Great Honeypot in the sky a thousand years before.

'In those days and times, these hills and valleys was covered in woods and forests and fields, and there was wild bears running around, and wolves and things.' He was only an ordinary man, but as he said it, I heard the making of a legend in his voice – he was only a hairsbreadth of self-restraint away from mammoths and sabre-toothed tigers, and he repeated his words ceremonially, like the ancient bards. The Durham accent is well-suited to incantation, especially if you are a southerner and can hardly make out what anybody is saying.

I met the ordinary man in the working man's club at Bearpark, which was as novel an experience for me as going to the Athenaeum, and probably less hassle for a man given to going around in sandals and bare feet. I count myself as being disqualified from being a member of most sorts of social club by being one of the middle classes. Working men, aristocrats (real and would-be) form clubs easily because they know where they belong: and middle classes centre their lives on homes and work instead, and know where everybody else belongs.

Thus a working man like the miners I met in County Durham is not any old man who happens to work with his hands, but one with a history, a community, an allegiance. As the clubman has a favourite armchair, he has his customary seat in the bar protected from usurping bottoms by the same invisible barriers of disapproval. His club, too, can be exclusive; women are allowed on sufferance, and a newcomer can remain an outsider for a long time – one man told me it had taken him ten years to become accepted.

Bearpark straggled its houses round the pit which, that evening, had the sun caught in its winding-gear as if it were trying to make the best of a grimy job. The pit was one centre of a community so close that it was a matter of comment that people had started to lock their doors instead of leaving them open for the neighbours to knock and walk in, as they used to: the Club was the other – and the more important, now that many of the miners came from other villages whose pits had been closed.

The club sprawled from a lounge with fine views at one end to a singing section at the other (which was not singing that night, but chattering with bingo) along a spine of bars. Jenny was allowed at either end but the bar and games room in the middle were for men only, so we saw little of each other until closing time. The hospitality was immediate: I had not been there a couple of minutes before a pint of beer was put into my hand, nor did anyone suffer me to buy a drink for the rest of the evening.

The club that was the ruination of the Dog and Gun down the road began as a wooden hut in the 1920s – a little bar where a miner could have a game of cards or dominoes and, more important, get drunk. 'Friday night, Saturday night and Sunday they came and got sloshed and forgot,' I was told by George the Treasurer, one of the three officials there that night, the others being Freddie and Bob. George was a compact, white-haired man who sat at the far end of his board-room table beneath a sun clock with a corona of golden rays as its surround, as if he were practising for the role of Louis XIV, for there is a good deal of pride in being one of those running such a successful community centre.

'Real good members, prepared to look on the club as their home,' said Bob.

'The devil of a club,' said George. 'A seven-nights-a-week job, this, a labour of love. You don't get a load of money out of it – and the missus has got to be tolerant, because if she starts, where are you?'

I said that it appeared it was not only missus who had to be tolerant: any woman had to. George replied that she was only excluded from the areas where the young lads went, to avoid trouble. 'We've never had to call the police, never since 1924. But when they've had a few drinks, they get a bit naughty with their language – it's not very nice if you're sitting with your daughter at the next table. Chauvinists, male chauvinists, aren't we?' He laughed quite heartily.

'The women are members,' Freddie pointed out, and qualified it immediately. 'Half-members, really, so that they can buy their own drinks. But they can't put up for committees or anything.'

'There *are* clubs where they're allowed in the bar,' said George. I felt myself obliged to adopt the expression of one just informed that bubonic plague has broken out in a city to which a dearly-loved relative is shortly to pay a visit. '*And* be put up for committees and everything.'

'There's one club, way down in the Midlands or south, has a woman *secretary*,' echoed Bob, lugubriously. It was quickly agreed that such a thing could never happen at Bearpark. 'We think men can run it best: it's been a man's club since it was first formed. Until recent years in a colliery village, the women were left in the house. They didn't come out to the club or the pub. You might mind the kids once a week while they went to the pictures.'

'You wouldn't want those days back, would you?' I asked, thinking of a friend who had told me how his father would take his mother out for a walk on Sunday morning, leave her outside the pub, and pass out a glass of lemonade for her to drink at the window-sill.

'Oh no, no. They come to the club now; they're half-members, as we said. I suppose that's progress. But this place was started by men, and jealously guarded by men until the last ten or fifteen years.'

'It's a refuge,' said George.

'First there was the odd one that was brave enough to come in when she knew she was going to get talked about all over the village for doing it, and it built up from there. Nobody bothers now.'

The bar was certainly more masculine and less comfortable than the carpeted, easy-chaired lounge where Jenny had joined the couples. It was an uncompromising place for drinking – bare, utility, like a Western saloon. Panelled walls bounced the conversation round like the snooker balls in the games room next door: a thick haze of tobacco smoke filled the air. The works – the bar itself – stretched right across the far end of the room, with Exhibition and Scotch ales, and Federation Bitter, for the clubs have their own brewery. One corner of the bar had been given up to the manipulation of a glass container of pink and white slips of paper in what was possibly some form of lottery. To me, the purpose of the jar and the men around it was incomprehensible: it might as well have been a group of eminent mathematicians attempting to discover the binomial theorem by writing all the numbers in the universe on separate little bits of paper and putting them through the kitchen blender until they achieved the right consistency.

I stood at the bar feeling exposed. 'They're very clannish here: they'll talk to you, but I don't think they'd like you to join the company,' said George encouragingly. 'However, ask them any question you like and you'll get a civil answer, unless of course you get a natural idiot. You know what I mean –

we've got some that you wouldn't class as idiots, but they behave like it at times.'

I looked around. Realities were written on the faces there more clearly than they would have been on the faces of a roomful of, say, teachers and bank managers – realities of hopelessness and cheerfulness alike. Some groups were full of loud vigour, some disturbingly withdrawn. A little old man with a blue suit, mottled red face and silver hair sat bolt upright before his pints, betraying no sign of their effects but for an increasing detachment from the room around him, and an ever more intense effort to frame his words on the few occasions when he spoke. I wondered why he was alone.

George, I learned, was a pigeon-racing addict. He and his son had topped the West Durham Amalgamation with a bird which flew the 519 miles from Tours in France in 13 hours 22 minutes.

'Just the same as owning a Derby winner,' George told me, doing his best to stop his voice soaring like a pigeon at the thought. 'They're a marvellous bird, for the size of them. There's no refuelling stops for them, no pull-up at a petrol station. She wasn't beat – could have gone another hundred mile, I think, though she'd flown a lot of weight off. You build them up, you see: a pigeon lives off itself when it's flying.'

'It doesn't work for cyclists,' I said.

'Well, you'll stop for a cup of tea and a snack, won't you?' He was not excited by cyclists, and quickly returned to his pigeon. 'She was liberated at six o'clock in the morning at Tours and was back home at twenty-two minutes past seven. Marvellous feeling, proud; you can't describe it – like scoring the winning goal at Wembley. You can't sleep until you know official – can't sleep, get irritable, and the wife'll say, "For Christ's sake, find out!" Oh, it's marvellous.'

After George had gone, standing in the middle of a strange bar trying to decide which group of people to talk to felt rather like being set down in the middle of a crowded vegetarian restaurant disguised as a lamb chop: an object of some curiosity value, but not really appropriate. I was a member of the middle classes off his own ground; the working-class working men and I looked at each other rather as the Yorkshire owl and I had the morning of my ride to Durham – unable to decide which of us was examining, and which of us was the specimen.

There was a gesture like a cavalry general waving a regiment or two to follow the Light Brigade from the other side of the room: it came from a large man who was almost square in shape except for his beer belly, which bulged out from his shirt like a pudding in a bag. I went over to him and his two solid companions and sat down beside them, but no question I could ask could elicit any further response from them. They stared – not at me, but into space: they were as silent, immovable and heavy as cushions stuffed with boulders – a hand would sometimes raise a glass to a pair of thick lips, and down the chin of the man who had beckoned, a thin drool of shining spittle trickled like the track of a snail. Abandoning any hope of divining what embryo curiosity or buried friendliness had caused them to beckon, I excused myself, and left them, both of which events they ignored.

After that, there was no use being shy – and looking round at the faces, I saw that by turns they were animated and rather serious and weary, but that there was a friendliness there, and as soon as I approached them, the groups opened up and let me in.

I learned that you could tell a man working on the Bearpark coalface by the scrub marks – the miner's equivalent of housemaid's knee, a white blaze of scar tissue along the forearm. The miner who showed me his had rather narrow eyes and very black eyebrows that turned up at the corners, so that it was rather like talking to Mephistopheles. He was indeed up from the underworld – and with a hangover which, the morning after the night before, sounded nothing short of hell.

'You think you're going to die, and you wish you could lie down and do it when you get into the twenty-two inches, and the rain's dripping on you – oh, it's killing,' said the miner.

'Why do it then?'

'I've worked in the pit since I was fifteen years old – I've two sons, but they'll not work down there. I'm the fifth generation at that colliery, and there'll not be a sixth.'

There was the click of brightly-coloured ivories from the games room next door. I thought it very unfair that my life should be so much more comfortable than his, even if more worried. On reflection, I thought I would much rather have the worry.

'They're grafters, real hard lads,' said the man with the jar containing the binomial theorem, who turned out to be a technician at Durham University, and introduced me to his group, and through them to a substantial part of the rest of the room – a cousin here, a dad there, a brother, an uncle, another cousin.

'Going back fifty years, Bearpark was dominated by half a dozen families, because the more children you had, the more money you had coming into the house.'

'I'm not bragging or anything, but one of them was the Corkers,' said his friend. As he said it, I noticed how careful everybody was to avoid any form of giving offence. Far from the language being lurid, it was decorous: no one wanted to boast, or show conceit. 'There's the saying – he's a proper corker – well I'm a Corker,' said the Corker. 'There were the Stones, too: they were like clans.'

'The Thompsons, the Shanks, the Lincolns – I'm Jimmy Lincoln,' said the university man. 'They had the biggest families of all, enormous: you're talking about ten or twelve in a family. My dad's family had seventeen, and then the children had offspring. But now they've dwindled down to twos and threes.'

'I'm glad to hear it,' I said, ''cos if they hadn't, they'd have taken over the world.'

'Too true, too true,' agreed Albert, who was the third member of the company.

'That was all the miners lived for: food, drink and – you name it. I'll let you say the word.'

There was a pause. Nobody said it.

'Fornication,' suggested Albert, as a compromise.

'Sex,' said the Corker. 'I'll say it was sex.'

'I'll say it was, too,' I replied. 'With that number of children, miners have got even more stamina than I thought. If they worked at the pit all shift, and then they went to the club and drank, and then . . .'

'. . . and then they went to bed,' finished the university man. 'Hence the families.'

'What did they eat to keep them going?' I asked.

'Stutty cake,' replied the company, unanimously.

'Study cake?' The accent was getting more difficult as the evening wore on.

'Totty cake. It's like days of old, the pitman's bread. If you was asking our wives, they could give you the ingredients: but we eat it. It's just beautiful – cut in half, buttered both sides, filled with onion, corned beef, meat, bacon and eggs, anything. Try one tomorrow.'

'Right, I will,' I promised, with little idea what.

'It's thin – about a foot round, and you cut it in half across.'

'Perhaps it's what I saw in the baker's this morning,' I said. 'That was round and had a hole as if someone had put their thumb in it.' The hole created great uncertainty.

'A gap at the end as if it didn't quite meet?'

'A thumb-sized hole.'

'Must have been an Old Fadge.'

'Fadge?'

'Brother to a study cake. An Old Fadge.' Everyone laughed – why, I couldn't make out. Was an Old Fadge an obscene reference? a hopeless anachronism? a secret sign of the Durham Underground Army of Liberation? I had no means of knowing. I decided to accept it as an Old Fadge, pure and simple. But the company had had enough of my gastronomic ignorance.

'Go into bloody baker's in the morning and ask for a stocky cake. The one where you found the piece with a hole in the middle.'

'But what's a Fadge?'

'The storry cake.' Everyone laughed. I gave up, and moved on.

'What's special round here?' I asked of a loud and lively group in the corner.

'The lakes and things like that.'

'The lakes?'

'We all grow lakes.'

'Oh, leeks.'

'We've got more than a hundred members, and we all have fine big leeks, you see.'

'But what's the special attraction of a leek?'

'There's not much attraction – it's just a competition, like.'

'Tricks of the trade there are to growing them, I expect.'

'Tricks of the trade to everything – and in leeks, aye there is.' (darkly) 'Mind, in villages just down the road, they've had them . . . sort of . . .' (we waited) 'sort of – pulled out.' Having uttered the blasphemy, he seemed relieved, and added, 'tops cut off' relatively cheerfully.

'We've never had it done in this club – it's noted for non-violence,' said the other leek-grower. 'You want to get on to him,' (pointing to a man across the bar). 'He judges all the shows and that.'

I got on to him but failed to get very far: 'You're a judge of leeks, they tell me,' I suggested, politely.

'I've got a grey nose, and I grow them,' replied the judge, a remark so cryptic that I was unable to concentrate on the rest of the conversation, thereby missing a great deal of useful information about rust marks, leek-girth norms, and standards of edibility. Only later in bed, as I was just about to drop off to sleep, did it flash upon me that 'grey nose' was Durham for 'greenhouse'.

I returned to the leek-growers. 'You are an amazing lot,' I said. 'They tell all these stories about you in the South, about your clubs, your leeks, your pits, your pigeons and your stubby cake –'

'Stotty cake . . .'

'Whatever it is – and so I come up to see what you're really like, and here you are with your cake, your leeks, your pits, your clubs and your pigeons. It's odd.'

'What's odd? There's no place like Durham. You may have been to Northallerton or Exeter or anywhere else but Durham's the best.'

I headed for the lounge to collect Jenny who said she had found a miner who was a poet and who had read her his poems.

'My evening wasn't quite like that,' I said. 'But I bet he didn't tell you about stubby cake.'

'The stuff we saw in the baker's? That's stotty cake: I thought you knew.'

As we passed the door to the bar on our way out, I looked in at the old man in the blue suit: he had gone off the pints, and was raising chasers mechanically and reverently to his lips.

Next day I rather tentatively wheeled my bicycle out into a fine morning to ride the few miles to the Tyne, conscious of a certain respect for Federation Bitter. In other respects, too, the club stayed in my mind for some while, partly because the life there was so different to what I knew and partly because I met Dickie Irwin, an entertainer professionally known as 'The Mouth of the Tyne'. He was a pensioner with twopence off his pint for life at his own club, the Little Empire, in Newcastle, but he had worked the clubs all over the country as a singer and comedian. His council flat was decorated with mementoes of his career in Variety, his conversation with patter from a lifetime of ad-libbing: he even smoked his cigarettes with a manic concentration.

'Went to the doctor's the other day, and people were saying, "Smoking Damages Your Health". A kipper said, "Well, it cured me".'

He was not one of the comedians he described to me as being sombre and sullen men, unable to tell a joke off-stage. His humour was so continuous and so ironic that it was difficult to tell where a joke ended and real-life began.

'I can remember my father sitting on the lawn, wishing he had a house to go with it. He used to stroke us and say "Rover" – he always wanted a dog, you see,' said The Mouth of the Tyne. 'When I was a kid, we used to think knives and forks were jewellery. If you were hard up, you used to get boots from the police fund stamped with a police stamp so that your mother couldn't pawn them.'

He had begun in the clubs after the war when they were just little wooden huts, he said, travelling by bus with his concert party. 'We had to have a good singer, our own piano player, maybe an accordion player, and a good clean comedian – you had to be clean, otherwise you were paid off. Even now, they won't tolerate blue comedians in the pit villages – and they'll not wear the strippers, except sometimes on a Sunday morning. The committee would meet you at the door, carry your bags to the dressing-room, get you a pint and a plate of pickled onions. The clubs were spit and sawdust, and people used to bring their sandwiches. Now it's grown into big business; the agents have stepped in – pickpockets with a licence. There are some huge clubs – they book the stars for a terrible fee, and the working man has to pay a cover charge in his own club. And now that they're spoon-fed with the gogglebox and the big acts, they expect the same from you, and if you're not as good, then you're out – immediate.'

The Durham and Sunderland working men's clubs were the hardest to work, he told me. 'They challenge you: they sit on their hands and say, "Make me laugh." If they like you, you're a king, but I've had some terrible experiences in clubs. They stop you in the middle of your act and say, "Now, ladies and gentlemen, we're going to pay this fellow off – he's nae good", and as you're walking through the audience with tears in your eyes, the women are shouting, "Do us a favour, don't come back." It's heart-breaking.'

Durham miners are traditionally militant, compared with the Northumbrian coalfield which was nicknamed 'the happy coalfield' for its lack of strikes. From what Dickie Irwin told me, the contrast seemed to have got into the clubs as well, with the Northumbrians particularly fond of music, while the demand in Sunderland was for 'a chap with a red nose and couple of balloons stuck up his jumper'.

The funniest thing he had ever seen in a club, he told me, was a rendering of the 'Indian Love Call' by two London artistes who began with the soprano singing, 'When I'm calling you-oo-oo-ooo, oo-oo-ooo' on stage while the man walked in from the back with 'I will answer you-oo-oo-ooo, oo-oo-ooo'. Halfway down the hall, a pitman got up and hit him right between the eyes, and said: 'Give us a bit of order, lad, there's a woman trying to sing.'

'I've had a concert chairman stop me in the middle of my patter, and call out, "The meat pies have come in the bar, if anybody wants one",' said The Mouth of the Tyne. 'Once, in a club beside Brancepeth, a little fellow stopped me and took the microphone. He wasn't used to speaking. He said: "Ladies and gentlemen, it gives me great pleasure to announce that your secretary, Mr Jackson, his wife and three kids, have all been killed in a motor accident on the way to their holiday in Blackpool. Now I want everybody in the club to be upstanding, remove your headgear, and sing 'Abide With Me' for your late secretary. And the Committee offer their deepest congratulations," (he meant condolences). So everybody stood up and sang "Abide With Me". Then they sat down, and

he give me the mike back. "Right lad," he says, "Carry on."
And that's a true story.'

There was enough morning wind to bunch up the clouds into
compact fluffs of white and grey as I set off round the Durham
ring road, for I had no idea of where any Roman road would be
likely to be until Chester-le-Street (Street in a town name is a
common giveaway of such things), and one route was as good
as the next. The road was prodigal with all the force of gravity
I had acquired climbing up from Yorkshire. For four miles or
so I sped down the slopes above the valley of the Wear, past the
village of Pity Me: the name is said to be a corruption of *petit
mer* and to have been bestowed by French monks because of a
nearby lake: there is another Pity Me in Northumbria near
Colt Crag Reservoir. As I squandered my hard-won altitude, I
could not escape a Puritan suspicion that what went down to
this side of the Tyne must go up again on the other and, on top
of that, I was wasting a following wind.

I came to Chester-le-Street, and turned off along it, stopping to ask a man pushing a shopping-bag on wheels what was
the big brown building I had seen in the valley. Whereupon he
pushed back his hairy pudding-basin of a hat, blinked his
watery grey eyes several times to aid concentration, and gave
me a run-down of every castle in the area that I ought not to
miss. I did not like to tell him that I had seen one already, and
was not going inside another until I had got over the shock,
but he dragged me round the corner to see the big brown castle
I had just told him I'd seen, bumping his shopping bag up and
down the kerbs so that I feared terribly for his groceries.

'Mind you, I'll tell you another place you don't want to
miss,' said the man in the hairy hat, eagerly. 'You want to go
into the church – oh, it's a beautiful place! And you'll see all the
Lumley warriors in stone, from years ago. Just up there, with
the big spire, and they'll be very pleased to see you . . .' And
the way he said it made me feel they really would, whether he
meant the verger or the Lumley warriors. It was all rather
pointless, but intensely welcoming, and I thought that I would
have been less spontaneously friendly to a stranger, and not the
better for it.

The town seemed to owe most of its being to nineteenth-century building and twentieth-century shop fronts: it was an untidy place, which made it all the more astonishing to come upon the Civic Centre which was all glass and curved metal frame like a modest and up-to-date version of the Crystal Palace. It was the only interesting piece of modern architecture that made me notice it in six hundred miles – but the man in the hairy hat had not mentioned it and a postman I stopped to ask whether people liked it said that opinions were divided, on account of the fact that it had cost money to build (far less than a conventional design, I discovered afterwards), and made it plain that he himself was most anxious to avoid having any sort of opinion on such an airy-fairy topic as the appearance of his surroundings.

It seemed, from my approach to Newcastle, that many local voters held that sort of view. Birtley was scrubby, Gateshead more together but surrounded by mediocrity, and I came over the Tyne on a ruthless road past the most hideous new office block, the Tyne Bridge Tower, which is opposite 'Rooley's for Scrap' and the blackened shell of St Mary's Church, and a great deal less worth having than either. I could not believe that it would have earned the tolerance of Richard Grainger who re-planned the centre of Newcastle as a spacious temple to Victorian commerce in the middle of the last century, giving it a practical elegance which re-development and traffic schemes have not yet been totally able to squeeze out of it.

The view over the river was the sort of pleasantly haphazard panorama that no town that has ever been a port can quite shake off. Newcastle is a split-level place: the Tyne Bridge of 1928 turns out to be rather higher than Stephenson's High Level Bridge, and the Swing bridge – where the Roman crossing was – is at the bottom of the cleft of the Tyne, at water level. I crossed the Tyne Bridge with the wind buffetting the arch of steel above me, the heavy lorries making the bridge shake. At the far end of the bridge was a public lift down. Intrigued, I locked up my bicycle and entered what was in effect a little panelled house, with pictures round the walls, including one of the liftman very proud with his lift. He was well suited to his job, being not only somewhat subterranean in appearance, but also rather small, which is no bad thing in a lift.

'It's all bridges, this place,' I said to the liftman – for I had counted five.

'Just as weel,' said the liftman, tersely: 'cannae swim across there.'

As he shut the lattice gates heavily behind me, I realised that I could not face calling him back without a proper excuse for having gone down, and would have to walk up. So I looked at the Swing Bridge, which lies in the river rather like a ship itself, although it has a domestic character to it as well, being so full of little gates and railings that if only someone would introduce a few dahlias and gladioli it would do perfectly well as a garden, and the glass control cabin above it as an elevated summerhouse: and walked up.

It was a long climb, but ungrudged, because the quayside still has something of the old Newcastle about it even if it no longer has the cosmopolitan crowd of Germans, Swedes, Dutchmen, Greeks and Norwegians it used to have when the ships came in. The Norwegians probably felt at home: where Durham often has French place names, the Geordie dialect has quite a lot of Norwegian in it, Dickie Irwin had told me. There is a love-hatred between Durham and Newcastle, and great rivalry between the football teams.

'My father was a Newcastle United supporter – he had black and white eyes. I remembered he promised to take my mother to the pictures, and she was getting dressed up and everything when the old man discovered that Newcastle were playing Grimsby at home. So out came his cap, his rattle and his muffler. My mother says: "Where are you going? What about the pictures?" He says: "To hell with the pictures." So she starts crying and says, "You think more of Newcastle United than you think of me." He says, "I think more of Sunderland, than I think of ye." '

Geordie humour is all its own, stemming, in Dickie Irwin's opinion, from the bitterness of a hard, dour life – self-knocking, like Jewish humour. 'They hadn't enough to go out, and their humour reflects that: it was either cry or laugh at themselves. Jokes about their grannies standing in front of the mangle taking the bones out of their corsets to make a pan of broth. People used to go to the butcher's and say, "Have you got a sheep's head, Jimmy? Leave the legs in." He'd say, "I'd better leave the eyes in – might see you through the week." I'm a fierce Geordie: I love my roots. I've travelled the world, but my heart jumps when I see those three bridges again.'

I lunched at one of Newcastle's many Italian restaurants, for – like Bedford and Soho – the city is lucky enough to have a substantial Italian population left over from the last war, although the thought of an Italian/Geordie dialect is quite alarming to contemplate. The Italian community seemed well assimilated: there was a notice on the wall advertising Christmas pudding. It being the second week in August, I asked for some since I could not work out whether this showed exceptional commercial acumen, or the opposite.

'It's a bit early, isn't it?' said the waitress, non-committally. I still could not work it out; nor did I get the pudding.

The other things Newcastle has of interest to the casually-minded tourist like myself, who will not be interested in what people tell him he ought to be interested in, are: the underground trains, extremely kitsch nudes which stand above the shops of Northern Goldsmiths (and are of course golden), and starlings, who come in from the surrounding country to spend the night. Windowsills and ledges in central Newcastle are black with them, screeching and jostling until they get settled down: there is always at least one quarrel per window-ledge, with a couple of birds standing on tip-claw, fluttering their wings into a blur and screaming their beaks off, looking for all the world like a couple of high-heeled middle-class matrons having a row. When they eventually drowse, they sometimes literally drop off, and fall up to ten feet before they wake up in great alarm and with a considerable fluttering of wings.

The Metro was very smart and very modern, automated to an extent which made the London underground seem Victorian.

'It's impressive, isn't it?' I said to a countryman who was debating with a ticket machine who should get the money and who should get the ticket, though the machine seemed to be winning both ways.

'When ye get to gnaw it,' said the countryman, grinding his teeth.

In Newcastle began my indubitably Roman experience: my journey west along Hadrian's Wall to Dere Street, where I could turn north. I have the greatest respect for Hadrian's Wall, which – as every Englishman knows – is like the Great Wall of China, only *much* bigger, because it is in England. Day and night for several hundred years, Hadrian's Wall was under unremitting siege by the Picts and Scots, who could be recognised by their blue uniforms, woad in the summer and cold in the winter, but who were always repulsed by the Roman legions, whose tactics were to hold their shields above their heads in imitation of tortoises, which made the Picts and Scots (who had never seen a tortoise) extremely puzzled. Then while they were thinking about it, other Roman legions could creep up undetected and massacre them horribly.

I began looking for Hadrian's Wall in the middle of Newcastle, but had some difficulty finding it because of all the other walls. At first, I had to walk along it, for Hadrian's Wall is one way the wrong way at the start, which must have been very confusing to the Picts and Scots, in addition to the imitation of the tortoise: moreover, it was heavily fortified by the Majestic Bingo and Social Club, the Newcastle Exchange and Mart, Adult Books, Newcastle Movie and Video Centre, a Chinese takeaway, Newcastle Model Railway Bargain Centre, the People's Bookshop, an undertaker, a re-upholstery specialist, a couple of dozen motorcycle shops, and the offices of the General and Municipal Workers' Union.

The road led very straight and very persistently up to the hills above the city: it had a feeling of disembodied purpose about it, as if it was going very firmly somewhere or other, and was not going to tolerate any stupid questions about where that might be. Romantic reminders of the Roman occupation were everywhere: a sign to Wallbottle; a stretch of rather tall crazy paving in front of a couple of semis, which was the Wall Itself, and in the care of the Ministry of Works. It was not as lofty as I had hoped: a notice said that it was an offence to injure or deface it, but it was difficult to see how anyone could have caused it much damage except by burrowing.

The Newcastle suburbs petered out, and I rode along the slopes above the valley of the Tyne with rain-clouds gathering on the hills of County Durham far across the river. The little village of Heddon-on-the-Wall boasted a more substantial

Roman remain, a hundred yards or so of garden-wall-size Wall, penned in on a Ministry of Works lawn: but the real garden walls and the houses seemed to have just as much dressed Roman stone in them. After Heddon, I was on the edge of the uplands, and the country was deserted.

The magic of Hadrian's Wall is in what is missing: past centuries had not a qualm in tearing down the original structure, some twenty feet high and ten feet across, and more than seventy miles long. It was a spendid quarry: more than that, it must have been no less inconvenient in its early days to the farmers than to the Picts and Scots – the same sort of problem as having your land cut in two by a motorway today. The locals gave the Wall plenty of assistance in picturesque crumbling for a millenium and a half, but at the end of that time quite a lot of it still remained, so the British government took a hand and ordered the construction of a new road between Newcastle and Carlisle – which in its way had a similar purpose to the Wall itself, the subjugation of the Scots, who were being inconveniently Jacobite at that time (Culloden had just been fought, but there was no telling that it was really going to be as decisive as it turned out to be). Whereupon, what had been useless above the ground was made useful below it, and became foundations.

So I rode, not so much along Hadrian's Walls as on it, and allowed my imagination to wander in the fields alongside, which were full of mysterious bumps of that conspicuous green smoothness with which sward covers ancient stones. It seemed to be more intensely green, perhaps because of the shading and shadowing of the bumps, perhaps because the stone beneath means the land can never have been ploughed but has been pasture for centuries. It was as if history was lying underground, waiting to get out: the bumps and ridges spoke of forts, mile-castles, and any kind of numinosity of the past you cared to imagine. As the road swept over the contours, I could see the whole landscape smoothed as well, into the unresisting curves of uplands close to the sky and winds: the crags do not actually begin until the North Tyne is crossed at Chollerford, and the remaining wall proper starts there too.

I met the man who built Hadrian's Wall. He had a face with strong edges, like the stones he worked with, and by Twice Brewed (which is fairly close to Once Brewed) I saw that both the builder and the wall were standing up well to the weather – the builder because he was still youngish, the wall because he was repairing it, as he was employed to do by the National Trust. True, the wall was not the twenty-foot barrier it had been before the last legionary left it for later generations to nibble at, but toppled stones had been unearthed and built up to head-height, with a turf cap to keep it all in place.

'Proper Roman stones: nice faces on them,' said the wall-builder whose name was Laurence Hewer, and rubbed his hand over them to feel that they were. The wall was a Roman sandwich, with two outer layers of long stones tapering into a middle section filled up with smaller stones: he and his men used mortar in the middle, but kept the original open joints on the outsides.

'Marvellous to work on something that's been here for such a long, long time,' he went on. 'Six years they reckon it took them to build it from coast to coast: it takes us as long to build a bridge as it took them to build these seventy-two miles. They certainly knew how to work.' -

He told me that the local stone would have been impossible to knock into shape, so this part of the wall was built of a freestone brought from quarries up to two miles away.

'All carried here: must have been a terrible job. Mind you, I always wonder why they needed a wall on these crags – the crags alone would stop anybody getting up.'

'Probably for the same reason soldiers polish the soles of their boots,' I suggested. 'Methodical, highly disciplined people, the Romans.'

The wall curled down into a dip, up the side of a hill, and along the edge of a minor precipice. A little file of tourists trailed up the path, getting in the way of proper walkers with big boots. The wall-builder confided to me that there trout in the pool below the crag: there were foxes, badgers, curlews, peewits, skylarks – what he called 'normal' wildlife. When he mended the wall, he thought of other things, and wrote poetry and songs in his head – 'not top of the pops, just local'.

'I'm still working for the Romans,' said the wall-builder. 'In this time of unemployment, they've even left us a job. Quite honestly, I've done that many sections of the wall in fifteen years, my men and myself, I reckon there's more of it mine than Hadrian's.'

There were still soldiers on the Wall it seemed, for I passed a sign to Albemarle Barracks which were some bare-looking buildings in dull red brick. It seemed, too, that there was a continuity among the local people, for at Harlow Hill I passed Tulip's Garage, and it was a Henry Tulip who, in 1801, had to be prevented from tearing down an especially good bit of wall by William Hutton, an antiquarian who walked it from end to end at the age of seventy-eight, and aroused Mr Tulip's historical conscience by crying all over him. Tulip's Garage had a sign which said National, but its ambiance was, at the best, parochial – for as well as selling petrol, sweets, pop, crisps, and ices, the garage was a Shoe Repair Agent – a logical, but unusual diversification. The village itself was rather wall-like, with all the buildings running into one another, so that it was difficult to tell where the church became a house, where the house became a farm, or where the farm became a row of cottages.

The sky was grey, but a solitary patch of sun moved slowly over the country to the north, making one field particularly green, another particularly gold, while to the south a dark net curtain of rain was falling over the Tyne, so that the hills across the river were as if I was looking at them through smoked glass. So I came to the country of many weathers, for as I passed the isolated Robin Hood pub, which was aromatic with a hayfield before it and a haybarn next door, the patch of sun swept over me and, following it, the rain. Fortunately, I had my Patent Cape – as I call it, on account of its several peculiar features.

Interesting aspects of the Patent Cape are the chin-strap which has a little roller that rolls one way but not the other to fasten it: but both ways, it pulls the hairs in your beard quite painfully. There are also straps to put over the handlebars, if you knew where, and a tail strap which is supposed to go under the saddle, I think, except that you are already sitting on the saddle, so that you have to stand up: when you do this, you naturally put your weight on the pedal, and the bike lurches forward, whereupon you move your left foot along a bit, and find yourself sitting on the saddle again.

When you eventually get to cycling through the rain in the Patent Cape, it makes you feel rather like a cow, in that you too are irrevocably out in the weather with a kind of thick skin round you – and doubtless a cow also suffers the same sort of continuous pattering in the ears that a cyclist gets when rained on in a cape. Another aspect of the Patent Cape – which does not afflict a cow – is that it is bright orange, and when you stop and shake the thing out to get rid of the water, it frightens the sheep.

At Carr Hill, which was most extraordinarily pockmarked by something in the past, the rain stopped, and the road bent round a little spinney: from the other side, I could see a line heading northward – Dere Street. I turned into a long stone inn at the crossroads, and drank a pint of Scotch Ale in honour of the north while I waited for Jenny: however, closing time came, and there was no sign of her so I got on the bike again, and left the Roman Wall to take my last Roman road. As I turned my back on the Tyne valley, I saw that the Wall was a frontier still, for straight away I was in hill country where beech trees grew small and bent before the wind, streams cut themselves deep into the earth, and grass took on golden-green-brown alpine colourings and grew reeds at the slightest opportunity. There were deep purple clovers, enormous scabious, and antirrhinums growing wild.

The rain had left a shining clarity in the air – clouds washed whiter, puddles gleaming by the roadside: it left it smelling of fresh earth, too, and shivering cold until the sun came out again. When the cars went over the cats-eyes, they said 'Plufffssht!' and shot out spurts of rainwater: when a cyclist experimented, exactly the same effect was found, except that the water went up his legs.

The top of the hill was a place to see whole counties: the land fell away down to Erring Burn, wandering its way to the North Tyne, and rolled expansively up over the far hills carrying Dere Street with it – tree-fringed, unswerving. Down the one-in-seven I went, helter-skeltering over the dips and across the grassy brook to find fields smiling with summer and tractors out haymaking. I headed up the long, straight hill ahead with the air still, but the road already almost dry for the sun was hot. The sky was so luminous that the trees darkened their green and became like silhouettes against it. Looking at the clouds was like lying on one's back on the bed of an impossibly crystal sea watching the hulls of great white ships passing over, among cirrus foam. It was absolute peace, except that from time to time a long drone would begin at one end of the straight and hum endlessly to itself until a car passed with a quick howl, the aural equivalent of going whoops! over a humped-back bridge.

At the brow of the hill, the rock was exposed on the surface and the course of the road had been changed to make the hill easier, the only detour in almost ten miles, but before I was round it the skies had darkened and the rain came pouring down again, making the valley silvery, and retreating over the cliffs of Reaver Crag in a gossamer shower. Whereupon, the sun came out again as if it had never been away, and turned the road to blue-black by reflecting the sky in its wet surface. The nearby sheep seemed not to mind the sudden chill, even though they had just been shorn, but ran away from the shaking of the Patent Cape as usual.

Past Colt Crag Reservoir it started to rain again, and out came the Patent Cape: this was ridiculous – I was still within line of sight of the place where I had been sweating into a T-shirt in the sun, and since then I had changed my clothes three times. It was like being a fashion model. It rained: it got dry: I frightened some more sheep.

They did not deserve such treatment, I decided, when I looked at them more closely. Whereas lambs have a good press – being the Lamb of God and the ultimate victim simultaneously with Spring and the quintessential baby all at once, not to mention a sign of a good roast – sheep are undervalued by the public at large, who are given to phrases such as 'mutton dressed up as lamb', 'and we like sheep have gone astray' & etc. & etc. There is not even a name for the individual animal – sheep for one, and sheep for all – but perhaps if they went about in ones they would be easier for the layman to appreciate, instead of being scattered over the hills, pointing in all possible directions like iron filings without a magnetic field. It is difficult to appreciate something which basically consists of a dumpy roll of shaggy carpet with sticks at the corners, a tail like a design fault, and a far too independent suspension on the behind and which is, moreover, frequently unpleasantly splotched with paint, grubby at the bottom edges, and rolls its jaw like a drunken sailor in the Bay of Biscay; however, if you look into their sheep's eyes, they are liquid and golden like pools of amber in black velvet. They are worth a second look, sheep, as any shepherd will tell you.

In this country, it had to be a close look, however, because there was no middle distance in it. The land had only two focal lengths – wide-angle and telephoto. Everything was as a piece – either the panorama, or the tiny and individual – the elaboration of lichens like brown and grey lace along the drystone walls, the wool caught in the reeds, the grass-flower. The road was the only individual thing in the landscape apart from the occasional clump of lonely trees, or a stone sheepfold: the animals themselves lost their identity and became a pattern on the land, the few plantations merged with the curve of the hill. It was a country in which earth and sky seemed equally important: the sky had battered the land with its associated weathers until it lay as flat as possible in passive resistance, after which neither had got anywhere so they had declared a truce.

We live in such a little, overcrowded island that there is something prodigal about Northumbria: in all my trip, it was the only place that had felt empty. There are three places in England in which I feel at home: the West Country, because it was my home; London, because it became so; and Northumbria, for no reason that I can possibly imagine – for I have no right there, no connection, and can often hardly understand the language that flows and laughs and reflects like a brook with waterfalls in it. Northumbria is England as I would see it – poor, deserted, honest, musical, kind-hearted, independent, straightforward, equal; a country of sheep that scamper instead of sheep that stodge.

It could not be said that Dere Street was easy cycling, for it had all its bends in the vertical plane rather than the horizontal, and every up seemed to be longer than the down that went before, so that momentum ran out – although when I sneezed in the middle of a pedal stroke up a particularly steep bit, I discovered that the convulsion gave an extra impetus. It then struck me that if only sneezes could be regularly induced, it would get one up hills much faster, and be the biological equivalent of the internal combustion engine. What was even more destructive to the momentum than hills, however, was coming upon a roadside grove of wild raspberries cooling their roots in the water of a ditch, and succulent accordingly: fortunately, a maniac sheep that jumped out under my front wheel provided me with a good excuse for stopping.

Past the Tone Inn and a corrugated iron sawmill which was methodically building up a model of the Great Pyramid out of wood scraps with the aid of a little conveyor belt, I came to a challenge – the modern road bent. Dere Street was barred by a heavy steel gate, which said. 'Vickers Ltd. Private Property. Trespassers Will be Prosecuted'. I was just thinking about trespassing when from the other side of the gate came a burst of machine-gun fire. I thought a bit more, and had not gone far up the main road when a little grey car came towards me and stopped.

'Oh, there you are,' I said. 'It's five o'clock, and you're late for lunch. Where have you been?'

'Newcastle, twice; and up and down this road several times. Where have *you* been?'

'I had the chance of taking part in a ballistics test, but decided not to participate. It's like the Falklands here, all sheep and guns.' A thunderstorm broke overhead. 'I have also been continually dressing and undressing in time with the weather, and for the moment I have had my sartorial fill.' I laid down the bicycle and sat out the thunderstorm in the car, eating tongue and stotty cake, which turned out to be bread baked soft, moist and flat, about the size and shape of a cowpat. The thunderstorm lasted just a bit longer than was necessary to give someone time to get into a Patent Cape: and stopped.

'But I still can't understand how we missed each other,' I said, getting out of the car and bouncing the bike to shake off the rain-drops.

'There was nothing on the road but cars – except just before I turned back, there was a man in the distance waving a red flag at the sheep.'

'Would it be this sort of colour, by any chance?' I asked, opening my bag. 'And why would anyone want to?'

'Why would anyone want to dress up like Red Riding Hood when they could have a perfectly ordinary and respectable yellow cape like everybody else?'

'You know,' I said, 'I've been wondering that myself.'

I set off to a musical trickling from the clear rivulets running along the roadsides in search of drains, and when they found one they gurgled into it, each with a different note. Round the curve of the hill, I came out above Ridsdale, a little grey village huddled into the slope of the dale and boasting the remains of a compact castle, the Gun Inn, and a combination grocer/draper.

There was a middle-distance again – the farmlands of the dale: beyond that, the view went on for ever over hills purple with heather, dark-green with scrub, greeny-brown with bracken, soft green with meadows. There were strange workings and heapings of stones along my route, but from a former quarry and the course of an old railway rather than from anything Roman, although the fort Habitancum was nearby. My brakes would hardly hold at first, but the gradient eased to a one-in-nine as I came to the village of West Woodburn, astride the pebbly river Rede at the valley bottom – although even this larger village, I saw, could no longer support its own school for it had been made into a private house and only a fading sign remained educational. As I neared the top of the hill out of the village, I stopped and looked back at the dale meadows sloping to the winding, tree-fringed river: the clouds had broken, the sun was coming down the fields, there was a perfect arc of colour in the sky, and the end of the rainbow was in the small, grey village. It felt like being part of a Turner painting of *The Wizard of Oz*, but as I walked up my hill, the rainbow rambled off to the remoteness on the other side of the dale.

Over the hill, the country was wild again, and skies too, for now I could see that day's weathers together; tumorous storm-clouds behind, black as slate pebbles, slate fronds, slate foam; brilliant white cumulus in patches of serene blue; and stretching between earth and sky as a tornado does, a storm on the horizon with the sun caught in the rain, looking like a piece of cosmic arc-welding. Coming to the top of a climb, I felt as if I were about to ride off the edge of the world.

I was almost in Otterburn before I realised it, for it was hidden among the folds of the moors: the fish were rising in the River Rede as I came over the hump-backed bridge below the village to the hotel, which was part medieval and had battlements. In the bar, a shepherd out for his birthday celebration shredded his buttonhole to provide myself and Jenny with a sprig of white heather. We agreed that Northumbria was a friendly world.

'A small world in a large landscape,' I said to Jenny. 'I've already had my luck for the day. I saw the End of the Rainbow, as in the well-known song, and am therefore in a position to acquaint you with the whereabouts of One Crock of Gold, Virtue for the Rewarding of.'

'Shall I pick it up now or tomorrow morning?' asked Jenny.

'Alas, even as I looked at the foot of the rainbow, it strode off into the hills again. It is the way with such things,' I added with sentiment.

'If it was a single foot, I would have thought it hopped.'

'Never mind,' I said, 'I'm telling you that for a few minutes today, the end of the rainbow was in the council houses of West Woodburn.'

X

PAST THE PIPER

TO MUSSELBURGH over CARTER BAR

The morning air was busy and rich: a bird with sun on its
wings wheeled past my window after an airy populace of little
flies, golden in the light. After breakfast, we pottered out into
Otterburn and into a vicarage coffee-morning cooing with the
rise and fall of Northumbrian voices – which lilt like their
wind-smoothed hills. In contrast with the harshness of the
land in winter, there is a gentleness among Northumbrians:
their bagpipes are indoor instruments, much softer than the
scrawny war-cry of the Scots: their music is still woven into
the life 'out-by' as they call it – the upland world of shepherds
and isolation, where a fiddle is hung on a string by the door in
every house and that door is always open.

273

There was a dignified old farmer sitting in state at the coffee-morning among the ladies with their home-made cakes. He had been to a hound-trail the previous day at which the singing had begun at nine o'clock and continued long into the early hours, and that had reminded him of his one regret in life – that he had not been musical. But although he had not noticed it, there was music in his voice and the voices around him, and harmony in the community such as is seldom found.

If you ask what the local people are like, you will get exactly the same reply anywhere in England. I can vouch for it: I asked the question for over five hundred English miles, and the answer was invariably: 'They're very friendly'. There was usually a qualification to this, however: 'Of course, you have to be here ten/fifteen/twenty years/you have to be born here before they'll show it/invite you into their homes/talk to you.' From this it seems to me that most of the English are not friendly at all, but have to convince themselves that they are. They do not want to love their neighbours, but to co-exist with them in a stable society. It is an eminently sensible attitude, rather cold, and not much fun.

In England, hearts appear to get warmer as the climate gets colder, and while I would put in a claim for the openness of Devon and Somerset people, it is certainly true that manners are warmer above the Humber, and that it was in the northernmost part of England that I found the closest community life. It was easy for them, of course, with so few people in so much beautiful emptiness, their life-line to the past uncut by greedy developers and insensitive planners.

Even in Redesdale, life was changing a little bit, one of the farmer's men told me: 'We're not keen on outsiders creeping in to buy up the houses as weekend cottages and spoiling the village community. One man, one house.'

'It's a nice number of people in the village,' said one of the ladies to me: and so it is, for Otterburn is something of a metropolis in Northumbrian terms, in that it not only has two shops, but a bank that opens on Tuesday and Thursday mornings for an hour and a half.

There are few tensions: economic problems must be simple in a place which hardly has an economy and there can be few racial difficulties in an area where 'a blackface man' means a shepherd of that particular breed. Jenny had found out about the crime rate the previous day in Hexham, where she had managed to lock the keys in the car, and had to call for help. 'What we need is a criminal,' was what the first member of the escape committee, a local garageman, had said to its second member, a local policeman. 'We're only a small place,' was the policeman's defensive reply: 'we haven't got very many of them here'.

Redesdale remains the sort of internally warm place that the English have in their mind's eye as an ideal, when they parrot their white lie about their own community being friendly. It even manages to be nice to the once-marauding Scots. 'We have no Harry Hotspurs in the district now,' said the farmer's man.

The farmer volunteered that his family had been in the dale since before the battle of Otterburn in 1388.

'It's a long time,' I replied.

'Well, it is,' said the farmer, musically, putting a peaceable cadence to half a millenium.

Leaving Otterburn, I headed upstream along the banks of the Rede, past the young spinney that surrounds Percy's Cross, commemorating the battle. As I looked at the monument with what I could remember of the 'Ballad of Chevy Chase' running through my head (which was not a lot, so that I was constrained to run it round in circles several times to produce a good effect), there came the solid thump of an artillery shell nearby. It reminded me that, whatever the rhetoric – and there had been a good deal of it that summer – the purpose and product of war had not changed since 1388.

Over the previous five hundred miles, there had crept up on me an astonishment at the extent to which Britain was an occupied country. It may have been that the roads I had chosen – the Fosse Way, Ermine Street and Dere Street – were still very much what they were originally – military routes; or, more likely, that a lot was going on in the aftermath of the Falklands' war, but there was a great deal more in the way of armed forces around than I had expected (or seen on my travels in France and Italy). I am sure they were all good chaps, but it did strike me that they were much more powerful chaps than I had given them credit for, and that it was just as well we all seemed to be sharing the same democratic principles for the time being. I suppose that indefinable concensus is what makes the difference between a tyranny or not but I had been thinking that, somehow, pottering, reasonable old Britain needed less force to bolster it up than a good many other countries, and I think I realised that I was naive to think so. There was so much for such a small island – a string of airfields from one end of the Fosse Way to another, the Admiralty at Bath, jet fighters over Yorkshire, convoy after convoy of khaki vehicles on the roads: I had passed a barracks and a couple of firing ranges only the day before, and now I had come to the real playgrounds – or 'Danger Areas' as they are cheerfully described on the map.

I came up to Dere Street again past a little farm in which a sheepdog was dashing in and out of the yard and jumping over the fences in sheer enthusiasm. It was the sort of energy that would have come in useful to a man beginning his journey late in the morning with a hike of getting on for twenty miles over questionable mountain paths wheeling a bicycle and luggage. I had no need of it: I was going on the main road instead, even without the large red flag blustering at the gate of the range to discourage me from following Dere Street through army country, into which it headed shortly afterwards. I was sorry to leave the Roman road, but I would have been sorrier to be on it, even without the holiday traffic that was going my way.

'Is this the way tae Scotland?' asked a raw-boned man in a little primrose-coloured car. He spoke with an air of great suspicion, as if he feared that: a) I might be English; b) I might therefore mislead him; c) I might organise the removal of his destination from the face of the globe while distracting his attention with my haverings.

'Ah yes, that's the place,' I said. 'Yes, certainly. Which other road were you thinking of taking?' There was no other road for miles.

It was odd to see the stream of cars go past looking at country in which nothing was happening, while the country ignored the road on which everything was: there seemed to be something the wrong way round somewhere. It was the right

way round for me, however: as I came through Rochester and
Redesdale Camp – hardly more than a line of grey houses by
the road, with the river in the valley below, brown, clear and
shining sometimes – I noticed a grasshopper sing for the first
time in many a hundred miles. It would have been more
pleasant without their cars, but they were capsules of people
that caused no trouble, so long as you did not break them
open.

The road began to climb up out of the dale. The sun was in
the grasses waving feathery by the road and reedy in the fields:
it lit the tops of the birch trees that began Redesdale Forest,
part of a concession to aesthetics which also included picnic
areas (one of which was at Raw, so that its sign read 'Raw
Picnic Area') and a fringe of larch and rowan along the
roadside. The berries were orange as yet, and blended with the
leaves more subtly than the brilliant red they were working
towards. The rowan is so bright that it ought to be vulgar, but
it just ends up being child-like.

The little grey car came along, and Jenny and I picnicked by
a brook on the edge of the forest: the stotty was still fresh. Pine
trees framed the glade.

'Would you say that this was a bower of any kind?' I asked.
'I've always wanted a bower, but you don't seem to get them
much nowadays.'

'I don't think it can be: bowers are meant to have leaves, and
all this has is needles.'

'Never mind, "wilderness were Paradise enow" – with a
flask of beer, a stotty cake, and thou,' I added, courteously and
lyrically: 'how about a song?'

'It's not wilderness and it's not paradise: it's the Forestry
Commission, which is the British compromise between the
two.'

Like the factory fields of Lincolnshire, a pine forest is an
example of the way money per se ought not to be allowed to
interfere too much in the real world of making things and
growing things. Money has only one purpose in life – to be got
rid of: only things are worth keeping for themselves alone. I
don't hate pines as much as many people do, but *only* pines
must be as bad as *only* sliced bread, *only* frozen peas, *only*
production line goods, *only* battery chickens and factory pigs.
A gift-wrapping of fancy trees along the edge is not enough, I

decided as I rode off: like money, apart from the psychological symbolism attached to it, pines are just *so* dull. The green is lack-lustre and the contours tediously uniform, whether you are close to, looking beneath the branches at the parade of straight trunks pallid with lichen, or whether you see the tops across the valley – for then the effect is of an inexpert stippling with lifeless colour, neither regular nor informal enough to be interesting, just untidy.

After Catcleugh Reservoir, gurgling and lapping against its barrage, the forest ends and the land becomes increasingly barer in the long wind up to Carter Bar. I was still at the bottom of the slope when the Alfa came screaming downhill and pulled up with a sharp spurt of gravel.'

'Hurry up!' said my producer.

'Hurry up this?' I queried, looking at the whole height of Cheviot ahead.

'There's a man on top playing the bagpipes, and he might go away.'

'The whole of bonnie Scotland is probably packed with people playing bagpipes who are just about to arrive. To say nothing of tossing cabers, cooking haggis, decorating their sporrans and waving membership cards for the White Heather Club.'

'Yes, but not on the Border. Just think of it in stereo: it's a really marvellous sound, and we'll get him to walk up and down.'

'It's just as well you never met Don Giovanni,' I said: 'you would have asked him if he had a good pair of ears, instead of –'

'Hurry up! I've promised I'll give him a lift back to Jedburgh afterwards, but I can't be sure he'll stay. He says he doesn't like the BBC.'

'Nor do I, much,' I said, engaging low gear. It was a long climb better taken in a leisurely manner. Halfway up I came to a strewing of dead bees all over the road which obviously lay between their hive and the flowers, so that one after another had been slapped out of the air by the cars.

'That's where it got you,' I said to the dead bees, panting: 'hard work and a sense of duty.' A live bee buzzed across, but I dodged it.

Carter Bar consisted of a little glister of cars and coaches rejoicing in the distinction between England and Scotland, a woman selling teas from a caravan, a large lump of stone, and Jenny jumping up and down metaphorically.

'Is he awa the noo?' I asked.

'What?'

'Have you no sense of regional identity?'

The piper had not gone: in the gaps between playing to the tourists, he had been whetting his whistle with the aid of a beer can. He wore a country jacket of green tweeds, a kilt with a fine and hairy sporran, and a beret edged with tartan and bearing a regimental favour, but when he played he abandoned the beret in favour of a bearskin. He was strikingly big and brawny, but softly spoken as if he were anxious not to alarm: his smile was not so much wide as warm, and the first thing he did was offer me his beer.

'It's a stiff hill. Never mind, it's all downhill from here on.' I laughed a pale sort of laugh, we got some more beer out of the car, exchanged hospitality for a while, and warmed to each other. 'It was the BBC television tried tae film me from behind a man putting 10p in the hat,' said Dave.

'Don't worry about it,' I said. 'I expect they had it on a string.' It is a hard life being a radio man working in a country increasingly dominated by television. You trail in the wake of interviews that went on all day and crews that departed leaving an ambience like the battle of the Somme, money that never got paid, mistakes that never got cut out of the finished film, and people suspect that you and your tiny tape-recorder are the advance guard of a battalion of directors, lighting men, sound men, camera assistants, grips, producers and continuity girls (there is something slightly suggestive about the title of 'continuity girls', which is probably why it sticks in people's heads after they have read it on the films). In fact, many television visits must be delightful, but it is a cumbersome, awkward medium that often has to ride roughshod over people to do its job – its own people much more than the public. Mistakes stand out because it is so much more literal a medium than radio, and since it is so much more important a medium, it attracts proportionately more tough and conceited people. Perhaps it is as well that people are becoming more conscious of the broadcast media even if it means that the many who are relatively trustworthy have to work just a little bit harder to prove it: scepticism is a fine thing in an imperfect world.

The piper – who called himself not just 'Dave Woods', but 'Dave Woods, Musician' as one might say 'Elizabeth, Regina' – told me that the inspiration of playing on Carter Bar had fallen from heaven in Bournemouth where he had been visiting his uncle, who was a long-distance coach driver.

'He said, "Dave, it couldn't be wrong if ye stood up on the Carter. I'll be in Jedburgh in a fortnight, and I'll meet ye. Remember and be there, Dave, because I'll be promising them on the bus that there's a piper to greet them." As ye ken, when ye're having a drink, one thing leads to another, so I kept my promise, for a promise made is a debt unpaid. They had a whip-round in the bus, and I had a fiver in about ten minutes, and since I was enjoying playing I kept playing for the rest of the day. And I realised this is what I should be doing. I can earn more money than my feyther, and I see him come home bent and knackered after a hard day's work. I'm not ashamed of what I'm doing.'

He toyed with his beer can, and continued toying with it until the contents were exhausted, whereupon we opened others, retreated over the road out of the way of the tourists, and sat ourselves in comfort either side of a stile.

'I started to play the pipes when I was ten years old. Then when I was sixteen, I became interested in women, heard Benny Goodman, and had to play the clarinet. There was no teacher around here, so I settled for six years in the Army – one of the best schools of music – and learned a classical repertoire, but I was out at nights playing jazz.

'When I got out of the Army, I decided it was to be either Jedburgh or London, so I went to London. At that time – 1963, 4, 5 – there was a difference of opinion between the British and American Musicians' Unions so that every American star that came to this country had to have a British band. So I was that band – with other guys, great guys, ye could throw anything in front of them: if a fly shat on the paper, they played a wrong note.'

'I played Brenda Lee, Roy Orbison, many times – Chuck Berry, Carl Perkins (mind, we came through the tradesman's entrance); and I went to Sweden for two weeks with Emile Ford, and stayed five years playing the bands. But it's a young man's game, living out of a suitcase all the time, so I called a halt and came home! I soaked up the sunshine in Spain for six months – more or less beach-combing, playing the pipes on the hotel steps and then going in and playing the band for a couple of hours, for which I got about 500 pesetas (but it was enough, ye ken). Then I came home to the Borders, and this is about as far as I've been since: I've got a cottage in the country with chickens, a couple of dogs, and a good woman, and I'll be doing this the rest of my life. I've found my little niche: it's nice and quiet, and I don't think they'll drop any atomic bombs on it, 'cos it's not that important. I don't have to go travelling any more: the whole world comes to *my* doorstep. I'm the guy that made it.'

'I used to be a sort of musician,' I said. 'I specialised in folk music.'

'All music is folk music. What the hell was Beethoven but folk? Mozart – what was he, some kind of Martian?' The corners of Dave's mouth were not quite managing to keep the beer in, some of the time.

'What do you think about, up here all day?' I asked.

'Every time, I think something different – sometimes, "Oh, what a rotten, shitty day this is," and sometimes, "Isn't life wonderful? I'm home and I'm able to earn a living by doing the thing I love to do. I must be one of the luckiest guys in the world." I've watched the view from here thousands of times, but I've never seen it the same twice: all ye have to do is to turn round, and it's changed. Look, the horizon is fifty miles. Ye're seeing the olden hills where the Romans lived.'

The Cheviots looked as if there was something living under the surface that had tried to force its way out of the depths of the earth and failed, leaving only lumps where it had put its fists, stuck its elbows, and stretched the grass up with its knees.

'Ye're seeing beauty, the fields turning golden this time of the year, the clouds going across country. Ye're seeing my home, Tom, that's what ye're seeing. It's a bit of real estate, belonging to three men – Buccleuch, Lothian and Home – but I own it all, because seeing is owning.' Fearing he had been talking too much about himself, he turned the conversation back to me. 'Where do ye live, Tom?'

'North London – Muswell Hill.'

'Oh, it's a nice wee village, Muswell Hill. It is a nice wee village, isn't it?' asked Dave, uncertain for a moment whether he might not be thinking of somewhere else.

'It's quite pleasant, actually.'

Dave got up from the stile and retreated with dignity into the little pine spinney beyond: 'for a piddle' he said, gravely.

'Who put that stone there, by the way?' I asked when he came back, pointing to the border marker thinking that it might be medieval or primeval.

'Ah, Tom, I can tell ye a wee story about that. All this was put up two or three weeks ago, or months maybe. It used to be just an old fence. Before that there was a sign saying "Scotland", but folk used to steal it to take to Welsh rugby matches, and the like. Now anybody that takes that boulder to a Welsh rugby match is welcome.'

'I should think you'd need about half the arms in Cardiff Arms Park to shift it.'

'That was the exact border there: so when Jimmy was placing the stone – my cousin Jimmy moved it, ye ken – he says, "I'll put it here" but I says, "Jimmy, no. Move it just a foot to the other side, one foot into England – you and I will know, but no one else will." Jimmy is the only guy that's stolen English ground for a good few hundred years – and a foot right the way across the border can add up to quite a few inches.'

Jenny took a photograph of Dave and myself standing either side of the border: then she had to take another one because we realised we were each standing in the wrong country.

'You weren't fooling when you said this place belongs to you,' I said. 'It's obviously being taken over by the entire Woods family.'

'When I see the grass grow, I think to myself, "it could be my ancestors' bones that's grown that grass," and when I see the heather bloom in August, I think, "I'm home. I'm not a lonely stranger any more: I'm Dave Woods, Musician, who . . ."'

I finished for him: '. . . who stands on Carter Bar.'

'Who stand on Carter Bar, and who's a piper –' He took his pipes and the regimental bearskin. 'Even though it's my day off, here I am. In February I come up here to stand and play in the mist: I've been up here with the snow billowing past me lugs. The open air is the only place to play the pipes. It's like creating a cathedral around ye – that's why I don't go to church on Sundays: this is my church. The thing about the pipes is looking at the horizon, and saying, "That's my top A," ' – he drew his hand in a line across the clouds, and again over the grass at his feet – ' "And that's my bottom A, and that's an octave between what ye're looking at and where ye are." And ye play the space in between.'

Then he tuned and he blew: people from the cars clicked pictures, and someone from a coach brought out a whole video system in his honour. The music was perhaps not unaffected by the level of the afternoon's entertainment, and as he played, he put his feet delicately one over the other as if he were walking over his own toes. With the white spats that he wore, it reminded me for some reason of a sheep. He had, too, a habit of turning his head down to one side and glancing out of the corners of his eyes that, with the pipes in his mouth, made me think of a bird with an extraordinarily long beak. Then he marched at me in a ceremonial send-off, nodded at me with his pipes, as if to say, 'Enough: back to the customers,' and I was away down the long hill, with the skirling of his music growing quickly fainter in the distance.

There was a gloriously swooping freewheel down from Carter Bar. I was no longer among the hills, as I had been on the other side of Cheviot: it was gentler, pastoral country to which the green-shaven hills were the background. A grey Rolls-Royce was having tea in a layby as I passed: the grey chauffeur outside, leaning at attention against the bonnet: the grey owner inside, upright – but they both drank out of the same plastic mugs. 'That is our democracy,' I thought. 'Two men, a Rolls and plastic cups, when it could be two men, two minis and porcelain.' Thus I formulated *Vernon's Third Principle of Social and Physical Geography*, viz:

> In any given democracy, Equality is the science of keeping the inequalities equal to what they were before: Stability the art of keeping the money where it always was, with the consent of all parties: and Progress the process of continually lowering the standard of taste to keep up appearances.

The whole landscape had a touch of class. I was travelling along a river valley, as I had been in Northumbria half an hour

before – though the Jed Water flowed north instead of south –
but the farms had no feeling of being beleaguered by the
weather; the air was warmer, the trees elegant and deciduous.
It was well cared for, prosperous, peaceful, and the incredible
downhill went on most of the ten miles to Jedburgh. I decided
that if I ever got as rich as the grey man in the Rolls and was
disposed to give myself up to the ultimate in self-indulgence, I
would have myself and the bike carried up to Carter Bar on a
motorised chaise longue, and freewheel down to Jedburgh
repeatedly, without ever having to cycle up.

There was a horn-blast behind me, and the Alfa flew past at
twice the normal speed with Jenny tense at the wheel and a big
brawny Scots arm extending from the window: it held a beer
can in lieu of a battle-axe and, as the car dwindled into the
distance, there dimuendoed with it a long Celtic lament of
'Where the hell have youuuu beeen?'

'Cheerio, Dave,' I shouted. As it disappeared, the car
seemed to give a violent lurch to one side, and there was a
prolonged hooting.

There were red cliffs above the river as I approached Jedburgh, and tiers of magnificent beeches cascaded down the
bank. In a field corner by the road an ancient oak had been
much operated on, with braces for its old branches and a
concrete transplant down its rotten trunk. A notice pinned to it
identified it as 'The Capon Tree – last survivor of ancient Jed
Forest'.

Jenny was waiting by the bridge near the Abbey which is a
cross between a Norman cathedral and something Roman,
like the Pont du Gard or the Coliseum, and very impressive to
come upon suddenly.

'Is Dave all right?' I asked, as we sat eating ice-cream in the
six o'clock sun on the grass by the pebbly river.

'He was sweet. I dropped him at the pub: he said to come
and have a drink if you had time.'

'Your driving seems to have gone off a bit. I thought you
were going off the road just after you passed me.'

'He gave me a fright. He put his hand on my thigh.'

'Did he really?'

'I almost crashed: jammed the brakes on. The man on the
other side of the road honked terribly.'

'I heard that. But what happened then? Let me guess: you

told him you were a simple radio producer, and only interested in ears.'

'No, I looked down and there was a bee on me. I'm sure I would have got stung, but he snatched it off and threw it out of the window. He never even noticed I was worried. He was a nice man after all.'

'The thing that worries me is the bee: I happen to know where it lives, and it's a long flight over the top of a mountain. In fact, it's in another country.'

Apart from the pastoral countryside, the evident differences of having crossed the border were in the accent, and in the architecture. There is a straight-up-and-down look to Scots houses which often stand as if they are holding in their tummies and their breath simultaneously, with their sharp roofs like caps firmly pulled down to keep the walls in place. I made my way out of Jedburgh past the local kilt-makers, took the road along Jed Water, and turned off across the Teviot to which it flows.

There were circles in the river as the trout rose to the evening flies, and splashes as they launched themselves into the air to get them. On the bank, three brown horses swished their tails vigorously to clobber the evening flies. The only thing in the landscape non-hostile to the evening flies appeared to be me: the evening flies drew the obvious conclusion, and came to be friendly, in clouds.

By the river, the evening damps were beginning to fall but the evening was golden and the road climbed into it through a gracious landscape, with a folly and a monument high on hills to the east. There were still the fine beeches, and once in a while a woodpigeon would flap out from them, making a fuss like a copy of *The Times* shaken out in the upper branches, arousing desultory caws from the rooks. There was a brook green with watercress, a farm with the farmer's wife splitting kindling in the last of the sun among a scratching, confused cluck of what used to be Brown Leghorns when I was a child among hens, but are probably some code-numbered hybrid now. But invisible among the fields, the course of Dere Street was edging towards me, and as Roxburgh District turned into

Ettrick and Lauderdale District – as signs told me it did – there was a long, distinctive straight ahead and, even more distinctive, the conical peaks of the Eildon Hills which, they say, were split into three by the power of an enchanter, and beneath which King Arthur and all his knights lie waiting for a faery trump to set them riding down upon St Boswells and Newtown St Boswells – where they will doubtless find the locals playing cricket, as I did. The road to Melrose lay below the northern flank of the Eildon Hills, and was in consequence rather over-hilly to come upon at the end of the day, but at last I saw the sun shining through a frill of smoke from the chimneys of a small town, and a ruined abbey purple in the evening light.

It was eight o'clock when I tied my bicycle to the kitchen drainpipe of the George and Abbotsford Hotel, and went round to the front to find that they had thoughtfully laid out a red carpet for me. 'Unless it's for you,' I said to a fellow-guest, a large Scot standing at the entrance, 'it must be for one of us.'

'Neither,' he said. 'I think it's for the wedding. But you're most welcome to come in though.' He and his wife were from Aberdeen, he told me, and had arrived at five o'clock, since when they had been on a pub crawl.

'Already?'

'Five pubs.'

'Which was the best one?'

'This one.' He went inside.

That evening, the hotel was all wedding guests, and waiters running about, and barmaids serving twice as many drinks as people ought to drink twice as fast as it was possible to serve them. Jenny and I were a little oasis of quiet in the middle of it all because we were coming to the end of the trip, and it felt odd.

'I was thinking in the bath,' I said.

'Better than singing, at any rate.'

From the bath, I had been able to look out to the ruins of the abbey, and the green hills beyond. There were swallows over the town; and sky, abbey and the trickling smoke from the fussy chimney-pot on the house opposite were all purple in the evening light. It struck me that what I was experiencing at that moment was peace, an unusual moment in a life normally spent rushing backwards and forwards like a pendulum – never getting anywhere, but moving with too much energy to stop. I felt as if I was in free-fall, and could float for a moment within the current of gravity. There was no stopping the restless pendulum, but by travelling for travelling's sake, I was moving with the swing and achieving the momentary illusion of a resting-point.

'There's a timelessness about this trip,' I said to Jenny later, with the wedding raging around us. 'It's only been days, but when you think back to the beginning, it seems like a year ago. The funny thing is that it all seems like the normal way of living, riding a bike up the Roman roads of Britain: it's the rest of the world that's crazy.'

And, for once, Jenny had no answer.

There was good solid porridge for breakfast, and shortly afterwards the lightest of scones in the warm kitchen of Abbotsford, where the sisters Maxwell-Scott keep up the heritage Sir Walter, their great-great-grandfather, built for himself on the site of a farm he had bought as a country retreat. Being the fifteenth of August, there was a little bunch of heather placed before his bust in the library.

'It's a tradition,' they told me. 'We were just working it out: it must be two hundred and eleven years since he was born. Didn't you realise you'd come on his birthday?'

The sisters were carefree ladies, two sides of the same coin. One was softer, one was brisker; one of a longer sort of shape, one of a chubbier: both were as cheerful as roses in a bowl. They had two loud little dogs to sit on the sofa like a whisky advertisement and a large black Labrador to pad along behind them on their rounds like an attendant priest – a failed guide-dog, they told me.

'Suddenly developed an aversion to heavy lorries, but fortunately we don't get many of those round here,' said the Longer Sister, gazing out on the gravel walks and lawns.

'Don't mind the dogs,' said the Chubbier Sister over the top of the barking. 'Elphin! Sir Walter always had so many, you know. About twelve. Elphin!'

Abbotsford must be the most domestic and personal stately

home in existence. Even the plantations of trees were laid out in the format of the battle of Waterloo because of Sir Walter's admiration for the military. (He could not become a soldier himself because one leg was shorter than the other, but was a territorial for years, and got into a great tizz over the prospect of a Napoleonic invasion.) Alas, many trees were cut down during the 1939 war, ruining the disposition of the troops of the previous one. The house itself is all grey turrets and would-be battlements on the outside, although it does not really have the height to support them, so that the effect is rather in the nature of an old baronial bungalow – of great quirky charm, and rambling, but nevertheless not the building it pretends to be.

Inside, Abbotsford is a high concentration of scaled-down history, for in the domesticity are all the trappings of a castle, a cathedral, a university and a prison. The yew lawn within the grey-walled garden would have done for Mary Queen of Scots to walk upon: the shining claymores, halberds, guns and armour would have equipped her guard, and the vaulted ceilings with bosses and gargoyles would have given her a suitably gothic place in which to pray after she had been locked in with the two-foot square lock Scott saved from the gate of the Tolbooth prison in Edinburgh when they were pulling it down, and which is the very lock in which the key turned on The Heart of Midlothian. She might even have managed to escape by disguising herself with the piece of Beardie's beard – Beardie being Scott's grandfather and extremely hairy, having vowed never to shave until the Stuarts were returned to the throne of Scotland – and vanish into the arboreal battle of Waterloo. Abbotsford was a good place for vanishing, the sisters told me.

'It is a marvellous, spooky house to play cops and robbers in and hide-and-seek – with two staircases, you can get round in a circle and avoid being caught.'

'Rather ghostly, especially by gaslight in the hall where the armour is: there was no electricity when we were children, though it was one of the first houses to be lit by gas. Sir Walter had his own gasworks at the side, the supply being made out of oil.'

'There were lovely places to hide in the woods and gardens – and in the snow, tobogganning on tin trays down the banks.

We had ponies and dogs and a very sweet French governess, didn't we?'

What with relics of Scott, and Scott's relics of other people, Abbotsford is like an etching for one of his books – with that Victorian quality of 'put-everything-in, providing it is goth-ically respectable'.

'There were gargoyles all round the dining-room, but fortunately my father had the sense to have them removed,' said the Chubbier Sister. 'He felt he just could not eat his lunch with gargoyles.'

Abbotsford is Scott's mind, and the mind of his age turned inside out, so that you can see into the corners. At the centre of the mind are the temples a writer built to himself and his craft: the library, with a little spiral staircase to a gallery you could preach from and a reading lectern with a powerful air of Mighty Abbey about it; and the study, the scholar's cell. It is a place of ritual and ceremonial fantasies, Abbotsford, but I could not decide whether they expressed an immense self-confidence, or an immense lack of it.

As a shrine, however, it could hardly be more suitable than if it had been built to be dead in rather than to live in: and a shrine it soon became. It is one of the oldest show houses in Britain, having been opened to the public in 1833, the year after Scott's death, in which it attracted a thousand visitors. Their number has greatly increased since, and with it the number of would-be relatives (i.e. anyone named Scott, espe-cially anyone named Scott from America).

'They're quite convinced about it, and you have to be very patient and polite, but I miss the visitors terribly during the winter,' said the Chubbier Sister. 'But then in March we hear the footsteps again.'

'Marvellous having our job in our own house! We don't have to go out to work, it comes in to us. Just occasionally at five o'clock, when we're hoping to get the house shut and we're worn out, another busload comes in and we wish we lived in a bungalow.'

'They're always dying to know if we've got a ghost, but we haven't.'

'Sometimes, they think it's Burns' Cottage and wonder why it's so big.'

'Or occasionally the Americans think it was Walter Raleigh's, don't they? Someone once thanked me for the family having brought over tobacco.'

'History is a kind of fairyland for people, isn't it?' I said. 'They don't need to be precise about it.'

'Then there was that sweet man who came and said to me that he couldn't find the bullet that killed Napoleon, that we had had it on show the last time, and he had brought his friend specially to see it. I couldn't say Napoleon died in his bed, so I told him we'd changed the exhibits and it had been put away for that year.'

'It must feel a bit like being royalty,' said Jenny: 'being a custodian of so much history.'

'We take it rather light-heartedly – sometimes we feel we ought to be paying more attention.'

It being the birthday, they were expecting a pipe band that afternoon, they said, by way of celebration. Jenny was ecstatic.

'But I've got to get all the way to the coast, and we've only just recorded a piper,' I objected.

'But this is a whole band: and we never got him to walk up and down, which –'

' – which is marvellous in stereo. And what about lunch?'

'I'll do them, and catch you up with the stotty cake.'

'Stotty, still?'

'I looked: it's still fresh. It's amazing stuff that stotty: they ought to give it to Arctic expeditions and things.'

'They ought to give it *all* to Arctic expeditions and things.'

Back at the main road, I crossed the Tweed by the most modern of the three bridges that lie next to each other – the old stone bridge below, and the slender viaduct that used to carry the railway alongside – and made my way north up the valley of the Leader Water, across which are the twin mounds of Black Hill and White Hill, although both were very green apart from the shifting white pattern made by a sheepdog tidying a distant flock of sheep. From this point, the course of the Roman road is uncertain: on the map, you can see a length of straight in the middle of nowhere continuing a line from the Melrose road below Newstead to the longer straight above

Lauder; or from the Leader Water, a lane running up the western slope of the valley becomes interestingly direct thereafter. I passed its fork, however, and kept to the valley road although I could see the lane going doggedly up over the hill after I had crossed the river by the long bridge at grey-roofed Earlston, and was climbing more gently myself along the other bank.

As I went gradually up through Lauderdale so I left the rural elegance of Roxburghshire behind me: the country became first more casually pretty, then open farmland. By the time I was five miles beyond the plain grey town of Lauder, I was at the foot of Lammermuir and beginning the long climb up Soutra Hill, with bracken and heather spreading on the bare hill, a single farm clinging to the slopes as if the last snows had pushed it halfway down and the next would be the end of it, and the river no more than a tiny rambling burn. It had turned cold and grey, and a strong smell of cabbages from the last of the arable below persisted for an unreasonable distance. I stopped for the third time just below the last winding of the hill and looked back many miles over Lauderdale to the greener country I had left behind: they still had the sun there. There was no sign of stotty cake upon the road.

The top of Soutra Hill was bare as bare – a desolation of heather and grass leading a hard, boggy existence. The only things that dared to stand upright were the snow-fences and one untidy little farm almost entirely surrounded by vehicles, as if the tenants were determined never to be cut off from a way of escape. On the other side, the view stretched far over the Firth of Forth: I was across the last hill of the many on which the Romans had placed their survey beacons, watching for the other lights ahead in the dark, throbbing minutely in a straight, straight line. It was at once exciting, and a bit glum.

I swept downhill into the farmlands of Lothian under leaden skies. Fala was a tiny village less grey than I had become used to, with a little church on a wooded hill; there were strange ruins by the road at Crichton Dean; Pathhead was a long town with single-storey cottages at one end and the long causeway up past Oxenfoord Castle at the other. At the end of the causeway, the main road bent west to Dalkeith, and I turned off through cornfields towards Musselburgh. After an initial kink it went straight, carrying on the line of the causeway:

then it twisted downhill past woodland, and went straight
again – a last display of Roman rectitude before the sea,
perhaps.

Although it was downhill, my pace grew slower: I felt that I
was losing the company of the road and that I would be glad to
see the little grey car again. I dawdled to the Whitecraig
roundabout, which was the last place where Jenny and I could
be sure of meeting each other, and hung about a bit, and a bit
longer, before I decided that I was going to get to the end of the
journey alone.

I headed straight off to Inveresk, which is the inland part
of Musselburgh, a town no longer celebrated for its mussels,
which are polluted, but still known for the wholesomeness
of its people who, six centuries ago, refused any reward for
their devotion to Randolph, Earl of Moray, in his last illness,
were dubbed 'honest fellows' by the Earl of Mar, who offered
it; and have been calling themselves honest ever since.
Honestas is the town motto, and an Honest Lad and Honest
Lass are chosen every year to represent the town at the Border
ridings, and lead the singing of the Musselburgh song:

> *Musselburgh was a burgh*
> *When Edinburgh was nane:*
> *And Musselburgh will be a burgh*
> *When Edinburgh's gane.*

which is almost the same as the rhyme I had heard at the start of
my journey:

> *Exeter was an airy down*
> *When Topsham was a busy town.*

Like Topsham, this was a harbour in Roman times, with a
fort and granaries to supply the soldiers on the Antonine Wall
further north. But even the dotted lines on my Roman road
map ran out here, at the kirk of St Michael, where there are
Roman stones in the walls, and the land-dead fisherfolk of
Fisherrow lie down in dirt the legionaries trod. They were
canny, poor, hard-working people, the fishers – and so separate a community that they even had their own gallery in the
church. However, there was still a working fishwife in Mus-

selburgh – as far as anyone knew, the last to carry the creel although she had taken to carrying it in a van.

Musselburgh is also part of golfing history for, though it is not the birthplace of the game, it is said to be the first links where holes were made – and there is an ancient hole-cutter in the Musselburgh Museum as a memorial to this vacuous invention. Certainly, the course has the only hole in the entire world where you can stand on the putting green and at the same time have a drink at the pub close by, through a window on to the green. A man had once won the hole after his ball had gone down the pub chimney and been retrieved from the fireplace.

On that grey afternoon of my arrival, I dawdled down the last stretch of Roman road to Inveresk church. Out of the flat cornfields I came into the village to discover houses and gardens of some style set behind high walls – and, on a corner, a house with Dutch gables, like the Dutch houses at Topsham. Inveresk was deserted: I was coming to a fork in the road, and there was no one to ask what went where. But at the join there were the gates to a large house, and at the gates a lodge, before which a young man was washing a car. He was a stranger here, himself, he said, but he would fetch the porter.

The lodge-keeper and his wife were middle-aged and friendly: the church was just down there: they kept the lodge for the scientific laboratory that had the big house now: I had come far? Exeter? What, on the Roman roads?

'But we've got the end of the Roman road here,' said the lodge-keeper. He took me by the arm and hustled me and the bicycle in through the gates. 'They found it when they were digging the foundations for the new laboratory.' We followed a winding path through the gardens: 'There.'

The new laboratory was a single-storey building made from modular units: whatever meaning had been buried beneath it was not expressed in its architecture, but I regarded it respectfully, there being nothing else to do with it. In front of it there was a stone seat, very rough, and grooved down the middle.

'They found that,' said the lodge-keeper. 'That was a piece of the road: a drain maybe, or some sort of gully.'

I looked down the drain, across the drain and – since it was now a seat – I sat on the drain. Then I leaned the bicycle against the drain and took a photograph of them together.

'It's not much, maybe, but . . .'

'Oh but it is,' I said. 'In six hundred miles on top of them, I think it's the first time I've seen a bit of the surface of a Roman road. I'll just go down to the church where the Romans had their temple, and then I'm done.'

I rode the last few hundred yards. At the church, there was nothing particularly Roman to be seen, and no way ahead. I stopped in the grey afternoon and considered: 'Was I really at the end? If so, why was there no endish feeling to it? Was not a drain – even if Roman – short on romance? In the absence of an endish feeling, ought I to do something to create one? But what?'

I might have had to stay there for some time, making up my mind – and it was getting cold – had it not been for the red setter. It came out of the drive of the house next to the church, waddling its hindquarters with the swings of its tail: walked straight up to me without a bark or a growl, and stood looking.

'So you are the welcome committee?' I said to the dog – aloud, since there was no one else about. 'Or are you just one curious individual looking at yet another curious individual?'

The setter did nothing except to give an indecisive wag to its feathery tail, but its eyes looked as solemn as if it grieved for every inch of my six hundred and ten and a half miles from Topsham.

'Since you *are* here,' I went on, 'and since there is no other end in sight, were you to feel so inclined, it does occur to me that you might be of some assistance. It would be ridiculously sentimental – in fact, I'm not really sure I could even bring myself to put it in the book – but for my own curiosity (just to see whether life really is like that, sometimes) I don't suppose . . .?'

The setter looked: I looked.

'Oh, very well, don't.'

The setter put out a healthy-sized tongue, and licked my hand.

'Well, well,' I said, 'how predictable. Yes, that was what I had in mind. I'm sure it will go down nicely with a nation of dog-lovers: thank you very much.'

I stroked the red setter, which seemed only *quid pro quo* in the circumstances, and cycled off to look for Jenny along an ordinary road that went nowhere in particular in a winding sort of way.

INDEX